The Boston University Cookbook

COOKING BY DEGREES

The Boston University Cookbook

Published in association with

BOSTONIA MAGAZINE

CBI

CBI Publishing Company, Inc.
51 Sleeper Street
Boston, Massachusetts 02210

COOKING
BY DEGREES

Edited by

Laura Freid

and

Terence Janericco

Editors: Laura Freid, Terence Janericco

Designer: Joe Kredlow

Printing (last digit): 9 8 7 6 5 4 3 2 1

Printed in the United States of America

Library of Congress Cataloging in Publication Data

Main entry under title:

Cooking By Degrees

    Includes index.
    1. Cookery.   I. Freid, Laura.   II. Janericco,
Terence.   III. Boston University.
TX715.C7833   641.5   81-3862
ISBN 0-8436-2216-4   AACR2

Dedicated to the late Mary Ross Finn,
beloved wife of Daniel J. Finn and
devoted mother of Debra, Daniel, Jr.,
Jeffrey, Kevin and Katherine Finn

Foreword

Cooking By Degrees symbolizes the creative strength of our alumni who have contributed their finest recipes to this collection. It is also inspirational as a team effort, the work of a dedicated committee of graduates whose families and friends tested all of the selections to assure high quality and variety.

Finally, *Cooking By Degrees* has a personal significance. My wife, Mary, was an enthusiastic member of the Boston University Cooks Committee prior to her sudden death in April, 1980. Mary was an excellent cook and an acclaimed hostess, and I am deeply gratified to learn that the alumni of Boston University chose to dedicate this book to her memory.

Daniel J. Finn
VICE PRESIDENT FOR UNIVERSITY RELATIONS
BOSTON UNIVERSITY

Contents

B oston University's Schools and Colleges line the south bank of the Charles River, a short distance from downtown Boston. Bordering the Charles River and Commonwealth Avenue, the University offers both the convenience and stimulation of a modern urban campus and the tranquility of nearby parks and river esplanades. The University provides its students with the advantages of a large contemporary educational complex while maintaining many of the traditional priorities of the liberal arts college. By granting its students access to the wide variety of courses offered within the institution, Boston University takes maximum advantage of its size and the range of its resources. By organizing its student body and faculty into 16 Schools and Colleges, the University maintains its human scale and sense of academic purpose. Boston University has long been devoted to the education of the total individual and continues to stress the virtues of liberal arts education in each of its undergraduate programs. The University is also responsive to the occupational needs of its students and the increasingly specialized demands they will face in the contemporary world. The University has launched innovative programs in science, engineering and other technical fields; in nursing, health care, communications, management and education; it has pioneered numerous interdisciplinary programs, the team method of teaching in its two-year college (the College of Basic Studies), the six-year Liberal Arts-Medical Education, the seven-year Liberal Arts-Dental Education Programs and the innovative Program in Artisanry.

The University's 63 acre Charles River campus provides ample space for its libraries and laboratories, gymnasiums and student centers, classrooms and residential units. Quiet quadrangles adjoin contemporary classroom and dormitory buildings, next to which stand traditional structures and the urban bow-fronted town houses of Boston's Back Bay. The large new dormitories offer a variety of opportunities for social exchange as well as cultural, intellectual and academic activities. The town houses provide administrative office space and also serve as dormitories for groups of twenty to thirty students. Some of these small dormitories are organized around students' common interests in Spanish, French, Russian, classics and music. Across town is the Boston University Medical Center, an impressive massing of contemporary buildings, containing the School of Medicine, the Henry M. Goldman School of Graduate Dentistry and the affiliated University Hospital.

Confirming the intention of its charter of 1869, Boston University has always been free of racial or religious discrimination in the admission of students and the hiring of faculty. Boston University was the first university to open all its departments to female students, and it has the distinction of graduating the country's first woman Ph.D. The School of Medicine was the first coeducational medical school. For the past decade, the student body has been divided almost evenly between men and women, and the University has attracted a sizeable and growing number of distinguished women faculty members.

Boston University has more than 134,000 alumni living throughout the world. The lives and meaningful social contributions of these men and women – teachers, nurses, lawyers, dentists, journalists, business people, legislators, musicians, actresses and actors, writers, occupational and physical therapists, engineers, doctors and others – are the true testaments to the lasting value of education at Boston University.

Cooking By Degrees belongs to the Boston University Community. Its richness and variety are reflective of the individual contributions of the University's alumni, faculty members, administrators, parents, students and friends.

We are particularly grateful to Committee Chairwoman Lorraine Wysoskie Hurley and Dr. Hélène Day, New England Consul for Monaco. Lorraine, a School of Education graduate, demonstrated remarkable organizational abilities and has since gone on to host a television program on children's cooking for Channel 10-TV in Connecticut. Each recipe included in the following pages has been tested by members of the prestigious Boston University Cooks Committee. We are indebted to the following executive committee members: Barbara Tomashefsky Abbott; Barbara Goulson Arceneaux; Helen Crawford Bander; Sterne Wallace Barnett; Andrea Bell; Nadine BeVille; Deborah H. Cohen; Kathleen Ruskey Cole; Mary Ross Finn (deceased), wife of Vice President Daniel J. Finn; Sharon Gamsin; Leah F. Gould; Rebecca J. Gourley; Gail Goodman Hamilton; Paulette Idelson; Terence Janericco; Elaine Spivack Katz; Lorraine Nelson Klein; Andrew Korn; Barbara Fearer Lanciani; Sandra J. Levine; Susan Freedman Mandel; Patti A. Marcus; Susan K. Moger; Dr. Linda Pollack Nelson; Carolyn Payne; Stanlee Lipkin-Quaytman; Mary Louise Redmond; Elaine Richman; Cynthia Rubin; Claire Shapiro Soja; Deborah Stearns Sullivan; Suzanne Pachter Wallach; Margaret Wilkerson; Carol Green Winer; and Dr. Matthew Witten. Our foreign representatives were particularly enthusiastic. Many thanks are extended to Shelley and Abe Tiber from Israel; Dr. Prakash Lulla from India; Patricia Bjaaland from Norway; and Ethel S. Chirinos from Peru.

During the past few years several Cook-In Demonstrations were held at the Boston University Castle. We would like to thank Hans Bucher, executive chef, Hyatt Regency Hotel; Richard Lucas, executive chef, Hotel Sonesta; Elvira Slezak, pastry chef, and Chuck Hemmerlin, day chef, Cafe Budapest; Gidon Apteker, former pastry chef for The Colonnade Hotel; Richard

Silver, proprietor of Black Forest Caterers, and Anthony Spinazzola, wine and food critic for *The Boston Globe,* for taking the time to demonstrate their talents during these occasions.

The unsung heroine of *Cooking By Degrees* is Mrs. Bert M. Hirshberg, who, in addition to guiding the committee and keeping track of thousands of minute details, has managed to maintain her energy and enthusiasm. Bert was assisted by Boston University students Kerrylee Dyroff, Sarah Jacobs, Christine Ann Leberer, Annette S. Racond, David Zizza and School of Public Communication intern Pamela V. Webster.

The *Bostonia Magazine* staff, in particular, Douglas Parker, Lori Calabro and Agnes Williams, helped to launch the book and remained as advisors throughout the project. Dr. Howard B. Gotlieb, director of Special Collections, Mugar Library, must be thanked for allowing us to use the Twentieth Century Archives list.

I am particularly grateful to Daniel J. Finn, vice president for University Relations, who has encouraged me to explore new ways for Boston University alumni to express themselves, and to President John R. Silber, whose enthusiasm for new projects and ventures has always been inspirational.

I would also like to thank co-editor Terence Janericco who transformed everyone's kitchen hieroglyphics to readily understandable and workable recipes.

Final credits are extended to Joe Kredlow, who designed the cover and text for *Cooking By Degrees,* a classic effort that you will enjoy as you use the book.

Laura Freid
EDITOR

I am pleased to have the opportunity to introduce this cookbook, which constitutes an important step in the continuing progress of Boston University's developing programs for, by and of alumni.

It is increasingly common to decry the state of cooking in the United States by pointing to the prevalence of fast-food restaurants. Even superficially, this is a dubious claim, given the fact that some fast-food restaurants — pizza and taco shops — have introduced a measure of diversity into the diets of many Americans who would otherwise have had little exposure to exotic cuisines that have the nutritional wisdom of peasant cooking everywhere.

But there is much greater ground for optimism about the state of the American kitchen and the American palate in the increasing diversity of superior cookbooks. In the year when my parents were married, a Fannie Farmer Cookbook was a standard wedding gift, and it provided the new bride with all she needed to know of technique and a lifetime of menus. Without denigrating what was and is a great cookbook, we can hardly imagine people serious about their food being content with a single cookbook, whether by Fannie Farmer, Joyce Chen, Julia Child or Escoffier himself.

The pursuit of cuisine is not at odds with the central mission of a university, for it involves developing an ability to make precise distinctions and to order things according to their preferability. They understand this very well in France, where cooking is esteemed as one of the fine arts, and the "philosopher of the table," Brillat-Savarin, spoke of the need to develop "a passionate and rational preference for all that flatters the palate."

In this country we are not ready to promote cooking quite that high, and I do not anticipate a fourth member of the School for the Arts. But as a nation we are increasingly learning that eating is more than consuming calories. We are moving further and further away from a once common vision of the future in which meals were to be reduced to a few bland but perfectly nutritious pills.

This cookbook has the potential to bring the 134,000 alumni of Boston University more closely together at their tables. All members of the Boston University community can be grateful to those who have made this possible.

John R. Silber
PRESIDENT, BOSTON UNIVERSITY

1 Appetizers

Appetizers

1

Barbara's Raw Vegetable Dip

1 qt. mayonnaise	
6 scallions	
6 sprigs parsley	
2 cloves garlic	
½ tube anchovy paste	

In a processor, combine mayonnaise, scallions, parsley, garlic and anchovy paste until finely minced. Serve with raw vegetables. Keeps one week. Makes 1 quart.

The only way for this to work is to use Hellman's mayonnaise. It just won't taste right if you use a cheaper brand.

Barbara Lanciani SED '66
Cookbook Committee
Leominster, Massachusetts

Low Cal Curry Dip

Helen K. Hickey
SAR '50/SED '54
Associate Dean
Sargent College of
Allied Health Professions

8 oz. low calorie cream cheese
2 tablespoons imitation mayonnaise
1/4 cup low fat milk (or more if needed for moisture)
2 tablespoons curry powder
1/2 teaspoon pepper
sprinkle of minced garlic

The day before using, combine cheese, mayonnaise, milk, curry powder, pepper and garlic. Serve with raw vegetables. Keeps one week. Makes about 1 1/2 cups.

Curry Dip

Phyllis Ratcliffe Hamilton
CLA '62
Libertytown, Maryland
Betsy Wilson
John Wilson
Associate Dean
School of Law

1 1/2 cups mayonnaise
2 tablespoons curry powder (or to taste)
1 tablespoon grated onion
1/2 teaspoon dry mustard
1/2 teaspoon salt
black pepper and cayenne, to taste

In a bowl, combine mayonnaise, curry powder, onion, mustard, salt and pepper. Mix well. Refrigerate for 2 hours to blend flavors. Serve with raw vegetables. Keeps one week. Makes 1 1/2 cups.

Curried Cream Cheese Dip

Diana Lin SMG'72
New York, New York

1 lb. softened cream cheese
1/3 cup milk
1 tablespoon Worcestershire sauce
1/4 teaspoon Tabasco sauce
1 tablespoon curry powder
1 tablespoon grated onion
1/2 teaspoon salt

In a processor, combine the cheese, milk, Worcestershire, Tabasco, curry powder, onion and salt. Cover and chill 6 hours to blend flavors. Serve as a dip with raw vegetables. Keeps one week. Makes about 2 cups.

Curry and Chili Sauce Dip

1	pint mayonnaise
3	tablespoons chili sauce
1	tablespoon curry powder
1	tablespoon minced garlic
1	tablespoon grated onion
1	tablespoon Worcestershire sauce
¼	teaspoon salt
¼	teaspoon pepper

If you do a lot of entertaining, this recipe is great because it keeps for a long time, and you can serve it to a number of different groups of people.

Leslie Miles
Associate Director
Admissions

Combine mayonnaise, chili sauce, curry powder, garlic, onion, Worcestershire, salt and pepper. Cover and chill. Keeps two weeks refrigerated. Makes about 2½ cups.

Dill Dip

⅔	cup sour cream
⅓	cup mayonnaise
1	tablespoon minced fresh dill (or to taste)
1	teaspoon grated onion (or to taste)

Phyliss Ratcliffe Hamilton
CLA'62
Libertytown, Maryland

Combine sour cream, mayonnaise, dill and onion. Mix well. Keeps three days. Makes 1 cup.

Pini Cheese Spread

7	oz. blue cheese
1	lb. cream cheese
2	tablespoons butter
1	heaping teaspoon paprika
1	teaspoon Worcestershire sauce
1	pimiento, minced
6	stuffed olives, minced
½	green pepper, minced
½	tablespoon minced parsley

This makes enough to last you through an entire box of crackers or a football game, whichever ends first.

Lori Calabro SPC'80
Managing Editor
University Relations

Combine the cheeses, butter, paprika, Worcestershire, pimiento, olives, pepper and parsley. Mix well. Serve with bread or crackers. Keeps one week refrigerated. Makes 3 cups.

Bibelkase

Terence Janericco CLA'61
Cookbook Committee Editor
Boston, Massachusetts

2 *cups small curd cottage cheese, sieved*
½ *cup heavy cream*
3 *cloves garlic, minced*
1 *tablespoon minced parsley*
salt and pepper, to taste

Combine cheese, cream, garlic, parsley, salt and pepper. Chill, covered, 3 hours. Serve with crackers. Keeps three days refrigerated. For a firmer cheese, place in a cheese cloth and sieve over a bowl. Drain for 24 to 36 hours. Makes about 2½ cups.

Southern Cheese Log

Diana Robbins CLA'64
National Alumni Council
Manderville, Louisiana

1 *cup finely ground pecans*
8 *oz. cream cheese*
1 *tablespoon Worcestershire sauce*
1 *clove garlic, ground with pecans*
2 *tablespoons chili powder*

Blend pecans, cheese, Worcestershire and garlic. Shape into a log, 5 x 1½ inches. Roll in chili powder. Chill until firm. Serve with crackers. Keeps three days refrigerated. Makes about 2 cups.

Herbed Cheese Spread

This is just like expensive fancy Boursin cheese, only you make it at home and it costs a lot less.

Margaret Wilkerson
Cookbook Committee

1 *lb. cream cheese*
8 *oz. butter*
2 *cloves garlic, crushed*
¼ *teaspoon dill*
¼ *teaspoon basil*
¼ *teaspoon oregano*
¼ *teaspoon marjoram*
¼ *teaspoon thyme*
¼ *teaspoon pepper*
¼ *teaspoon salt*

In a mixer, combine cheese, butter, garlic and herbs. Mix well. Serve with crackers. Can be frozen. Makes 3 cups.

Hot Chili Pepper Spread

10 oz. Cheddar cheese, grated
3 cans chopped green chili peppers
3 eggs, beaten
3 tablespoons milk

Preheat oven to 325°. Grease a 9 inch pie pan. Combine cheese, peppers, eggs and milk. Pour into prepared pie pan. Bake 45 minutes. Serve immediately with crackers. Serves 8.

Barbara Goulson Arceneaux
PAL'54
Cookbook Committee
Jacksonville, Florida

Cheese Ball

1 lb. Cheddar cheese, grated
1 lb. Swiss cheese, grated
1 lb. American cheese, grated
1 orange rind, grated
1 tablespoon mayonnaise
½ cup crushed walnuts

In a 3 quart bowl, combine cheeses and rind, fold in mayonnaise and mix well. Shape into a ball and roll in walnuts. Chill 1 hour. May be made two to three days ahead. Cannot be frozen. Makes 6 cups.

When you serve this, make it the center attraction, surrounded by small party rounds.

Sterne Barnett CBA'35
Cookbook Committee
Chestnut Hill, Massachusetts

Pistachio-Gruyère Cheese Spread

8 oz. gruyère cheese, grated
⅓ cup mayonnaise
3 to 4 tablespoons dry white wine
¼ teaspoon dry mustard
⅛ teaspoon minced garlic
½ cup chopped pistachio nuts
2 tablespoons chopped parsley
1 teaspoon grated lemon rind

Combine cheese, mayonnaise, wine, mustard and garlic. Mix well. Combine nuts, parsley and lemon rind. Layer cheese and nut mixtures in a glass container. Chill. Keeps one week refrigerated. Makes about 1⅔ cups.

Nancy Marsh Hartman
SFA'52
Former Trustee
Needham, Massachusetts

Caponata (Eggplant Spread)

1 large eggplant, ½ inch cubes
salt
⅓ cup olive oil
2 medium onions, minced
1 cup diced celery
1 lb. can solid pack tomatoes
½ cup wine vinegar
1 tablespoon sugar
2 teaspoons salt
1 teaspoon basil
½ teaspoon oregano
¼ teaspoon pepper
several dashes cayenne
5¾ oz. black olives, sliced
2 tablespoons capers
2 tablespoons pine nuts

Sprinkle cubes of eggplant with salt and let drain for 20 minutes. Sauté eggplant in half the oil, stirring for 8 minutes. Remove to a bowl and sauté onions in remaining oil until soft but not brown. Stir in celery and tomatoes. Simmer 15 minutes, stirring often until reduced by ⅓. Stir in vinegar, sugar, salt, basil, oregano, pepper and eggplant. Cook covered 10 minutes. Add olives, capers and pine nuts. Simmer 10 minutes uncovered. Correct seasoning with salt and pepper. Serve hot or cold on melba toast or rye bread. Keeps one week refrigerated. Makes about 3 cups.

Elaine Spivack Katz
SAR '76
Cookbook Committee
Oak Lawn, Illinois

Pickled Eggplant

1 qt. white vinegar
2 to 3 eggplants, peeled, ¼ inch thick slices
salt, to taste
2 cloves garlic, crushed
black pepper, to taste
red crushed pepper, to taste
oregano, to taste
olive oil

William Henneman
Professor
Department of Mathematics
College of Liberal Arts

Boil 1 quart white vinegar and 1 quart water. Add about 10 slices of eggplant and cook 1 to 2 minutes. Remove and place in strainer. Press out vinegar and place in bowl. Repeat process until all slices are cooked. Layer each batch of eggplant seasoned with salt, garlic, black pepper, oregano and red crushed pepper. Cover with oil, cover the bowl and refrigerate. Serve as appetizer or on sandwiches. May be kept one week in refrigerator. Makes about 1 quart.

Eggplant Antipasto

1 medium eggplant, peeled, 1 inch cubes
½ cup olive oil
1 onion, chopped
1 carrot, diced
1 small bunch celery, ½ inch pieces
⅓ cup wine vinegar
½ cup canned Italian plum tomatoes
salt and pepper, to taste

For variety, tuna fish, olives and anchovies may be added.

Joan Schilder GRS '77
Herbert Schilder
Professor
Assistant Dean
Goldman School of
Graduate Dentistry

Cook eggplant in ¼ cup olive oil until tender. Cook onion, carrot, celery in remaining olive oil in another skillet until onion is soft but not brown. Remove eggplant and add vinegar to skillet. Reduce by ½. Add tomatoes and simmer 10 minutes. Add salt, pepper and carrot mixture. Chill. Serve with crackers. Keeps one week refrigerated. Makes about 2 cups.

Baba Ganooj *(Eggplant Spread)*

Serve this with pieces of
raw onion and make sure
everyone else is eating it
the same way.

Peg Mitchell CLA '67
Assistant Director
Reunions

1 lb. eggplant
1 tablespoon olive oil
1 clove garlic
1 teaspoon salt
¼ cup finely chopped onions
2 to 3 tablespoons tahini (sesame seed paste)*
¼ cup fresh lemon juice

Prick eggplant and cook under broiler, 4 to 5 inches
away from unit, 15 to 20 minutes, turning occasionally
to cook on all sides. When cool, pull skin off. Gently
squeeze out as much of the juice as possible. Place
eggplant in bowl and mash with fork. Add oil gradually
while beating eggplant. Crush garlic with salt and add to
eggplant with onions. Add tahini and lemon juice alternately. Blend well. Taste and add more salt, lemon or
tahini as needed. Place in serving bowl and garnish with
chopped parsley and black olives. Serve with pita bread
and raw onion wedges. May be made one day ahead.
Makes 1½ cups.
*Tahini is available in Middle Eastern markets and larger
supermarkets.*

Marinated Mushrooms

Judy Spellissey SFA '75
West Chelmsford,
Massachusetts

1 lb. cleaned button mushrooms
⅔ cup olive oil
½ cup vinegar
1 tablespoon lemon juice
1 clove garlic, minced
1 teaspoon tarragon
½ teaspoon sugar
salt and pepper, to taste

Combine mushrooms, oil, vinegar, lemon juice, garlic, tarragon, sugar, salt and pepper. Mix well. Refrigerate covered, overnight, stirring occasionally. Keeps two weeks refrigerated.

Marinated Carrots

8 carrots, ¼ inch thick, 2 inches long	
1 green pepper, chopped	
1 red onion, sliced	
1 can tomato soup	
½ cup salad oil	
¾ cup sugar	
⅓ cup vinegar	
½ teaspoon salt	
1 teaspoon French mustard	
1 teaspoon Worcestershire sauce	

Mary Anne Gannam
Nicholas Gannam
CLA '40/GRS '41
National Alumni Council
San Francisco, California

Blanch carrots in boiling, salted water until tender crisp. Drain and run under cold water to stop cooking. Combine carrots, pepper, onion, tomato soup, sugar, salad oil, vinegar, mustard, Worcestershire and salt. Mix well. Marinate in a covered container for 12 hours. Keeps one week refrigerated. Makes about 40 sticks.

Peruvian Causa *(Potato Balls)*

Place in avocado halves
for a dramatic display.

Ethel S. Chirinos SED '75
Cookbook Committee
Lima, Peru

| 2 lbs. potatoes, unpeeled |
| 6 tablespoons salad oil |
| ¼ teaspoon cayenne (or to taste) |
| 3 tablespoons lemon juice |
| ½ teaspoon salt |
| ¼ teaspoon pepper |

Boil the potatoes until tender, drain and peel. Mash the potatoes. Stir in the salad oil, cayenne, lemon juice, salt and pepper. Shape into small balls and garnish with parsley leaves.

Sauce

| 2 tablespoons lemon juice |
| 2 onions, chopped |
| salt and pepper, to taste |
| ¼ cup vinegar |
| 1 tablespoon oil |
| 1 aji or chili, cut in strips |

Combine lemon juice, onions, salt, pepper, vinegar, oil, aji or chili. Serve with causa. Causa can also be used to fill peeled avocado halves and garnished with mayonnaise and hard cooked eggs.

Caviar Mold

Gail Goodman Hamilton
SON '66
Cookbook Committee
Winston-Salem,
North Carolina

| 8 oz. cream cheese |
| ¼ cup sour cream |
| ½ medium onion, grated |
| Worcestershire sauce |
| 4 oz. caviar |

Mix cream cheese, sour cream, onion and Worcestershire. Shape into round flat cake. Spread caviar over top and sides. Refrigerate for at least 1 hour before serving. Can be made two days ahead. Makes 1 cup.

Tabbouleh *(Middle Eastern Salad)*

¾ cup fine Burghul (cracked wheat)*

1 large onion, finely chopped

salt and black pepper

1 cup finely chopped parsley

3 tablespoons chopped fresh mint, or
1½ tablespoons dried mint, crumbled

5 tablespoons olive oil

5 tablespoons fresh lemon juice

1 medium fresh ripe tomato, diced

lettuce leaves

Serve on lettuce leaves.

Peg Mitchell CLA '67
*Assistant Director
Reunions*

Place Burghul in bowl and completely cover with cold water. Let soak for ½ hour or until soft. Drain and squeeze out moisture. Spread on a clean cloth to dry. Place Burghul in large bowl. Add onions and mix by hand. Season to taste with salt and pepper. Add parsley, mint, olive oil and lemon juice. Mix together. Taste and add salt and pepper and/or lemon as needed. Add diced tomato. Tabbouleh is eaten with lettuce leaves or in pita bread. Can be made one to two hours ahead. Makes about 4 cups.

Burghul available at Middle Eastern markets.

Taramosalata *(Greek Caviar Dip)*

2 slices stale bread

¾ cup water

4 ounces tarama* (fish roe)

1 cup olive oil

juice of 1½ lemons (or to taste)

Carol Cicma CLA '70
Providence, Rhode Island

Combine bread, water, tarama*, olives and lemon juice in a processor. Process until dip takes on the consistency of mayonnaise. Serve with toasted pita bread or crackers. Keeps one week refrigerated. Makes about 3 cups.

Tarama can be bought in Greek or Middle Eastern markets.

Choomis and Chapati

(Chickpea Spread and Flat Bread)

A favorite recipe from the
Total Loss Farm—agricul-
tural/artists commune,
Guilford, Vermont

Douglas Parker SFA '67
Senior Designer
University Relations

Choomis

1 cup chickpeas

½ lb. sesame seeds

juice of 2 lemons

4 cloves garlic

salt, to taste

dash paprika

sesame or peanut oil

Soak chickpeas overnight. Cook chickpeas in water until
tender. Combine chickpeas, sesame seeds and peeled
garlic in a processor or grinder. Add lemon juice, salt,
paprika and enough oil to make it spreadable.

Chapati

Mix 1 teaspoon salt for each cup of flour. Add cold
water, a little at a time, to make a stiff dough. Knead out
flat and shape into thin rounds. Cook in lightly oiled
skillet or griddle.

Cheese-Clam Log

Gail Goodman Hamilton
SON '66
Cookbook Committee
Winston-Salem,
North Carolina

8 oz. cream cheese

1 can smoked clams, chopped

1 tablespoon minced onion

1 tablespoon lemon juice

⅛ teaspoon ground pepper

chopped parsley

Roll cream cheese between 2 sheets of plastic wrap to
form a 4x8 inch rectangle. Combine clams, onion, lemon
juice and pepper. Spread on cheese. Fold long sides into
middle and overlap slightly. Roll over onto serving plate.
Garnish with parsley.

Jane's Herring Stuff

1 jar herring tidbits, drained, onions removed
1 large red onion, chopped
1 green pepper, chopped
1 small can chopped black olives
8 oz. bottle chili sauce

Combine herring, onion, pepper, olives and chili sauce. Marinate 3 hours. Serve with crackers. Keeps three to four days refrigerated. Serves 4 to 6.

A perfect hors d'oeuvre to serve with drinks or take on a picnic.

Natalie McCracken
Assistant to the Dean
College of Liberal Arts

Cranberry Herring Spread

8 oz. herring tidbits in wine sauce, drained
8 oz. whole cranberry sauce
1 medium red onion, thinly sliced
½ pint sour cream
rye bread or crackers

Drain herring, discard onions and slice herring. Combine herring, cranberry sauce, sliced onion and sour cream. Mix well. Serve with bread or crackers. Keeps two days. Makes 3 cups.

Sue Lavien
David Lavien
LAW '29/SMG '30
Former Trustee
Boston, Massachusetts

Herring Dip

14 oz. herring in wine sauce, drained
½ pint sour cream
½ cup mayonnaise
1 tablespoon lemon juice
1 green pepper, chopped
3 scallions, chopped
1 teaspoon celery seed
1 teaspoon sugar

Combine herring, sour cream, mayonnaise, lemon juice, pepper, scallions, celery seed and sugar. Mix well. Chill. Keeps one week in refrigerator. Makes 3½ cups.

Sue Lavien
David Lavien
LAW'29/SMG'30
Former Trustee
Boston, Massachusetts

Cucumber and Mussels Vinaigrette

Diana Lin SMG '72
New York, New York

4 *lbs. mussels, well scrubbed*
½ *cup vinegar*
¼ *cup sugar*
1 *cup sliced cucumbers*
salt and pepper, to taste

In a large kettle, steam the mussels, covered until they open. Discard any mussels that do not open. Remove the mussels from their shells and put aside. Combine the vinegar, sugar, cucumbers, salt and pepper. Toss with the mussels. Refrigerate for 4 to 6 hours. Serves 4.

Salmon Mousse

Excellent on canapés or with crudités.

Dr. Linda Nelson CLA '74
Cookbook Committee
Lansdale, Pennsylvania

2 *envelopes unflavored gelatin*
2 *tablespoons lemon juice*
1 *small onion, sliced*
½ *cup boiling water*
½ *cup mayonnaise*
¼ *teaspoon paprika*
1 *minced fresh dill*
1 *lb. can salmon, drained*
1 *cup heavy cream*
1 *grape or black olive*

Pour gelatin, lemon juice, onion and boiling water into blender. Cover and blend at high speed for 40 seconds. Add mayonnaise, paprika, dill and salmon. Blend covered at high speed. With cover off, add cream, a little at a time, blending for a few seconds each time. Blend 30 seconds more. Pour into 5½ cup mold, preferably shaped like a fish. Chill. Unmold and insert a grape or black olive for an eye. Can be made two days ahead. Serves 20.

Kipper Spread

3 cans kipper snacks, minced
5 eggs, hard boiled, minced
2 onions, minced
2 stalks celery, minced
1 teaspoon pickle relish
1 teaspoon salt
mayonnaise

Dr. Matthew Witten
CLA '72
Cookbook Committee
Los Angeles, California

Combine kippers, eggs, onions, celery, relish and salt. Mix well. Fold in mayonnaise to taste. Chill. Serve on lettuce, crackers or as a sandwich spread. Keeps two days. Makes 3 cups.

Salmon Balls

1 lb. can red salmon, cleaned
8 oz. softened cream cheese
1 tablespoon lemon juice
2 teaspoons grated onion
1 teaspoon horseradish
1 teaspoon salt
1 teaspoon liquid smoke (optional)
drop of Tabasco sauce
1/2 cup chopped nuts
3 tablespoons minced parsley

Barbara Goulson Arceneaux
PAL '54
Cookbook Committee
Jacksonville, Florida
Nancy Marsh Hartman
SFA '52
Former Trustee
Needham, Massachusetts

Combine salmon, cream cheese, lemon juice, onion, horseradish, salt and tabasco. Shape into a ball, wrap in plastic wrap and chill. Roll ball in walnuts and parsley. Make one day ahead, can be frozen. Serve with crackers. Makes about 3 cups.

Terrine de Campagne
(Country Pâté)

This variation is much lower in fat than traditional pâtés. It's great served with French bread.

Carl Ruck
Professor
Department of
Classical Studies
College of Liberal Arts

2	*medium onions, minced*
¼	*cup butter*
2	*cloves garlic, crushed*
	rosemary, thyme, basil
1	*chicken breast, deboned*
1	*lb. chicken livers*
3	*eggs, beaten*
¼	*cup cognac (optional)*
1	*cup medium cream*
1½	*teaspoons salt*
	pepper, to taste
½	*lb. boiled ham, sliced*
4	*bay leaves*

Preheat oven to 350°. Sauté onions in butter. Add crushed garlic and liberal pinches of herbs. Grind chicken breast with skin and chicken livers in a processor and add to onion and herb mixture. Mix in eggs, cognac and cream. Season with salt and pepper. Pour an inch layer of mixture into a loaf pan. Cover with a layer of ham and alternate layers until mixture is used. Insert bay leaves along sides of the loaf pan. Seal pan with foil, and place it in several inches of water in a larger pan. Bake for 2 hours. Uncover and bake 30 minutes longer. Remove from oven and weight with 2 food cans. Chill overnight before serving.

Pâté de Foie de Porc
(Pork Liver Pâté)

Richard Lucas
Executive Chef
Hotel Sonesta
Cambridge, Massachusetts

1	*lb. pork liver, 1 inch cubes*
½	*lb. fat back, 1 inch cubes*
½	*lb. pork butt, 1 inch cubes*
1	*cup port wine*
½	*cup cognac*
6	*shallots, sliced*

1 clove garlic

4 bay leaves

3 tablespoons salt

1 tablespoon peppercorns

1 tablespoon thyme

1 lb. fat back, thinly sliced

Combine liver, fat back, pork, port, cognac, shallots, garlic, bay leaves, salt, peppercorns and thyme. Cover and marinate in refrigerator 24 to 48 hours. Discard bay leaves. Remove the meat from the marinade and place the ground meat into a terrine or mold that has been lined on the bottom and sides with fat back. Cover top of mold with another thin slice of fat back. Preheat the oven to 350°. Place the terrine in a roasting pan half filled with water in oven for 1 hour, until juices run clear or it registers 165° on a meat thermometer. Remove from oven and chill. Keeps two weeks refrigerated. Serves 12.

Red Headed Pâté

3 tablespoons gelatin

6 tablespoons cold water

2 10¾ oz. cans consommé Madrilène

2 tablespoons lemon juice

½ teaspoon Worcestershire sauce

¼ teaspoon ground nutmeg

½ teaspoon thyme

12 oz. liverwurst, mashed

1 lb. softened cream cheese

3 oz. softened cream cheese

Marguerite E. White
Acton, Massachusetts

In a small saucepan, soften the gelatin in water, then dissolve over low heat. Stir in the consommé, lemon juice, Worcestershire, nutmeg and thyme. Pour ½ cup of the broth in the bottom of an 8 cup loaf pan. Chill until firm. Mix the liverwurst and cream cheese until well blended. Fold in the remaining consommé mixture and pour on top of the set layer of consommé. Chill until firm. Unmold onto a serving platter. Place the remaining cream cheese into a pastry bag and decorate the pâté with the cheese. Serve with crackers. May be made three days ahead. Makes 8 cups.

Liverwurst Ball

Mrs. Francis S. Doody
Francis S. Doody
*Professor
Department of
Finance/Economics
School of Management*

1 lb. liverwurst
1 ½ teaspoons minced garlic
1 teaspoon minced onion
1 teaspoon sweet basil
8 oz. softened cream cheese
3 tablespoons mayonnaise
½ teaspoon Tabasco sauce
salt and pepper
1 cup minced parsley

Combine liverwurst, garlic, onion and basil in a processor until smooth. Shape into a ball and chill. Beat cheese, mayonnaise, Tabasco, salt and pepper together. Spread on chilled ball. Sprinkle with parsley. Make 2 days ahead to develop flavor. Keeps six days. Makes 1 ½ pounds.

Stuffed Grape Leaves

A Mediterranean
specialty

Daphne S. Palmer
Friend of Boston University

1 jar grape leaves, rinsed, drained
2 onions, chopped
2 tablespoons olive oil
1 ½ to 2 cups rice
salt and pepper, to taste
1 lb. lean hamburger

Simmer grape leaves 15 minutes in boiling water, covered, drain. Sauté onions in olive oil until golden. Add rice, hamburger, salt and pepper to taste. Place 1 teaspoon on the broad end of each leaf, fold over the sides, then roll to form a neat log. Serve hot or cold. Can be kept one week in refrigerator or frozen for two months. Serves 20.

Beef Roll-Ups

2 *small jars sliced dried beef*
8 *oz. softened cream cheese*

Spread beef slices with cream cheese. Roll the slices and chill until serving time. Decorate platter with parsley and place a small bowl in the center filled with black pitted olives. May be prepared two days ahead. Keep covered in the refrigerator. Makes about 48.

Serve on a round platter and alternate beef roll-ups with stuffed deviled eggs.

Mary Ross Finn
The late wife of
Daniel J. Finn
Vice President for University Relations

Mock Blintz Appetizers

1 *lb. small curd cottage cheese*
3 *eggs*
3 *tablespoons sour cream*
½ *cup Bisquick*
½ *cup butter, melted*

Preheat oven to 350°. In a bowl, beat cottage cheese, eggs, Bisquick, butter and sour cream together. Spray tiny muffin pans with oil *and* dot generously with butter. Fill ¾ full with mixture. Bake for 35 to 40 minutes until golden. Can be frozen. Makes 48.

Use minced green pepper or mushrooms for variety.

Bert M. Hirshberg
Cookbook Coordinator

Cheese Puffs

1 *cup butter*
4½ *oz. sharp Cheddar cheese*
3 *oz. cream cheese*
2 *egg whites*
1 *loaf firm, unsliced bread (such as Pepperidge Farm), crusts removed, 1 inch cubes*

Preheat oven to 375°. In a double boiler, heat the butter, cream cheese and Cheddar until well blended. Beat egg whites until stiff. Fold into cheese mixture with a fork. Dip bread cubes into cheese mixture and place on buttered cookie sheets. Chill 2 hours or overnight. Bake 8 to 10 minutes or until golden brown. Makes 35.

These hors d'oeuvres are my absolute favorites. They make a hit at any cocktail party.

Mary Simpson
John B. Simpson
SED '50/'54
Director of Athletics

Hot Cheese Puffs

Gertrude E. McGuire
SED '42/'44
Portland, Connecticut

1 cup grated Cheddar or gruyère cheese

1 teaspoon horseradish

mayonnaise

6 slices bread, crusts removed

Preheat oven to 400°. Combine cheese and horseradish. Add enough mayonnaise to bind. Spread on bread. Bake until puffy and golden. Cut into quarters. Serve immediately. Makes 24.

Cheese Cocktail Cookies

Patti Marcus SAR '72
Cookbook Committee
Brighton, Massachusetts

½ lb. softened butter

½ lb. Cheddar cheese, grated

2 cups flour

2 cups Rice Krispies

salt, to taste

cayenne pepper, to taste

Preheat oven to 300°. Combine butter, cheese, flour, Rice Krispies, salt and pepper. Mix well. Shape into 1 inch balls, place on buttered baking sheet and bake 30 minutes or until golden. Can be frozen. Reheat to enhance flavor. Makes about 60.

Chili Con Queso (Hot Dip)

Diane M. Dodendorf
SON '72
Omaha, Nebraska

½ onion, minced

2 tablespoons butter

2 medium tomatoes, chopped

4 oz. can chopped green chili peppers

½ teaspoon salt

8 oz. cream cheese

corn chips

Sauté onion in butter until soft. Stir in tomatoes, chili peppers and salt. Simmer uncovered 10 minutes. Stir in cream cheese until melted. Pour into chafing dish to keep warm. Serve with corn chips. Can be reheated. Serves 8.

Parmesan Rounds

12 bread rounds
12 thin onion slices
4 tablespoons mayonnaise
4 tablespoons Parmesan cheese

Toast bread rounds on both sides. Cut onions to same size and place on top of toast. In a bowl, combine mayonnaise and cheese. Spread on top of onions. Broil until puffed and browned. Serve immediately. Makes 12.

The ingredients in this recipe are usually those you have right on hand. It's a great hors d'oeuvre and men in particular love them.

Margaret Wilkerson
Cookbook Committee

Broiled Stuffed Mushrooms

40 large mushroom caps, washed
½ cup chopped onion
2 tablespoons bread crumbs
¼ cup butter
3 tablespoons sour cream
Tabasco sauce
¼ teaspoon curry powder
salt and pepper, to taste
¼ lb. Cheddar cheese, thinly sliced

Remove stems from the mushrooms and mince finely with the onion. Stir in the bread crumbs, butter, sour cream, Tabasco, curry powder, salt and pepper. Fill the mushroom caps and top with thin slices of cheese. Broil until cheese is melted, about 2 minutes. Serve hot. Makes 40.

Edith Stearns
Professor
School of Music
School for the Arts

Champignons Grand'mere
(Stuffed Mushrooms)

A vegetable, appetizer or
hors d'oeuvre

Sylvia Brussel
GRS '74
Professor
Graduate Psychiatric Nursing
School of Nursing

24 *medium to large mushrooms*
2 *cloves garlic, minced*
8 *tablespoons butter*
1 *cup fresh bread crumbs*
½ *cup freshly grated Parmesan cheese*
½ *teaspoon salt*
¼ *teaspoon freshly ground black pepper*
2 *tablespoons chopped parsley*

Preheat oven to 350°. Remove stems from mushroom caps. Chop stems finely and sauté with garlic in 4 tablespoons of the butter. Add the crumbs, Parmesan, salt, pepper and parsley. Sauté the caps briefly in 3 tablespoons of remaining butter. Fill the caps with the stuffing and place in shallow, buttered casserole dish. Melt remaining butter and drizzle over tops. Bake 15 minutes and serve very hot. May be prepared for baking the day before. Makes 24.

Seafood Stuffed Mushrooms

Norma Calabro
Parent
Pawtucket, Rhode Island

¾ *cup cracker crumbs*
½ *cup minced langostinos, shrimp or crabmeat*
½ *cup bread crumbs*
1 *tablespoon lemon juice*
1 *tablespoon mayonnaise*
1 *tablespoon butter*
¼ *teaspoon minced garlic*
salt and pepper, to taste
48 *mushrooms, caps cleaned, stems removed*

Preheat oven to 350°. Combine cracker crumbs, langostinos, bread crumbs, lemon juice, mayonnaise, butter, garlic, salt and pepper. Fill mushroom caps. Bake 20 minutes. May be prepared two days ahead. Bake just before serving. Makes 48.

Onion Olé

1	cup mayonnaise
1	lb. sharp Cheddar cheese, grated
½	cup sliced scallions
¼	cup drained, chopped, pimiento-stuffed green olives
1	teaspoon capers
6	English muffins, split
2	tablespoons grated Parmesan cheese

Preheat oven to 375°. Combine mayonnaise, Cheddar cheese and onions, and beat until fairly smooth. Stir in olives and capers. Spread cheese mixture evenly over each muffin half. Sprinkle with Parmesan cheese. Cut into quarters. Bake 15 minutes or until cheese is bubbly. Serve hot. May be refrigerated for two days before baking. Makes 48.

Helen Haft Goldstein
SSW '48
Cary, North Carolina

Zucchini Artichoke Squares

2	jars marinated artichoke hearts
1	onion, minced
1	clove garlic, crushed
1	cup grated zucchini
4	eggs
¼	cup bread crumbs
½	teaspoon salt
½	teaspoon pepper
½	teaspoon oregano
½	teaspoon cayenne
½	lb. sharp Cheddar cheese, grated
2	tablespoons minced parsley

Preheat oven to 325°. Drain oil from one jar of artichokes into frying pan. Sauté onions and garlic in artichoke oil over low heat for 5 minutes. Add zucchini and cook 5 minutes more. Add minced artichokes. Beat eggs in a bowl. Add bread crumbs, salt, pepper, oregano, cayenne, Cheddar, parsley and vegetable mixture. Butter a 7x11 inch pan. Pour in mixture. Bake 30 minutes until set. Cut into squares. This may be made in advance and heated. Serve warm. Makes about 75.

These are the simplest, tastiest hors d'oeuvres. They may be made ahead of time so you aren't fussing with cheese puffs or pieces of dough at party time.

Carla Kindt SED'75
Development Office
Bill Beckett
SED'76/SSW'78

Kugeli

Lorraine Wysoskie Hurley
SED'67/'69
Chairwoman
Cookbook Committee
Newtown, Connecticut

6 *large potatoes, peeled, grated, drained*
1 *onion, chopped*
½ *cup bacon drippings*
3 *tablespoons flour*
½ *teaspoon baking powder*
3 *eggs*
salt and pepper, to taste
sour cream

Preheat oven to 350°. In a skillet, sauté the onion in bacon fat. In a bowl, combine the potatoes, onions, flour, baking powder, salt and pepper. Mix well. Beat the eggs and stir into the potatoes. Butter a 12x7½x2 inch baking dish. Add the potato mixture and bake 1 hour or until golden. Cut into 50 squares to serve as an hors d'oeuvre or larger pieces if served as a main dish. Serve with sour cream. Can be frozen and reheated. Serves 6 or makes 50 hors d'oeuvres.

Zucchini Sticks

Nancy Marsh Hartman
SFA'52
Mason Hartman CLA'49
Past President
Friends of the Libraries
Needham, Massachusetts

3 *cups thinly sliced zucchini*
1 *cup Bisquick baking mix*
½ *cup minced scallion*
½ *cup grated Parmesan cheese*
2 *tablespoons minced parsley*
½ *teaspoon salt*
½ *teaspoon dried marjoram or oregano leaves*
dash pepper
¼ *teaspoon minced garlic*
½ *cup vegetable oil*
4 *eggs, slightly beaten*

Preheat oven to 350°. Butter a 13x9x2 inch baking pan. In a bowl, combine zucchini, Bisquick, scallion, Parmesan, parsley, salt, marjoram or oregano, pepper, garlic, oil and eggs. Mix well. Spread in pan. Bake 35 minutes or until golden. Cut into 2x1 inch rectangles. Can be reheated. Makes about 48 pieces.

Clam Stuffed Shells

30 Ritz crackers, crumbled
10 oz. can whole baby clams, juice reserved
3 tablespoons minced onions
3 tablespoons Worcestershire sauce
1/3 cup butter, melted
1/4 teaspoon minced garlic

Barbara Lanciani SED'66
Cookbook Committee
Leominster, Massachusetts

In a 2 quart bowl, mix crackers, clams, onion, Worcestershire, butter and garlic. Add enough reserved juice to make moist. Place in 8 small, warmed clam shells or china substitutes. Bake at 350° for 25 to 30 minutes. May be made a day ahead. Bake just before serving. Makes 8.

Clams Casino

1 can minced clams, drained, juice reserved
1/4 cup Italian bread crumbs
2 tablespoons minced onion
1 tablespoon oil

Judy Walker Tait SPC'62
Rockville, Maryland

Preheat oven to 350°. In a bowl, combine clams, bread crumbs, onions and oil. Add just enough reserved juice to moisten. Fill 20 small clam shells or 10 large shells. Serve hot. May be prepared a day before and heated just before serving. Makes 10 to 20.

White Wine Clam Puffs

8 oz. cream cheese
1/4 cup dry white wine
7 oz. minced clams, drained
24 toast rounds
4 slices bacon, cut in squares

This is scrumptious.

Denise Obertie SON'73
Danville, Pennsylvania

Preheat broiler. Blend cream cheese with wine until smooth. Stir in clams. Spread on toast rounds. Top with bacon squares. Broil 5 minutes or until bacon is crisp. Mixture may be made ahead, but do not spread on toast or broil until just before serving. Makes 24.

Baked Stuffed Clams

Originated and enjoyed in
Boston's North End
waterfront

Douglas Parker SFA '67
Senior Designer
University Relations

12 littlenecks or cherrystone clams
½ cup bread crumbs
4 tablespoons olive oil
2 tablespoons minced fresh Italian parsley
1 tablespoon grated Parmesan cheese
1 clove garlic, pressed
¼ teaspoon oregano (or to taste)
salt and pepper, to taste
2 pieces of bacon, cut to 2 inch lengths
pimiento or sweet roasted red peppers, cut in strips
lemon wedges

Shuck clams and place meat on larger half-shell. Combine bread crumbs, olive oil, parsley, Parmesan cheese, garlic, oregano and salt and pepper and cover clams with a layer of the mixture. Garnish with a small piece of bacon on each stuffed clam and a strip of pimiento on top of the bacon. Bake in hot oven (375° to 400°) for about 6 minutes or until crumbs are brown and the bacon is cooked. Serve with cocktail forks and wedges of lemon.

Crab Meat Fondue

Mary Ross Finn
The late wife of
Daniel J. Finn
Vice President for
University Relations

2 cups thick, hot white sauce
1 lb. crab meat, flaked
1 lb. mild Cheddar cheese
¼ cup dry sherry (or to taste)
1 teaspoon dry mustard (or to taste)
1 teaspoon Worcestershire sauce (or to taste)
1 teaspoon cayenne
½ teaspoon paprika
salt, to taste
French bread cubes

In a chafing dish, combine sauce, crab, Cheddar, sherry, mustard, Worcestershire, cayenne, paprika and salt. Serve warm with French bread. May be made the day before and reheated. Makes about 4 cups.

Crab Meat Won Ton

1	lb. crab meat
1	lb. cream cheese
1	egg yolk
1	teaspoon salt
1/2	teaspoon white pepper
1	package won ton or egg roll skin
	oil for deep frying

Don Batting SPC'57
Vice President
General Alumni Association
Medfield, Massachusetts

Sauce for dipping

1	cup salad oil
1/2	cup ketchup
1/3	cup vinegar
1/3	cup honey
2	tablespoons lemon juice
2	tablespoons soy sauce
2	teaspoons Worcestershire sauce
1	teaspoon salt
1	large onion

In a bowl, combine crab meat, cheese, egg yolk, salt and pepper. Place ½ teaspoon of mixture in center of square won ton skin. Fold diagonally into a triangle. Seal with raw egg yolk or milk along edges. Heat oil to 375°. Fry until golden brown and crisp. Serve hot with dipping sauce. In a blender or processor combine salad oil, onion, ketchup, vinegar, honey, lemon juice, soy sauce, Worcestershire and salt. Serve with won tons. Can be frozen and reheated. Makes about 75.

S. White ENG'68

Saté Ajam *(Indonesian Skewered Chicken)*

1 clove garlic, minced
2 teaspoons lime juice
1 teaspoon salt
1 teaspoon brown sugar
1 teaspoon water
1 teaspoon imported soy sauce
½ teaspoon molasses
dash pepper
dash coriander
2 chicken breasts, skinned, boned, 1 inch squares
2 tablespoons vegetable oil

In a bowl, combine garlic, lime juice, salt, sugar, water, soy sauce, molasses, pepper and coriander. Add chicken and marinate 1 hour at room temperature or overnight, refrigerated. Preheat broiler. Thread chicken on skewers. Brush with oil and broil 5 minutes on each side or until brown and crisp. Serve with Katjang Saos. May be prepared for broiling 24 hours before. Serves 6 to 8.

Katjang Saos (Indonesian Peanut Sauce)

½ cup salted peanuts
2 tablespoons vegetable oil
¼ cup chopped scallions
1 clove garlic, minced
1 teaspoon lemon juice
4 teaspoons soy sauce
¼ teaspoon ground ginger
dash Tabasco sauce (or to taste)

In a blender, combine peanuts, oil, scallions and garlic. Blend until smooth. Add lemon juice, soy sauce, ginger and Tabasco. Blend. Pour into saucepan and heat. Keeps one week refrigerated. Makes 2 cups.

Barbecued Chicken Wings

3 *lbs. halved chicken wings, without wing tips*
½ *cup soy sauce*
½ *cup honey*
⅓ *cup lemon juice or vinegar*
4 *or 5 slices gingerroot*
½ *teaspoon dry mustard*
⅛ *teaspoon chili powder*
2 *tablespoons sherry*
salt, to taste

Preheat oven to 375°. In a saucepan, combine soy sauce, honey, lemon juice, gingerroot, mustard, chili powder and salt to taste. Simmer 2 minutes. Place wings in a shallow pan. Pour on half the sauce. Bake 45 minutes, basting often with remaining sauce until the wings are a deep mahogany. Serve hot or cold. May be made two days ahead. Makes about 24.

These are definitely finger foods and should be served with plenty of extra napkins.

Sterne Barnett CBA '35
Cookbook Committee
Chestnut Hill, Massachusetts

Chinese Chicken Wings

2½ *lbs. or more halved chicken wings, without wing tips*
¼ *cup soy sauce*
2 *scallions, cut in ¼ inch pieces*
¼ *teaspoon ground ginger*
2 *tablespoons sherry*
1 *clove garlic, crushed*

Combine the soy sauce, scallions, ginger, sherry and garlic. Add chicken wings. Cover and marinate overnight. Preheat oven to 350°. Drain chicken and place in baking dish. Bake 30 minutes. Put under broiler to crisp. Can be frozen. Makes about 24.

Carol Ekster SED '73
Andover, Massachusetts

Sweet and Sour Chicken Wings

Never fails to win
applause

Elizabeth Latour Freeman
CLA '61
Waltham, Massachusetts

3 lbs. halved chicken wings, without wing tips

½ cup soy sauce

4 tablespoons sweet and sour sauce

4 tablespoons cooking oil

2 tablespoons sugar

salt and pepper, to taste

Preheat oven to 350°. In a baking pan, combine soy sauce, sweet and sour sauce, oil, sugar and salt and pepper. Add chicken wings. Bake 40 to 45 minutes, or until done.

Rumaki

Mary Ross Finn
The late wife of
Daniel J. Finn
*Vice President for
University Relations*

1 cup soy sauce

1 cup chicken broth

¼ cup dark brown sugar

½ teaspoon powdered ginger

1 pound chicken livers, halved

1 pound bacon, halved

Preheat oven to 375°. In a saucepan, combine the soy sauce, chicken broth, sugar and ginger. Simmer 5 minutes. Add livers and simmer 10 minutes. Cool. Wrap each piece of liver in a piece of bacon and hold together with a wooden toothpick. Place in pan and bake until bacon is cooked but not crunchy. May be prepared for baking the day before. Makes about 48.

Variation: Marinate 1 can water chestnuts, sliced in half, for 6 hours, then wrap in bacon, as above, instead of using livers.

Sweet and Sour Meatballs

1 lb. ground beef
1 small onion, minced
½ cup bread crumbs
1 egg, lightly beaten
1 teaspoon salt and pepper
1 teaspoon mustard
⅛ teaspoon minced garlic
1 8 oz. can tomato sauce
1 can water
juice of 1½ lemons
¼ cup sugar

Mrs. Samuel Wexler
Friend of Boston University
Chestnut Hill, Massachusetts

Combine beef, onion, bread crumbs, egg, salt, pepper, mustard and garlic. Mix well and shape into 30 to 40 meatballs. In a saucepan, combine the tomato sauce, water, juice and sugar. Add meatballs and simmer until cooked through, about 40 minutes. Can be frozen.

Sweet and Sour Meatballs

2 lbs. round steak, ground
1 large potato, peeled, grated
1 large onion, grated
2 eggs
8 oz. bottle chili sauce
8 oz. jar grape jelly
1 cup water
1 clove garlic
½ teaspoon thyme
1 teaspoon salt
pepper
parsley

The chief entertainment value of this hors d'oeuvre is having your guests try to figure out what flavors are in the sauce.

Natalie McCracken
Assistant to the Dean
College of Liberal Arts

Preheat oven to 350°. In a bowl, combine ground steak, potato, onion and eggs. Shape into small balls and place on baking sheet. Bake until cooked through, 10 minutes. In a saucepan, simmer chili sauce, grape jelly, water, garlic, thyme, salt and pepper, 30 minutes. Add meatballs and simmer 20 minutes. Can be made ahead and frozen. Makes about 60.

Swedish Meatballs

This can be used as an
hors d'oeuvre, or if you
make the meatballs big-
ger, it makes a terrific
main dish.

Lenore Ryan
Administrative Secretary
School for the Arts

1 lb. ground round
½ lb. pork tenderloin, ground once
3 eggs, beaten
2 tablespoons flour
1 teaspoon salt
¼ teaspoon pepper
¼ cup salad oil
2 tablespoons flour
1 can undiluted condensed consommé
1 teaspoon Bovril or Kitchen Bouquet
½ cup sherry

Mix meats, eggs, salt, pepper and 2 tablespoons flour
until blended. Form very lightly into 50 meatballs. In a
hot skillet, brown meatballs and remove. Stir 2 tablespoons flour until smooth into oil left in skillet. Cook
until medium brown. Add consommé and Bovril.
Return meatballs to skillet. Simmer covered 5 minutes.
Add sherry. Can be frozen and reheated. Makes 50.

Kuo-Teh *(Potstickers)*

These are called Pot-
stickers in San Francisco
and because I'm from Cal-
ifornia, that's the term I
use. On the East Coast,
people call them Chinese
ravioli.

Carla Kindt SED '75
Development Office
Bill Beckett
SED '76/SSW '78

48 round won ton skins
vegetable oil
¼ cup beef or chicken stock

Place a won ton skin on the counter top with 2 teaspoons of filling, moisten edges and fold over to make
a half moon. Traditionally, one side of the turnover is
pleated and pressed against the other. Set aside. Can be
frozen for a month. To cook, pour a film of oil in the
bottom of a frying pan with a tight lid. Heat medium
high. Add potstickers with seam side up. Cook until bot-
toms are dark brown. Pour in stock. Cover tightly and
simmer 10 minutes, 15 minutes if frozen. Serve with
dipping sauce. Makes about 48.

Shrimp Filling

½ lb. raw shrimp, minced
½ lb. pork, ground
1 cup shredded Chinese cabbage

¼	*cup minced scallion*
¼	*cup minced onion*
2	*tablespoons soy sauce*
1	*clove garlic, minced*
½	*teaspoon salt*

Combine shrimp, pork, cabbage, scallion, onion, soy sauce, garlic and salt. Mix well.

Pork and Onion Filling

1¼	*lb. pork, diced*
2	*tablespoons soy sauce*
1	*tablespoon honey*
2	*cloves garlic, minced*
2	*tablespoons minced scallions*
1	*tablespoon vegetable oil*
2	*tablespoons sherry*
2	*teaspoons cornstarch*
	salt and pepper, to taste

Simmer pork, soy sauce, honey, garlic and scallions in oil until well browned. Combine sherry and cornstarch and stir into pork mixture. Simmer until thickened. Season with salt and pepper.

Beef and Ginger Filling

¾	*lb. ground lean beef*
1	*cup chopped bean sprouts*
1	*onion, minced*
1	*tablespoon minced ginger*
½	*teaspoon salt*
¼	*teaspoon cayenne*

Combine the beef, bean sprouts, onion, ginger, salt and cayenne.

Chili Dipping Sauce

½	*cup soy sauce*
2	*tablespoons beef stock*
1	*teaspoon hot chili oil*
1	*teaspoon sesame oil*

Combine soy sauce, beef stock, chili oil and sesame oil.

Hot Salami and Cheese in Phyllo Triangles

Neila Straub SED '70
Beverly, Massachusetts

½ lb. phyllo leaves
¼ lb. butter, melted
10 oz. frozen chopped spinach, thawed, well drained
½ cup chopped salami
½ cup shredded Cheddar cheese
1 egg, beaten

Preheat oven to 400°. Place 1 sheet phyllo on work surface. Brush with melted butter and top with second sheet. Cut into 6 strips, each 2 inches wide. Combine salami, cheese, spinach and egg. Place rounded teaspoonful of filling at 1 end of strip. Fold 1 corner to opposite side, forming a triangle shape. Continue folding, keeping triangle shape, to other end of strip. Brush with melted butter. Repeat with remaining strips. Arrange pastries on lightly buttered baking sheet. Bake 10 minutes or until golden. Serve hot. Can be frozen and reheated. Makes about 24.

Spiced Pecans

Carolyn Payne
*Cookbook Committee
Coordinator
University Functions*

1 lb. pecans, shelled
1 egg white, beaten stiff with 1 teaspoon water and ½ teaspoon salt
½ cup sugar, mixed with ½ teaspoon cinnamon

Preheat oven to 200°. Thoroughly coat pecans with egg white mixture, then with sugar mixture. Spread on a greased cookie sheet in a single layer. Bake 1 hour, stirring every 15 minutes. Can be frozen. Makes 1 pound.

Miniature Reuben Sandwiches

36 slices party rye
Thousand Island salad dressing, to taste
4 oz. cooked corned beef, thinly sliced
8 oz. sauerkraut, drained, minced
6 slices Swiss cheese

Preheat oven to 400°. Spread each slice of rye with a little of the salad dressing, top with a thin slice of corned beef and cover with a teaspoon of sauerkraut. Cut each slice of cheese into 6 pieces and place on top. Bake 6 to 8 minutes or until cheese melts and appetizers are heated through. Serve immediately. May be prepared for baking two hours ahead. Makes 36.

Perfect for a party

Barbara Goulson Arceneaux
PAL '54
Cookbook Committee
Jacksonville, Florida

Shrimp Toast

½ lb. raw shrimp, minced
4 water chestnuts, chopped
½ teaspoon sugar
1 tablespoon cornstarch
1 egg, lightly beaten
2 tablespoons minced shallots
6 slices wheat bread, crusts removed
oil (to fill center of wok; use as little as possible)

Mix shrimp, chestnuts, sugar, cornstarch, egg and shallots. Spread each slice of bread with ⅙ of mixture. Heat oil in wok. Lower slice of bread, shrimp side up and cook until golden on all sides. Drain very well. Repeat for each slice. Chill until firm. Slice each piece into 4 triangles. Heat in oven. Serve with duck sauce. Thirty minutes preparation time. Makes 24.

Laura Freid
Editor
Bostonia Magazine

Mock Kahlua *(Coffee Liqueur)*

Amy Glick Korman
CLA'74
Pittsburgh, Pennsylvania
Debbi Calabro
Friend of Boston University
Pawtucket, Rhode Island

3 cups sugar
3 oz. instant coffee
2 cups water
1 quart vodka
2 vanilla beans, split lengthwise

In a 2 quart saucepan combine sugar, water and coffee. Heat over low heat until the sugar has dissolved. Cool. Put in a 1 gallon glass jug. Add the vodka and vanilla beans. Let steep for 30 days. Remove vanilla beans. Keeps indefinitely. Makes 2 quarts.

Hot Buttered Rum Cider

Patti Marcus SAR'72
Cookbook Committee
Brighton, Massachusetts

My father taught me how to make this. I grew up going to football games and this was a special treat at halftimes.

1 cup brown sugar
1 cup boiling water
3 quarts cider
1 quart dark rum
2 tablespoons butter
cinnamon, to taste

Dissolve sugar in water. Add cider and bring to a boil. Add rum and butter. Ladle into cups. Sprinkle cinnamon on top. Keep warm in chafing dish. Serves 16.

Minted Lemon Orange Iced Tea

10	mint leaves
¾	cup sugar
7	tea bags
2	cups boiling water
1	can frozen lemon juice, thawed
1	cup orange juice
6	cups water

Betsy Wilson
John Wilson
Assistant Dean
School of Law

In a bowl, combine mint, sugar, tea and water. Let macerate for 2 hours. Strain. Stir in lemon juice, orange juice and water. Keeps three days refrigerated. Serves 8 to 10.

Golden Cooler

2	cups orange juice
1	ripe banana
2	heaping teaspoons chocolate flavored coffee
	juice of 1 lime
	lime slices

Amy Glick Korman
CLA'74
Pittsburgh, Pennsylvania

In a blender, purée the orange juice, banana, instant coffee, and lime juice. Serve in tall glasses garnished with lime slices. Keeps 24 hours. Serves 2.

Scotch Eggs

These are ideal for brunches, after theater suppers and picnics and can be served either hot or cold.

Danny Staples
CGE'68/CLA'72/GRS'78
Boston, Massachusetts

7 eggs
1 lb. sausage meat
1 medium onion, minced
1 clove garlic, crushed
1 tablespoon minced parsley
1 teaspoon salt
½ teaspoon crushed thyme
fresh ground pepper, to taste
2 cups bread crumbs
1 teaspoon paprika

Hard cook 6 of the eggs. Chill under cold running water and peel. Combine sausage meat, onion, garlic, parsley, salt, thyme, pepper and remaining egg. Mix thoroughly. Divide into 6 equal parts and shape into thin patties. Encircle each hard cooked egg with the sausage so that it is evenly covered, as if you were making a snowball. When all 6 eggs have been encased, roll them liberally in the bread crumbs. Set in an ungreased baking dish an inch or so apart and sprinkle tops with paprika. Chill in refrigerator for 1 hour. Set oven at 325° and bake for 45 minutes or until golden brown (or heat oil for frying to 375° and fry until golden). Serve, at room temperature, whole or cut the eggs in half, exposing the yolk, white and sausage. Can be kept four days. Serves 6 to 12.

2 Soups

Soups

2

Cold Spicy Avocado Soup

1 large ripe avocado, peeled, seeded
1½ cups chicken broth, heated
1 small clove garlic, minced
¼ teaspoon Tabasco sauce
1 tablespoon lemon juice
¾ cup heavy cream
¾ cup sour cream
fresh dill or chopped chives
salt and pepper, to taste

It is important to use ripe, soft avocados, preferably Californian.

Andrea Bell SAR '77
Cookbook Committee
Manhattan Beach, California

Cut avocado into pieces and place in blender with chicken broth. Blend until smooth. Add garlic, Tabasco and lemon juice. Blend again. Combine with cream, sour cream, salt and pepper to taste. Chill. Serve in chilled glass bowls with a dollop of sour cream and sprinkle of dill or chopped chives for garnish. May be made a day ahead. Serves 6.

Cold Avocado Soup

Gail Ucko CLA '78
Fort Lauderdale, Florida

2 cups peeled, sliced avocado
2 cups chicken stock
½ teaspoon onion juice
1 cup light cream
1 cup sour cream
salt and pepper, to taste
paprika, parsley, finely sliced scallion

In a blender, combine avocado, chicken stock and onion juice. Purée. Put into bowl and beat in creams, salt and pepper. Chill. Serve sprinkled with paprika, parsley and scallion as garnish. May be made ahead. Serves 6.

Cold Cucumber Soup

Always serve this soup in chilled bowls. It's a delightful summer specialty.

Andrea Bell SAR '77
Cookbook Committee
Manhattan Beach, California

½ onion, diced
2 large cucumbers, unpeeled, diced
¾ cup diced raw potatoes
1 sprig parsley
2 tablespoons butter
2 stems fresh dill
2¼ cups chicken broth
¼ teaspoon white pepper
½ cup heavy cream, sour cream or yogurt

In a 2 quart saucepan, sauté onion in butter until soft. Add cucumbers, potatoes, parsley, dill, chicken broth and pepper. Simmer until tender. Purée in blender or processor. Chill. Correct seasoning with salt and pepper. Stir in heavy cream. May be prepared two days ahead. Serves 4.

Cucumber Soup

3 *cucumbers, peeled, grated*

3 *cups yogurt, sour cream and/or buttermilk*

3 *cloves garlic, crushed*

3 *tablespoons minced fresh dill*

1 *tablespoon salt*

Drain excess water from cucumbers. Put in a bowl and stir in yogurt, sour cream or buttermilk or a combination. Stir in garlic, dill and salt. Chill 24 hours. Keeps four days refrigerated. Serves 6.

My mother's cooking policy was to make things that needed only one dish to prepare. Her cucumber soup recipe requires no work, and it tastes wonderful.

Arlene S. Ash
Professor
Department of Mathematics
College of Liberal Arts

Gazpacho, Malaga-style

4 *oz. blanched almonds*

2 *cloves garlic*

1 *teaspoon salt*

4 *slices day old bread*

6 *tablespoons olive oil*

3 *tablespoons red wine vinegar*

4 *cups ice water*

croutons

48 *seedless grapes, peeled*

Blend almonds, garlic and salt in a blender or processor until the almonds are finely ground. Soak the bread in cold water. Squeeze to extract most of the moisture. Add bread to almond mixture and blend. Add oil and vinegar. Beat in 1 cup of water. Transfer soup to a large bowl. Stir in the remaining 3 cups of water. Add more salt and vinegar if desired. Chill. Serve very cold, garnished with croutons and grapes. May be prepared two days ahead. Serves 6.

Cookbook Committee

Gazpacho

Susan K. Moger CLA '73
Cookbook Committee
Los Angeles, California

2 *cloves garlic, minced*
2 *tablespoons vegetable oil*
2 *medium fresh tomatoes, peeled, seeded, diced*
½ *green pepper, grated*
½ *onion, grated*
½ *cucumber, grated*
2 *tablespoons red wine vinegar*
2 *tablespoons lemon juice*
24 *oz. tomato juice*
4 *oz. bay shrimp, cooked*

Sauté garlic in oil. Add list of ingredients, except shrimp, and chill for 4 hours. Serve in soup bowls and garnish with a few bay shrimp. May be made two days ahead. Serves 6.

Cold Orange Soup

An excellent soup for the afternoon

Dr. Prakash Lulla SGD '71
Cookbook Committee
Bombay, India

24 *oz. orange juice*
3 *cups water*
3 *tablespoons sugar*
1 *tablespoon lemon juice*
1 *tablespoon cornstarch*
1 *teaspoon orange or lemon rind*
1 *egg white*
2 *teaspoons powdered sugar*

In a 1 quart saucepan, combine orange juice, water, sugar, lemon juice, cornstarch and orange or lemon rind. Simmer 10 minutes. Chill. When ready to serve, whip the egg white until stiff, beating in the powdered sugar. Put soup into bowls and top with meringue. May be prepared a day ahead. Serves 8.

Melon Soup

1	large ripe cantalope or honeydew, peeled, seeded, chopped
2	cups orange juice
2	tablespoons lime juice
½	teaspoon cinnamon
	fresh mint, chopped

In a blender, combine melon, orange juice, lime juice, and cinnamon. Purée, correct seasoning. Garnish with mint. Serve cold. May be made a day ahead. Serves 6.

Peg Wallace LAW '76
Brookline, Massachusetts

Canadian Cheese Soup

½	cup butter
½	cup chopped celery
½	cup minced green pepper
½	cup minced onion
½	cup minced carrot
1	pint chicken stock
6	tablespoons flour
3	cups milk
1	cup light cream
2	cups grated Cheddar cheese
1	teaspoon salt
	pinch pepper

In 3 tablespoons of butter, sauté the celery, pepper, onion and carrots for 5 or 6 minutes. Add chicken stock and simmer until vegetables are just tender. Purée vegetables and stock in blender. Melt remaining butter and stir in flour; blend well and gradually add milk and cream. Cook, stirring constantly, until thickened and smooth. Add cheese and stir until melted. Season and combine with vegetable mixture. Serve hot. Can be reheated. Serves 6.

I got this recipe from a woman who worked in the cafeteria of the John Hancock Building in Boston. How she reduced the portions I'll never know.

Claire Shapiro Soja CLA '68
Cookbook Committee
Harvard, Massachusetts

Cream of Curried Barley Soup

This is a complete meal in itself. The milk and the barley provide total protein requirements.

Claire Shapiro Soja
CLA '68
Cookbook Committee
Harvard, Massachusetts

1 stalk celery, finely chopped
1 small onion, finely chopped
1 carrot, finely chopped
½ stick butter
¼ cup vegetable oil
3 tablespoons flour
2 tablespoons dry chicken bouillon powder
½ cup barley
3½ cups milk
¼ cup white wine
2 oz. pimientos, chopped
½ teaspoon curry powder
½ teaspoon white pepper

In a 3 quart saucepan, sauté celery, onion and carrot in butter and oil until tender crisp. Stir in flour, bouillon powder and barley. Add milk, wine, pimientos, curry and pepper. Just barely simmer until the barley is cooked and the soup has thickened, about 45 minutes. Do not allow to boil. Can be reheated. Serves 4 to 6.

Wild and Crazy Stew

Good for large groups

Nancy Barton SED '77
Rehoboth, Delaware

¼ lb. bacon, chopped
1 medium onion, chopped
2 cups water
4 medium potatoes, diced
1 can tomato purée
1 lb. can kidney beans
salt and pepper, to taste

In a large casserole dish, sauté bacon and onion until browned. Add water and potatoes and simmer until tender. Stir in purée and beans. Correct seasoning. Simmer 20 minutes. May be made ahead. Serves 6.

Big Momma's Busytime Bean Soup

1 cup chopped onion
1 clove garlic, crushed
10 cups water or vegetable stock
1 cup black turtle beans, rinsed
1 cup white navy beans, rinsed
1 cup kidney beans, rinsed
¾ cup brown barley, rinsed
½ cup brown rice, rinsed
1 bay leaf
1 tablespoon celery seed
1 cup chopped carrot
1 cup chopped potato
½ cup chopped green pepper
½ cup chopped celery
1 tablespoon oregano, thyme or dill
salt and pepper, to taste
1 head Swiss chard or lettuce, chopped

A favorite recipe guaranteed to turn you into an overnight 'bean nut'!

J. A. Pollard Garrett
SFA '56
Waterville, Maine

In a large kettle, preferably iron, sweat the onion and garlic until soft. Add the water or stock to the turtle beans and navy beans. Simmer 1 hour. Add the carrot, potato, pepper and celery. Stir in the thyme, salt and pepper to taste. Simmer 45 minutes. Stir in the chard or lettuce. Simmer 15 minutes longer. Serve with salad and homemade bread. Makes about 10 servings

Chili Bean Soup

This is a hearty whole-meal soup. Serve with steamed corn tortillas.

Andrea Bell **SAR** '77
Cookbook Committee
Manhattan Beach, California

2 large onions, diced
2 cloves garlic, minced
2 tablespoons corn oil
1 heaping tablespoon chili powder
2 quarts beef stock
2 cans chili beans or kidney beans
1 lb. can plum tomatoes
3 tablespoons sugar
1 cup Monterey Jack cheese (optional)
3 tablespoons minced onion

Sauté onions and garlic in 2 tablespoons corn oil until golden. Mix in chili powder. Add beef stock, beans, tomatoes and sugar. Simmer for 50 minutes. Before serving, add 1 cup finely grated Monterey Jack cheese, if desired. Mix well so cheese is completely melted. Top with a teaspoon of raw chopped onion. Serves 8.

Lithuanian Borsch

Lorraine Wysoskie Hurley
SED '67/'69
Chairwoman
Cookbook Committee
Newtown, Connecticut

16 oz. can whole beets
1 cucumber, peeled, grated
1 small onion, minced
2 tablespoons minced dill
salt and pepper, to taste
3 to 4 tablespoons vinegar
2 to 3 tablespoons sour cream

Drain beets, reserving the juice, and grate into a bowl. Combine with cucumber, onion and dill. Measure beet juice and add enough water to make 1½ quarts. Add to beets. Season with salt and pepper. Chill. In a separate bowl, combine vinegar and sour cream. Add shortly before serving. Keeps two days refrigerated. Serves 6.

Cream of Broccoli Soup

1 bunch broccoli, cut into florets, slice stems
1 onion, chopped
4 cups stock
3 tablespoons butter
3 tablespoons flour
1 cup milk
1 cup medium cream
salt, pepper and nutmeg, to taste

Lorraine Nelson Klein
GRS '76
Cookbook Committee
North Kingston,
Rhode Island

Steam onion and broccoli until tender. Purée in blender, using as much stock as necessary. In a saucepan, melt butter and stir in flour. Add milk and blend until smooth. Do not boil. Add broccoli purée, remaining stock and cream. Add salt, pepper and nutmeg to taste. May be made two days ahead. Serve hot or cold. Serves 4.

Variation: Stir in ½ cup yogurt.

Corn Chowder

½ cup butter
1 medium onion, minced
½ cup minced carrot
4 tablespoons flour
1 qt. milk, scalded
1¼ teaspoons salt
¼ teaspoon pepper
½ teaspoon parsley
2 16 oz. cans cream style corn

Sandra J. Levine **SED '59**
Cookbook Committee
Newtonville, Massachusetts

In a saucepan, melt butter. Sauté onion and carrot until soft but not brown. Add flour and corn until bubbling. Stir in milk, salt, pepper and parsley. Bring to a simmer, stirring. Add corn and reheat. May be made two to three days before. Serves 4 to 6.

Linsensuppe

Recipe from an embassy
wife who has lived abroad
most of her life

Pat Bjaaland
CLA '67/GRS '68
Cookbook Committee
Oslo, Norway

2 cups lentils
1 qt. water
2 large onions, chopped
6 slices meaty bacon, diced
2 tablespoons butter
4 cups beef stock
1 cup dry red wine
2 carrots, sliced
2 bay leaves
1 clove garlic
1½ teaspoons thyme
1½ teaspoons oregano
2 potatoes, peeled, diced
salt and pepper, to taste
croutons

Soak lentils in water overnight. In a large casserole dish,
sauté onions and bacon in butter until onions are
golden. Stir in the lentils and beef stock, wine, carrots,
bay leaves, garlic, thyme and oregano. Simmer covered
for 45 minutes. Add potatoes and more wine, if desired.
Simmer 2 to 3 hours. Correct seasoning with salt and
pepper. Serve with croutons. Can be frozen. Serves 6
to 8.

Cream of Mushroom Soup

Lorraine Nelson Klein
GRS '76
Cookbook Committee
North Kingston,
Rhode Island

2 onions, minced
3 tablespoons butter
3 tablespoons oil
3 cups minced mushrooms
4 tablespoons flour
4 cups chicken stock
½ cup light cream
salt, pepper and nutmeg, to taste
¼ cup heavy cream

Sauté onion in oil and butter until transparent. Add mushrooms and cook 3 minutes. Blend in flour and cook 1 minute. Add chicken stock and bring to boil. Blend until smooth and cook over low heat for 5 minutes. Add light cream, salt, pepper and nutmeg. Cook 5 minutes; do not boil. Add heavy cream, blend and serve. May be made two to three days ahead. Serves 4.

Cream of Mushroom Sherry Soup

4 cups chicken stock
1 lb. mushrooms
2 tablespoons butter
3 tablespoons flour
1 teaspoon salt
dash white pepper
dash dry mustard
dash cayenne
2 cups heavy cream
1/3 cup dry sherry
3 tablespoons whipped heavy cream
3 teaspoons sliced toasted almonds
paprika

Canned cream of mushroom soup has become an institution in the United States. This soup will prove to be a vast improvement.

Andrea Bell SAR '77
Cookbook Committee
Manhattan Beach, California

Place stock, mushroom stems and ½ mushroom caps in blender. Purée and place in saucepan. Cook for ½ hour. Strain, reserving stock. Melt butter in 3 quart saucepan. Whisk in flour, salt, mustard, pepper, cayenne. Cook 1 minute. Add stock, stirring rapidly. Thinly slice remaining mushroom caps and add to soup. Simmer 8 to 10 minutes. Stir in cream and sherry and heat. Serve hot garnished with 1 tablespoon whipped cream, a dash of paprika and slivered, toasted almonds. May be made two days before and reheated. Serves 6.

Onion Soup

Joy Honig SED '76
Chestnut Hill, Massachusetts

6 large onions, sliced

4 tablespoons butter

3½ cups chicken broth

3½ cups beef broth

3 tablespoons Madeira wine

12 thick slices French bread, dried in the oven

¾ cup gruyère cheese

In a kettle, brown the onions in butter until golden. Cover with broth; simmer 40 to 45 minutes. Add wine. Put 1 slice of bread in each soup bowl; top with ½ tablespoon cheese and fill with soup. The bread will float to the surface. Immediately top it with another slice. Sprinkle on additional cheese and brown 2 to 3 minutes under the broiler. May be prepared for broiling several hours ahead. Serves 6.

Onion Soup Gratinée

Formerly a large wholesale market serving the entire city, Les Halles in Paris leaves a glowing tradition, Onion Soup Gratinée being part of that tradition.

Andrea Bell SAR '77
*Cookbook Committee
Manhattan Beach,
California*

6 tablespoons butter

8 onions, sliced

salt and fresh ground black pepper, to taste

2 qts. brown stock

½ cup Madeira wine

½ cup butter

1 clove garlic, minced

6 ⅜ inch slices French bread

6 thin slices gruyère cheese

Melt 6 tablespoons butter and sauté onions until they are soft and golden not browned. Season with salt and pepper. Add stock and simmer for 20 minutes. Add Madeira and lower heat. Melt butter in skillet. Add garlic and sauté until golden. Remove garlic and discard. Sauté bread turning pieces over when browned. Remove bread. Put soup in individual flame-proof bowls. Place on top of each a piece of French bread and a slice of gruyère cheese. Place under broiler until cheese bubbles. Serve immediately. May be prepared for oven several days ahead. Serves 6.

Gule Erte Suppe
(Norwegian Yellow Pea Soup)

2 qts. water
2 teaspoons salt
1 lb. whole yellow peas
1 to 2 qts. beef, chicken or ham stock
1 onion, diced
1 carrot, diced
1 potato, diced
1 cup diced celery
½ lb. pork fat, diced
salt and pepper, to taste
marjoram or thyme, to taste

Pat Bjaaland
CLA '67/GRS '68
Cookbook Committee
Oslo, Norway

In a large kettle, bring water and salt to a boil. Add peas. Boil 10 to 15 minutes. Let sit overnight. Next morning, return to a boil until skins burst. Skim off the skins. Add the stock, onion, carrot, potato, celery and pork fat. Season with salt, pepper, marjoram or thyme. Simmer until the peas are tender. Can be frozen. Serves 6 to 10.

Cream of Potato Soup

4 cups sliced potatoes
2 cups water
2 teaspoons salt
1 small onion, sliced
3 tablespoons butter
4 to 5 sprigs parsley
2 tablespoons flour
3 cups milk
salt and pepper, to taste

Amy Glick Korman
CLA '74
Pittsburgh, Pennsylvania

In a saucepan, simmer potatoes, water and salt until tender. In a skillet, sauté onion in butter until soft. In a blender or processor, combine the potato mixture, onion, parsley and flour. Process until smooth. Put soup into a saucepan, add milk and heat to a simmer. Correct seasoning with salt and pepper.

Velouté Potiron
(Cream of Pumpkin Soup)

I first tasted this soup on the isle of Jamaica and made up my own variation. It's a fancier soup than the work indicates, and it's just as good served cold or hot.

Carol M. Winer CBA '58
Cookbook Committee
Framingham, Massachusetts

1 qt. chicken stock

1 qt. canned pumpkin

1 pt. water

2 cups heavy cream

½ cup crumbled, crisp bacon

In a kettle, combine stock, pumpkin and water. Bring to a boil. Lower heat and slowly add cream, stirring continuously. Serve topped with crumbled bacon. May be made two days ahead. Serves 12 to 14.

Squash Bisque

Beulah Freeman Katz
Friend of Boston University

1 cup minced onion

¼ cup minced carrot

3 tablespoons butter

salt and pepper, to taste

2 potatoes, diced

1½ lbs. squash, diced

4 cups chicken stock

1 cup light cream

cayenne, to taste

In a kettle, sauté the onion and carrot in butter until soft but not brown. Sprinkle with salt and pepper. Add potatoes, squash and chicken stock. Simmer 25 minutes until vegetables are tender. Force through a sieve or food mill. Place in a saucepan; add cream and heat. Correct seasoning with salt, pepper and cayenne. Can be reheated. Serves 6.

The Misses' Parker Tomato Soup

3 qts. ripe tomatoes, sliced
2 qts. water
6 onions, finely sliced
6 tablespoons sugar
3 teaspoons salt
½ teaspoon pepper
30 whole cloves (Yes, that's right, 30!)
sprigs parsley
6 tablespoons cornstarch
1 cup cold water
6 tablespoons butter
½ cup cream, whipped

A favorite of my mother, who got it from two elderly New England spinsters, the Misses Parker, of East Haddam, Connecticut. It is best made in August, when tomatoes are plentiful and inexpensive.

Irene Kampen
20th Century Archives
Mugar Library

In a kettle, combine tomatoes, water, onions, sugar, salt, pepper, cloves and parsley. Boil, then lower heat and simmer until tomatoes are soft. Strain. Dissolve cornstarch in the cold water and stir it back into the hot soup. Cook, stirring until thickened and smooth. Stir in the butter. Correct seasoning with salt and pepper. Serve topped with the whipped cream. Can be frozen. Serves 12.

Scallion Soup

4 cups chicken stock
1 bunch scallions
grated Parmesan cheese

Helen Crawford Bander
SED '31
Cookbook Committee
Paris, Arkansas

In a saucepan, simmer broth. Cut scallion tops in thin slices, reserving white part for another use. Simmer in broth 10 minutes. Sprinkle each serving with grated cheese. Serves 4 to 6.

Fresh Vegetable Minestrone

Helen Crawford Bander
SED '31
Cookbook Committee
Paris, Arkansas

½ cup chopped onions

1 clove garlic, minced

1½ cups diced green peppers

1 cup diced celery

1½ cups chopped tomatoes

¼ cup butter

1 cup diced carrots

1 cup fresh green peas, cooked

2 qts. chicken stock, boiled

¼ cup minced parsley

½ teaspoon pepper

½ teaspoon marjoram

salt, to taste

1 cup diced potatoes

grated Parmesan cheese

In a large kettle, sauté onion, garlic, pepper, celery and tomatoes for 10 minutes, stirring. Add, carrots, peas, stock, parsley, pepper, marjoram. Simmer 45 minutes. Add potatoes and simmer 30 minutes. Taste for seasoning and add salt, if needed. Serve with cheese. Keeps three days refrigerated. Serves 8.

Spinach Soup

Carla Marcus Schair
SED '70
Scarborough, Maine

10 oz. fresh or frozen chopped spinach

2 tablespoons butter

2 tablespoons flour

salt

½ cup chopped onion

1 qt. milk

cayenne, to taste

In a 2 quart pot, melt butter and stir in flour, salt and onion. Cook 5 minutes. Add milk slowly, stirring constantly. In another pan, cook spinach until wilted; drain. Add spinach to milk; season to taste. Mix in blender until smooth. Serve hot or cold. May be served with a dollop of plain yogurt or sour cream. Can be frozen. Serves 6.

Minestrone

½ lb. dry white beans, soaked in water overnight
3 qts. water, salted
¼ lb. bacon or salt pork (optional)
1 clove garlic, minced
1 leek, diced
1 large Spanish onion, chopped
1 tablespoon chopped parsley and stems
¼ lb. mushrooms, sliced
1 green pepper, diced
1 teaspoon olive oil
2½ qts. water
2 potatoes, diced
1 cup shredded cabbage
3 medium tomatoes, chopped
1 cup sliced zucchini
1 small turnip, peeled, diced
2 carrots, finely sliced
3 stalks celery, chopped
3 spinach leaves, chopped
2 cups tomato purée
1 teaspoon oregano
1 teaspoon chopped basil
½ teaspoon rosemary
salt and fresh black pepper, to taste
1 cup macaroni or ditali
grated Parmesan cheese

Called the national soup of Italy, minestrone varies tremendously and has specific regional varieties.

Andrea Bell SAR '77
Cookbook Committee
Manhattan Beach, California

Drain beans and boil them in salted water for 1 hour. Drain. Sauté the salt pork (or bacon), garlic, onion, leek, parsley, mushrooms, green pepper in olive oil until lightly browned. Add 2½ quarts water, potatoes and tomatoes. Cook for 45 minutes. Add the beans and macaroni and cook until macaroni is al dente. Sprinkle Parmesan and serve. May be made ahead and reheated. Serves 8.

New England Clam Chowder

Very rich and satisfying

Roger Caras
20th Century Archives
Mugar Library

5 *lbs. onions, diced*
1 *cup vegetable oil*
4 *(No. 10) cans chicken broth*
5 *lbs. potatoes, peeled, diced*
144 *steamer clams, cleaned*
2 *qts. milk*
1 *qt. heavy cream*
1 *lb. butter*
salt and pepper, to taste
minced chives

Sauté onions in oil until soft but not brown. Drain onions. In a huge kettle, simmer chicken broth, potatoes and onions for 3 hours. In another large kettle, place clams and 1 cup of water. Cover and steam until clams open. Discard those that do not open. Reserve broth. Remove clams from shells. Discard shells. Mince clam meat. Set aside. Add 1 quart of clam broth to chicken broth. Be sure sand is not carried with the clam broth. Simmer 1 hour. One hour before serving, add milk, cream and butter; 30 minutes before serving, add clams. Correct seasoning with salt and pepper. Serve topped with chopped chives. Can be reheated. Serves approximately 50.

Note: Serve with garlic bread, salad and dry, cold wine. Soave is good.

Cape Cod Fish Chowder

| 3 lbs. fresh cod fillets, cut into 2 inch pieces |
| 1 qt. boiling water |
| 1 qt. milk |
| ¼ lb. salt pork, diced |
| 3 large yellow onions, thinly sliced |
| 4 cups thinly sliced raw potatoes |
| salt and pepper, to taste |
| Pilot crackers |

Thomas P. O'Neill, Jr.
HON '73
*Speaker, United States
House of Representatives*

In a soup kettle, fry pork fat until crisp; remove cracklings and save. Cook onions in fat until soft but not brown. Add potatoes and water. Simmer until tender. Add fish and cook for 15 minutes. Add milk and season with salt and pepper. Heat but do not boil. Serve sprinkled with pork cracklings and Pilot crackers. Can be reheated. Serves 8.

Haddock Fish Chowder

| 1 onion, minced |
| 1 tablespoon butter |
| 2 medium carrots, sliced |
| 2 small potatoes, diced |
| 1 lb. haddock, cut into 2 inch pieces |
| 1½ qts. milk |
| salt and pepper, to taste |
| 1 teaspoon minced parsley |

Bernice Lipman
*Friend of Boston University
Wayland, Massachusetts*

Sauté onion in butter until soft but not brown. Place fish on onion. Cover, cook over low heat for 15 minutes. In separate pan, boil carrots and potatoes in a little water until soft. When done, add drained vegetables and milk to fish. Add salt, pepper, parsley. Simmer. Can be reheated. Serves 6.

California Cioppino (Fish Stew)

Nancy Bechtel SED '69/'73
Buzzards Bay, Massachusetts

1 medium onion, chopped

2 cloves garlic, chopped

2 tablespoons chopped parsley

4 medium tomatoes

¼ cup tomato juice

2 lbs. fish (rock, cod, red snapper), cut into bite size pieces

salt and pepper, to taste

Sauté onion, garlic and parsley in oil until lightly browned. Add the tomatoes and juice. Simmer about 15 minutes. Add fish and cook gently 20 to 30 minutes. Season with salt and pepper. Serve immediately in soup plates. Serves 6.

Clams and Prawns Bianco

Jean Solomon
Parent
Cataumet, Massachusetts

3 scallions, thinly sliced

4 cloves garlic, crushed

2 tablespoons olive oil

3 6 oz. bottles clam juice

18 cherrystones or littleneck clams

¾ cup dry white wine

1½ lb. large shrimp (prawns), shelled and deveined

¼ cup chopped parsley

In a Dutch oven or large saucepan, sauté scallions and garlic in olive oil until tender but not brown. Stir in the clam juice and add clams and shrimp. Heat to boiling, then cover. Lower heat and simmer 10 to 12 minutes until clams open. Clams may be added 2 to 3 minutes before the shrimp, if desired. Transfer to a serving bowl or individual large soup plates and sprinkle with parsley. Best if served immediately. Serves 6.

Lobster Bisque

5	tablespoons butter
1	medium onion, finely diced
⅓	cup diced carrots
1	stalk celery, finely diced
½	bay leaf
	pinch of thyme
2	sprigs parsley
1¾	lb. live lobster, split, cleaned and cut into 4 or 5 pieces with cracked claws
3	tablespoons brandy
⅓	cup dry white wine
½	cup fish stock or clam juice
5	tablespoons flour
2	cups milk, scalded
2	cups heavy cream
1	tablespoon Madeira wine

This is a classic. It can become a comfortable part of your cooking repertoire.

Andrea Bell SAR '77
Cookbook Committee
Manhattan Beach, California

Melt 2 tablespoons butter and sauté onion, carrots and celery until onion is translucent. Add bay leaf, thyme, parsley and lobster. Sauté until the lobster turns red or about 5 minutes, stirring occasionally. Flame 2 table-spoons brandy and pour over mixture. Add the wine and stock and simmer 20 minutes. Remove the lobster, cool, and remove the meat from the shell. Dice the meat and set aside. Reserve the shell and broth. Melt the remain-ing butter in a saucepan, add the flour and blend with a whisk. Stir in the milk vigorously. Add the lobster shell and the vegetable mixture. Cover and simmer for 1 hour. Strain through a fine sieve. Add remaining brandy and cream. Correct seasoning. Add lobster and serve. Can be frozen. Serves 4.

Chupe de Camarones

(Peruvian Shrimp Soup)

Ideal for winter—this
hearty recipe is from
Chaquipa, Peru.

Ethel Chirinos SED '75
Cookbook Committee
Lima, Peru

2	tablespoons oil
½	cup onion
	salt and freshly ground black pepper, to taste
½	teaspoon cumin seeds
8	cups water
½	cup diced carrots
½	cup peas
½	cup fresh corn kernels
½	cup diced green beans
8	small potatoes, diced
½	cup rice
½	teaspoon oregano
8	large shrimp, shelled, deveined
1	cup milk
½	cup farmer cheese
8	eggs (if serving 1 per person; if not, only 3 will be necessary)
½	cup minced parsley

Heat the oil in a large pan. Add onion, salt, black pepper,
cumin seeds and sauté until soft but not brown. Add
water, carrots, peas, fresh corn, beans and potatoes. Simmer 15 minutes or until the vegetables are almost done.
Add the rice and oregano. Simmer 15 minutes. Add the
shrimp until it turns pink. Stir in the milk and cheese.
You can poach 1 egg per person in the soup, or you can
beat 3 eggs lightly and add, stirring for a few minutes
until eggs form strings.
Decorate with parsley or slices of yellow, fresh hot pepper that have been toasted. May be prepared two days
ahead. Serves 8.

La Soupe aux Écrevisses
(Shrimp Soup)

24 medium shrimp, uncooked
3 tablespoons salted butter
2 carrots, thinly sliced
1 onion, minced
bouquet garni (parsley, bay leaf, 6 peppercorns, pinch of thyme and tarragon)
¼ cup cognac
3 cups water
3 cups dry white wine (Muscadet)
1 teaspoon tomato paste
crème fraîche

I came across this recipe when I was studying at the Sorbonne in Paris. It's a variation of a soup served at a two-star restaurant and is great as a first course for Sunday dinner.

Francis X. J. Coleman
Professor
Department of Philosophy
College of Liberal Arts

Peel and devein shrimp, reserving shells. In a 3 quart saucepan, melt and sauté carrots and onion until golden, about 6 minutes over medium heat. Add bouquet garni. Toss in cognac; light it with a match to burn off the alcohol. Add tomato paste and equal parts of water and wine. Simmer 15 minutes. Strain and return the soup to a clean saucepan and let simmer over a very low heat for 1 minute. Add shrimp and simmer for 5 minutes. Serve in separate bowls and at the last moment, swirl a tablespoon of crème fraîche into each bowl. Can be frozen.

Crème Fraîche

2 cups heavy cream
1 cup sour cream

In a saucepan, combine ingredients and warm very gently over low heat, not exceeding 80°. Remove from heat and leave covered overnight in a 75° room. It will thicken into a nutty heavy substance. Refrigerate 6 hours before serving. Keeps up to two weeks refrigerated. Makes 3 cups.

Old Fashioned Chicken Soup

Chicken soup has been legended to do some incredible things—almost guaranteed to cure the common cold!

Andrea Bell SAR '77
Cookbook Committee
Manhattan Beach, California

1 4 to 6 lb. stewing chicken, cut into pieces
4 carrots, cut into 1 inch sections
3 stalks celery, cut into 1 inch sections
2 large onions, quartered
sprig parsley
small bay leaf
8 peppercorns
⅛ teaspoon thyme
1 tablespoon salt

Cover the chicken pieces with cold water. Bring to a full boil and discard water. Rinse chicken. Cover again and bring slowly to a boil. As the liquid simmers, carefully skim the fat and foam. Add the carrots, celery, onions, parsley, bay leaf, peppercorns, thyme and salt; bring to full boil and skim again. Simmer 2 hours, adding more water to pot if needed. Strain, cool thoroughly and refrigerate. Remove fat. Reheat, adding noodles or matzo balls. Can be frozen. Makes 3 quarts.

Matzo Balls

Could chicken soup be complete without matzo balls? Feel free to experiment with seasonings.

Cookbook Committee

¾ cup chicken stock, boiled
1 cup matzo meal
1 small onion, minced
3 tablespoons chicken fat, reserved from stock
2 eggs, slightly beaten
1 teaspoon salt
black pepper, to taste
1 teaspoon minced parsley
dash nutmeg

Pour hot chicken stock over matzo meal. Sauté onion in
1 tablespoon chicken fat until soft but not brown. Add to
matzo meal mixture. Add remaining fat. Mix well. Add
eggs, salt, pepper, parsley and nutmeg with matzo mixture. Chill thoroughly. Form into balls and drop into
boiling soup about 15 minutes before serving. Simmer in
an uncovered pan. Serve immediately. May be made
ahead. Serves 6.

Chicken Bouillabaisse

1 onion, thinly sliced
¼ cup olive oil
1 teaspoon minced garlic
1½ cups chopped, peeled tomatoes
3 lb. chicken, cut up
salt and pepper, to taste
2 pinches saffron
1½ cups dry white wine
2½ to 3 cups chicken stock
1 bay leaf
½ teaspoon thyme
½ teaspoon crushed fennel seeds
2 1 inch pieces orange rind
Tabasco sauce, to taste

Mrs. Francis S. Doody
Francis S. Doody
Professor
Department of
Finance/Economics
School of Management

In a casserole dish, sauté onion in oil until soft but not
brown. Add garlic and tomatoes and cook 10 minutes.
Lightly season chicken with salt and pepper and add to
pan. Simmer covered 10 minutes, turning once. Add
wine and enough stock to cover. Add bay leaf, thyme,
fennel, orange rind and saffron. Correct seasoning with
salt, pepper and Tabasco. Cover and simmer until tender,
about 20 minutes. Can be frozen. Serves 4 to 6.

Mnemiopsis* Mische

This is a recipe originally invented by Dr. Sebastian Beroë of Naples. It is a very tasty seafood recipe that we often use here during the summer and early fall when the ctenophores are available.

Sidney L. Tamm
Professor
Department of Biology
College of Liberal Arts

3 buckets fresh Mnemiopsis
½ gallon milk
paprika, to taste
garlic, to taste

Strain the ctenophores, then blend at low speed for 3 to 5 minutes. Slowly mix in pot with ½ gallon of milk, add pinch of paprika and garlic to taste. Simmer for 10 to 15 minutes. Excellent brothy soup with tangy sea taste. Serves 12.

*Mnemiopsis is a large, succulent ctenophore which is abundant in the plankton.

3 Fish

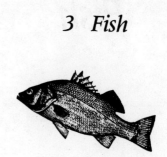

Fish

3

Scalloped Fish

1 lb. fish fillets, cut in small pieces
36 Ritz crackers, crumbled or 3 cups cracker crumbs
2 eggs, lightly beaten
1 cup milk
1¼ cups cream of mushroom soup
¼ cup butter

Marion A. Parsons
GRS'20/'35
Alumni Award Recipient
Gloucester, Massachusetts

Preheat oven to 350°. In a bowl, combine fish, crackers, eggs, milk, mushroom soup and butter. Place in a greased 1 quart casserole. Bake 50 minutes. May be prepared one day ahead. Serves 4.

Fish Fillets and Eggplant Caviar

Susan Freedman Mandel
SED '70
Cookbook Committee
Oakland, New Jersey

1 large eggplant
⅓ cup Italian salad dressing
3 tablespoons sugar
½ red onion, diced
1 cucumber, diced
2 tablespoons lemon juice
4 fish fillets

Preheat broiler. Broil eggplant in a pie plate, turning often, until charred on all sides. Remove from oven, peel off skin and put pulp in a bowl. Beat in salad dressing, sugar, onion, cucumber and lemon juice. Place fish in greased baking dish. Spread eggplant over the top. Bake for 25 minutes or until fish flakes easily. May be prepared for baking one day ahead. Serves 4.

Norwegian Fried Herring

Pat Bjaaland
CLA '67/GRS '68
Cookbook Committee
Oslo, Norway

2 lb. fresh herring, cleaned
salt and pepper, to taste
1 cup parsley (optional)
½ cup flour
4 tablespoons vegetable oil
juice of ½ lemon

Salt the fish lightly and pack cavities with parsley, if desired. In a pie plate, combine flour, salt and pepper. Roll the fish in the flour. In a skillet large enough to hold the fish in 1 layer, heat the oil over medium heat. Fry the fish until golden, 10 minutes per inch of thickness. Sprinkle with lemon juice before serving. Best if served immediately. Serves 4.

Fish Cakes with Egg Sauce

½ *lb. salt codfish*

2 *onions, thinly sliced*

2 *peppercorns*

1 *bay leaf*

1 *cup mashed potatoes*

1 *egg, well beaten*

½ *tablespoon soft butter*

⅛ *teaspoon pepper*

vegetable oil for deep frying

Cookbook Committee

Soak fish in cold water for several hours, changing water once or twice. Simmer onion, peppercorns and bay leaf in 1 cup water for 5 minutes; add drained fish and enough water to cover fish. Bring to a simmer (do not boil); remove from heat and let stand for 15 minutes. Drain, reserving poaching water. Flake the fish and beat in mashed potatoes and egg. If mixture is too stiff, beat in cream or milk, 1 teaspoon at a time. Add the butter and pepper. Heat oil to 385°. Fry 1 tablespoon of the mixture at a time until golden. Drain. Serve with egg sauce. Can be frozen. Serves 6.

Egg Sauce

2 *tablespoons butter*

2 *tablespoons flour*

1 *cup strained poaching liquid*

1 *egg, hard cooked, chopped*

salt and pepper, to taste

Melt butter and blend in flour. Cook over low heat until frothy. Pour in liquid and stir to blend. Simmer 2 minutes. Fold in the chopped egg. Correct seasoning with pepper. Add salt only if needed.

Fish Pudding
with Fresh Tomato Sauce

Best bet for cod, schrod, halibut, sole

Terence Janericco CLA '61
Cookbook Committee Editor
Boston, Massachusetts

2 lbs. white fish fillets, cut in 1 inch pieces
1½ cups medium cream
1½ tablespoons cornstarch
2 teaspoons salt
⅛ teaspoon white pepper
¼ cup minced onion
2 tablespoons butter
4 cups tomatoes, peeled, seeded, chopped
1 tablespoon minced fresh basil
salt and pepper, to taste

Preheat oven to 350°. Butter inside of a 1½ quart oven-proof pudding mold or 8½x4½x2½ inch loaf pan. Set aside. In a processor or blender, purée the fish with the cream in batches. You may, for a silkier texture, force it through a sieve. Beat in the cornstarch, salt and pepper and mix well. Pack the mixture into the prepared pan. Cover with foil. Place the mold in a baking pan and pour hot water into the pan; put it in the middle of the oven. Lower the temperature to 300° and bake 1 hour or until a knife inserted in the center comes out clean. Remove from the oven and the water bath and let rest for 10 minutes. Tilt the mold to drain off any liquid. Unmold onto a serving platter. May be prepared a day ahead and baked shortly before serving. Serves 6.

Sauce

Sauté the onion in the butter in a 1½ quart saucepan until soft but not brown. Add the tomatoes; cook, stirring over high heat until they start to give off their liquid. Add basil, salt and pepper. Boil over high heat, 10 minutes. Do not overcook the tomatoes. If the sauce is too thin, drain off the excess. The tomatoes should retain their shape. The sauce may be made a day ahead and reheated.

Fish Custard Mold

1¾ cups milk	Cookbook Committee
2 extra large eggs (or 3 medium)	
1 stalk celery	
1 lb. haddock or cod fillets, ground	
2 teaspoons salt	
⅛ teaspoon pepper	
pinch of tarragon, basil, saffron or cumin	
½ cup chopped onions	
1 carrot, thinly sliced, cooked	
¼ cup matzoh meal	
butter	

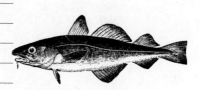

Preheat oven to 350°. In a blender, liquify eggs, milk, onion and celery. Mix with fish, salt, pepper and tarragon. Stir in matzoh meal. Melt butter in a 1 quart fish mold and pour excess into fish; cut carrot circles in half for scales; cut some in strips for fins; leave 1 circle for eye. Arrange in mold. Spoon the fish mixture into mold. (NOTE: If any mixture left, place in separate buttered dish.) Bake 1 hour in a water bath. Let stand for about 10 minutes before unmolding. Serve warm or cold with cucumber sauce or horseradish sauce. May be prepared ahead and reheated in a water bath. Serves 4 for meal and 8 for buffet snack.

Broiled Flounder

1 lb. flounder fillets	Mrs. John M. Sinclair John M. Sinclair SMG '62 *Brookline, Massachusetts*
2 tablespoons mayonnaise	
1 tablespoon Dijon mustard	
2 teaspoons finely chopped parsley	
lemon or lime wedges	

Preheat broiler to high. Arrange fillets on oiled baking sheet, sprinkle with salt and pepper. Blend mayonnaise, mustard and parsley; brush evenly over fillets. Place fillets under broiler about 3 or 4 inches from heat. Broil until golden brown on top and fish is just cooked. (You don't need to brown the bottom of the fish.) This will take from 1 to 4 minutes, depending on broiler and thickness of fish. May be prepared for broiling several hours before. Serves 3 to 4.

Oven Baked Flounder or Sole

Deborah Cohen CLA '69
Fort Lauderdale, Florida

1	large whole flounder
1	cup dry white wine
2	tablespoons minced shallots
2	tablespoons minced parsley
3	tablespoons bread crumbs
1	tablespoon melted butter
	salt and pepper, to taste
2	tomatoes, halved (optional)

Preheat oven to 375°. Place fish in a large, flat baking dish with white side up. Pour on wine and sprinkle with shallots, parsley, bread crumbs, butter, salt and pepper (also tomatoes, if desired). Bake 10 minutes, basting twice. Raise heat to 400° and bake 10 more minutes. May be prepared for baking hours ahead. Serves 4.

Sautéed Flounder Parmesan

With thanks to Jerry Smith of the College Club of Boston

Elsbeth Melville CLA '25
Dean of Women Emerita
National Alumni Council

12	flounder fillets
	milk
½	cup flour
½	cup grated Parmesan cheese
1	teaspoon salt
½	cup peanut oil
½	cup melted butter
	lemon juice

Marinate fillets in milk for 30 minutes. Drain and pat dry. Mix flour, Parmesan and salt. Coat fillets in flour mixture, shaking off the excess. Sauté fillets in oil until golden on each side. Transfer to a serving platter, baste with melted butter and sprinkle with lemon juice. Serves 12.

Baked Haddock Au Gratin

3 lbs. fresh haddock fillets
1 tablespoon minced thyme or 1 teaspoon dry thyme
1 lb. tomatoes, peeled, seeded, chopped (or 1 lb. canned tomatoes, drained)
1 clove garlic, minced
4 tablespoons grated Parmesan cheese
salt and pepper, to taste

M. Allen
Friend of Boston University

Preheat oven to 350°. Place fillets in greased baking dish. Cover with tomatoes, garlic, cheese, thyme, salt and pepper; bake until fish flakes easily (approximately 45 minutes). May be prepared for baking the day before. Makes 6 servings.

Paul's Poisson

2 shallots, minced
1 cup dry white wine
dash lemon juice
¼ cup fish stock or clam juice
1 tablespoon butter
¾ lb. fresh sole
2 tablespoons grated Parmesan cheese
1 tablespoon fresh bread crumbs
1 tablespoon minced parsley

My husband, Paul, improvised on a dish he first tried at the Palace Hotel in Madrid, Spain. He spent hours trying to duplicate the recipe, until he came up with this variation.

Dr. Jane Norton
SED '70/'74
President
Women Graduates' Club

In a saucepan, simmer wine, stock, lemon juice, shallots and butter for 4 minutes. Place fish in a baking dish and pour on sauce. Sprinkle on the cheese and bread crumbs. Broil 6 minutes, without turning. Sprinkle on parsley. Serves 2 to 3.

Salmon Croquettes

A reliable and quick
method

Mark Premack
DGE '73/CLA '75
Omaha, Nebraska

2 7 oz. cans salmon

1 egg

1 medium onion, minced

¾ cup bread crumbs

vegetable oil

Drain salmon; reserve juice. Discard skin and bones, mash. In a bowl, combine salmon, egg, onion and bread crumbs. Shape into small cakes. Cover bottom of skillet with a thin layer of oil. Sauté croquettes until brown on both sides. Serve with buttered spaghetti, if desired. Can be reheated or frozen. Serves 4.

Fillet of Sole with Crab

Irene Howard
Staff
School for the Arts

1 lb. sole fillets

6½ oz. crab

½ cup mayonnaise

½ cup milk

½ teaspoon salt

½ teaspoon pepper

Preheat oven to 400°. Drain fillets. Divide the fish into 4 portions and place each on a square of aluminum foil. Combine crab, mayonnaise, milk, salt and pepper. Spoon over the fillets. Wrap and seal foil packets. Bake 15 minutes. May be prepared for baking the day before. Serves 4.

Alaskan Baked Swordfish

| 1 small can evaporated milk |
| 1 teaspoon salt |
| 4 6 oz. fish fillets (salmon, swordfish, halibut, etc.) |
| 1 sleeve Saltine crackers, finely crumbed |
| 6 tablespoons butter, melted |

Preheat oven to 550°. Combine evaporated milk and salt. Dip fillets in milk and dredge both sides in cracker crumbs. Sprinkle with butter. Place in baking dish and bake 10 minutes per inch of thickness until golden but moist inside.

This recipe was developed in the 1940s by an Alaskan chemist who was asked to find the best possible recipe for salmon. The project was backed by the Alaskan Fishing Industry. This recipe is excellent for swordfish and other fish.

Ellen Kwait
Friend of Boston University
Marblehead, Massachusetts

Calimari

| 2 lbs. fresh squid |
| 2 cloves garlic |
| 3 tablespoons oil |
| 2 medium onions, minced |
| 1 lb. 13 oz. can whole Italian tomatoes |
| 1/2 cup dry white wine |
| salt and pepper, to taste |
| red pepper flakes, to taste (optional) |
| 1 lb. pasta, cooked al dente |

Clean, gut and skin the squid. Slice into rings. Sauté the garlic in the oil until golden. Remove garlic and discard. Then, sauté onion in oil and add squid. Sauté until white. Add tomatoes and simmer, breaking up tomatoes. Add wine. Simmer 30 minutes, seasoning to taste. Serve with pasta noodles (spinach or regular) or a vegetable such as steamed eggplant or zucchini. May be prepared and reheated. Can be frozen. Serves 6.

Ellee Koss CLA '78
Auburndale, Massachusetts

Baked Stuffed Squid

Anna E. Bessette
SON '63/'65
Attleboro, Massachusetts

2 lbs. squid, 6 to 7 inches long (about 18 large squid)

6 tablespoons cooking oil

1 onion, chopped

4 cloves garlic, minced

5 oz. fresh cooked shrimp, peeled, chopped

2 tablespoons minced parsley

½ teaspoon salt

⅛ teaspoon pepper

10 threads saffron, crushed

2 eggs, hard boiled, chopped

¼ cup sherry

½ cup bread crumbs

½ cup milk

1 raw egg

⅛ cup water

1 medium clove garlic

1 small bay leaf, crushed

⅛ teaspoon chervil

⅛ teaspoon basil

12 oz. Italian tomato sauce

1 carrot, thinly sliced

Preheat oven to 325°. Pull heads off squid and discard. Cut tentacles into ¼ to ½ inch lengths. Place in bowl and reserve 5 unbroken ink sacs; discard remaining ink sacs. Rub skin from squid with hands and discard. Cut off wings. Chop and place with tentacles. Turn body tube inside out. Remove soft gelatin substance and spine from inside. Wash tube and reverse. Slit opening down into body about ½ inch. Refrigerate until ready to stuff. In a skillet, sauté tentacles and wings in 2 tablespoons oil for 2 minutes. Set aside. Sauté onion (except 1 teaspoon) and minced garlic in the same oil until soft. Add to tentacles and wings. Add 2 more tablespoons oil to skillet.

Add the shrimp (and/or ham, pork), parsley, salt, pepper, 5 threads saffron and hard boiled eggs. Sauté 2 minutes and add to tentacles. Add sherry; mix and cool. Reserve skillet oil and juices for next step. In a separate bowl, mix bread crumbs, milk, raw egg. Add to squid mixture; stir well. Stuff squid tubes, leaving room at neck end to pin with toothpicks. Add last 2 tablespoons oil to skillet; sauté stuffed squid tubes gently, turning until tubes are opaque (no longer than 10 minutes). Remove each piece to lightly oiled casserole. Puncture sacs, drain ink into skillet, dilute with ⅛ cup water. Omit ink and water for squid without ink. Add remaining saffron, garlic clove, reserved onion, bay leaf, chervil and basil. Simmer 5 minutes. Discard garlic clove; add Italian tomato sauce and carrots. Simmer 5 to 8 minutes. Pour over squid in casserole; cover; bake in 325° oven 50 minutes. May be made ahead and baked before serving. Serves 6.

Clams en Gelée
Special Collections

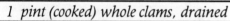

1 pint (cooked) whole clams, drained
1 pint minced clams, drained
½ cup Grand Marnier liqueur
10½ oz. clear beef consommé
6 thin slices lemon
1 cup sour cream

In a medium size crystal or silver bowl, combine the whole and minced clams. First, pour Grand Marnier on top of clams and then the consommé. This should fill the bowl to the top. Place in refrigerator for 4 hours until contents have jelled. Frost the top of the mold with sour cream and adroitly decorate with lemon slices. Use a large cold silver spoon to serve. Serves 6.

This dish, which may be utilized as an hors d'oeuvre or as a sumptuous first course, has been frequently served to visiting authors and film personalities. It is designed to bring the muse to the fore and the psyche to contentment.

Dr. Howard B. Gotlieb
Director
Special Collections
Mugar Library

Clam Casserole

Barbara Tomashefsky
Abbott CLA '59
Cookbook Committee
Hudson, New Hampshire

1 cup cracker crumbs
6 oz. can minced clams, liquid reserved
1 egg
¼ cup melted butter
1 cup milk

Preheat oven to 350°. In a bowl, combine cracker crumbs, clams, egg and butter. Let set 1 hour in refrigerator. Mix in milk and place in 1 quart casserole. Bake until set (45 minutes to 1 hour). Can be reheated. Serves 4.

Hot Cross Tuna Casserole

Mark Premack
DGE '73/CLA '75
Omaha, Nebraska

2 7 oz. cans tuna, drained, flaked
1 10 oz. package frozen peas, thawed
1 cup shredded Cheddar cheese
1 cup sliced celery
1 cup salad dressing
½ cup bread crumbs
¼ cup chopped onion
¼ teaspoon salt
⅛ teaspoon pepper
1 8 oz. package refrigerated crescent rolls

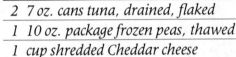

Preheat oven to 350°. In a bowl, combine tuna, peas, cheese, celery, salad dressing, bread crumbs, onion, salt and pepper. Mix well. Put into 10x6 inch baking dish. Separate dough into 2 rectangles; press perforations to seal. Cut dough into 4 long and 8 short strips. Place strips over casserole in a lattice design. Bake 35 to 40 minutes, or until crust is golden brown. May be prepared for baking the day before. Serves 6.

Causa Stuffed with Tunafish

1 recipe causa mixture*
1 small can tuna fish
1 cup mayonnaise
1 egg, hard cooked, chopped
1 large avocado, peeled, sliced
6 ripe olives, minced
minced parsley
½ red pepper, minced

Ethel Chirinos SED '75
Cookbook Committee
Lima, Peru

Divide the causa into 3 portions. Place 1 portion in a small serving casserole. Combine the tuna and mayonnaise. Spread ½ of the tuna mixture over the causa; top with ½ of the remaining causa and cover with remaining tuna. Arrange avocado slices, chopped egg and olives over the tuna and top with remaining causa.
*See recipe under appetizers.

Crab Stuffed Avocado

1 cup drained crab meat
1 cup stuffing mix
¾ cup milk
⅓ cup minced onion
¼ cup yogurt
¼ cup mayonnaise
½ cup stuffing mix tossed with 2 teaspoons melted butter
4 to 6 ripe avocados

Barbara Christ Stone
SED '67
Tucson, Arizona

Preheat oven to 400°. Pick over the crab meat, discarding any cartilage. In a bowl, combine the stuffing, milk, onion, yogurt, mayonnaise and crab meat. Mix well. Place in a greased 1 quart baking dish. Sprinkle buttered stuffing mix on top. Bake 25 to 30 minutes or until bubbly. Cut avocados in half, remove seed and fill centers with hot crab mixture. May be prepared for baking the day before. Serves 8 to 12.

Crab Chesapeake Bay

This recipe was inspired by a Southern specialty enjoyed during one of my trips south.

Dr. Hélène R. Day GRS '71
Co-Chairwoman
Cookbook Committee
Belmont, Massachusetts

1 *small green pepper, minced*

1 *strip red pimiento, minced*

½ *tablespoon dry English mustard*

¾ *teaspoon salt*

¼ *teaspoon white pepper*

1 *egg*

1 *cup margarine*

2 *lbs. crab meat, picked over*

1 *cup mayonnaise*

Preheat oven to 350°. In a bowl, combine pepper, pimiento, mustard, salt, pepper, egg and ½ cup mayonnaise. Add crab meat and mix well. Heap into crab shells or individual baking dishes. Bake 18 minutes. May be prepared for baking 1 day ahead. Can be served hot or cold. Serves 4 to 6.

Crab Meat Casserole

Anna E. Bessette
SON '63/'65
Attleboro, Massachusetts

1 *lb. crab*

2 *eggs, hard cooked, chopped*

1 *onion, grated*

½ *cup mayonnaise*

½ *cup chopped parsley*

¼ *cup salad dressing*

¼ *cup dry sherry*

3 *tablespoons lemon juice*

2 *tablespoons Worcestershire sauce*

1 *tablespoon prepared mustard*

1½ *cups fresh bread crumbs, cubed*

3 *tablespoons butter, melted*

Preheat oven to 350°. In a bowl, combine crab meat, eggs, onion, mayonnaise, parsley, salad dressing, sherry, lemon juice, Worcestershire and mustard. In a separate bowl, combine bread crumbs and butter. Mix well. Combine ½ bread crumbs with crab meat and mix well. Turn into greased 1½ quart baking dish. Sprinkle with remaining crumbs. Bake 40 to 45 minutes. Garnish with fresh parsley. Can be frozen and reheated. Serves 6.

Cheese and Crab Meat Casserole

¼ cup butter
2 tablespoons minced onion
¼ cup flour
2 teaspoons salt
1 teaspoon paprika
⅛ teaspoon pepper
3¼ cups milk
1½ cups macaroni shells, cooked
1 lb. mushrooms, sliced, sautéed
¾ cup crab meat, shredded
1½ teaspoons cooking sherry
1 cup shredded sharp Cheddar cheese

Norma Calabro
Parent
Pawtucket, Rhode Island

Preheat oven to 350°. In a 1½ quart saucepan, melt butter, sauté onion until soft, but not brown. Stir in flour, salt, paprika and pepper. Cook until bubbly. Stir in milk and cook, stirring until thick and smooth. In a greased 2 quart casserole, combine shells, mushrooms, crab meat and sherry. Mix well. Pour on sauce. Sprinkle with cheese. Bake 20 minutes, or until bubbly. May be made a day ahead. Bake at last minute. Serves 6.

Cape Scallops Supreme

1 lb. Cape scallops
½ cup cornmeal
¼ teaspoon salt
1 tablespoon flour
dash pepper
1 tablespoon minced parsley
butter

John Alton Rose
SED '41/'43/'73
Ernestine Dakin Rose
SED '40/'41/'70
Lynnfield, Massachusetts

Preheat broiler. Mix cornmeal, salt, flour, pepper and parsley flakes in a large plastic or paper bag. Put scallops into bag and shake to coat with cornmeal mix. Place scallops in shallow baking dish or on cookie sheet side by side. Dot with butter. Place under broiler 4 to 5 minutes or until golden brown, turning once. Do not overcook! May be coated one to two hours ahead. Serves 4.

Scalloped Scallops

Elaine Hatch Laverty
CBA'72
Philadelphia, Pennsylvania

¾ to 1 cup cracker crumbs

¾ lb. scallops

½ package frozen peas (optional)

½ to ¾ cup milk

¼ cup dry white wine

¼ cup butter, melted

salt and pepper, to taste

Preheat oven to 350°. In buttered 1 quart casserole, layer crumbs, scallops and peas. Combine milk, wine, butter, salt and pepper. Pour over the top. Bake for 20 to 30 minutes or until scallops are just cooked. May be prepared for baking a day before. Serves 4.

Scallops and Brussels Sprouts

Diana Lin SMG'72
New York, New York

½ lb. brussels sprouts, halved

1 tablespoon oil

½ cup chicken broth

1 lb. Bay scallops

salt and pepper, to taste

2 teaspoons cornstarch

¼ cup cold water

Place the sprouts in a 10 inch skillet with the oil; add the broth and simmer until just tender. Remove the sprouts. Simmer scallops in the pan for 2 minutes and return the sprouts to the pan. In a small bowl, combine the cornstarch and water. Add to the skillet and cook, stirring until the mixture comes to a boil and thickens. Correct seasoning with salt and pepper. Serve at once. Serves 6.

Coquilles Isle de Chevre

1 lb. Bay scallops
1 cup dry vermouth or white wine
½ cup julienne strips of ham
1 cup fresh peas
½ cup heavy cream
½ cup Swiss cheese, cut in strips

Preheat broiler. Poach scallops in vermouth. Remove scallops and set aside. Simmer ham and peas in broth for 10 minutes. Transfer to casserole; add scallops, cream and place Swiss cheese strips on top. Broil just long enough to melt cheese. May be prepared for broiling the day before. Serves 4.

Isle de Chevre is French for Goat Island, which is where I was in Rhode Island, when I first made the dish. I was entertaining a guest during a bad storm and all that was in the refrigerator were some scallops, peas and the rest of the ingredients.

Donis Dondis
Dean
School of Public Communication

Broiled Scampi

2 lbs. jumbo shrimp, peeled, deveined
½ cup olive oil
1 teaspoon dry mustard
6 tablespoons lemon juice or vinegar
4 tablespoons chopped parsley
2 or more cloves garlic, crushed
2 teaspoons salt
¼ teaspoon pepper

Preheat broiler. In a bowl, combine shrimp, oil, lemon juice, parsley, garlic, salt, mustard and pepper. Marinate 2 to 24 hours. Drain and broil until just cooked. May be made a day before. Serves 4 to 6.

Denise Oberti SON'73
Danville, Pennsylvania

Shrimp Creole

Serve over your
favorite rice.

Esperanza Tomé
Staff

1 onion, chopped
1 green pepper, chopped
½ cup chopped mushrooms
¼ cup chopped celery
1 tablespoon vegetable oil
1½ cups tomato sauce
8 slices tomato
1 lb. large shrimp
1 tablespoon salt
1 tablespoon minced garlic
1 tablespoon black pepper

In a large saucepan, sauté onions, green peppers, mushrooms and celery in oil until browned. Add tomato sauce and tomato. Bring to a boil. Reduce heat and add shrimp, salt, garlic and black pepper. Simmer until shrimp are pink. Serve over white rice. Can be prepared ahead and reheated or frozen. Serves 4 to 6.

Sweet and Pungent Shrimp

Carol Lowe
Philip L. Lowe
Former Member
Board of Visitors
School of Management

¼ cup brown sugar, firmly packed
2 tablespoons cornstarch
½ teaspoon salt
¼ cup vinegar
1 tablespoon soy sauce
1 teaspoon minced gingerroot
2½ cups pineapple chunks, juice reserved
1 green pepper, cut into strips
2 small onions, cut into rings
1 lb. shrimp, peeled, deveined

In saucepan, combine sugar, cornstarch and salt. Stir in soy sauce, vinegar, ginger and syrup drained from pineapple and cook until slightly thickened, stirring constantly. Add pepper, onions and pineapple and simmer 2 minutes more. Add shrimp and simmer, stirring until shrimp just turns pink. Serve immediately over rice. Sauce may be made ahead and shrimp added just before serving. Serves 4 to 6.

Shrimp Curry

3 lbs. shrimp, peeled, deveined
¾ cup butter
¼ cup minced onion
¾ cup flour
3 tablespoons curry powder (or to taste)
2 cups milk
2 tablespoons minced ginger
3 tablespoons lemon juice
salt and pepper, to taste
boiled rice
chutney
grated coconut
raisins
eggs, hard cooked, chopped
cashews, chopped

Gwendolen Rochester
Office of Housing

In a saucepan, cook shrimp in boiling salted water until just cooked. Drain shrimp, reserving 1 cup of liquid. In a saucepan, melt butter and sauté onion until golden. Stir in the curry powder. Cook, stirring for 3 minutes. Stir in shrimp liquid and milk. Cook, stirring until thickened and smooth. Stir in shrimp, ginger, lemon juice and salt. Cook until shrimp are warm. If desired, more curry may be added to taste. Serve with rice, chutney, coconut, raisins, eggs and nuts. Sauce without the shrimp can be made ahead and frozen. Shrimp can be added when ready to use. May use chicken or lamb instead of shrimp. Serves 6.

Homard au Porto
(Lobster with Port Wine)

Demonstrated during a
Cook-In at the Boston
University Castle

Richard Lucas
Executive Chef
Hotel Sonesta
Cambridge, Massachusetts

2½ lb. lobster, cooked
4 tablespoons butter
½ cup port wine
¼ cup brandy
1 cup heavy cream
1 egg yolk
dash cayenne
12 toast points

Remove lobster from shell. Melt butter in a skillet. Add port wine and reduce by half. Add brandy and flambé. While flaming, add lobster, heavy cream and the egg yolk. Cook, stirring until lightly thickened. Add cayenne and salt to taste. When sauce has thickened, remove from heat and place in a casserole with toast points. Can be reheated. Serves 6.

Chinese Lobster Sauce

You don't need a wok to make delicious Chinese food. I use a regular saucepan for the sauce and then serve it with rice, spare ribs and egg rolls, if I can find them.

Phyllis Drector
Development Office

2 lbs. ground beef or pork
2 eggs, beaten
2 tablespoons minced garlic
2 tablespoons sugar
4 bouillon cubes
2 cups hot water
4 tablespoons cornstarch
2 tablespoons soy sauce, imported
4 teaspoons Gravy Master (optional)

In a skillet, brown the meat, breaking it up. Add the egg, garlic and sugar. Stir in bouillon cubes and water. Simmer 2 minutes. In a small bowl, combine the cornstarch, soy sauce and Gravy Master. Simmer until sauce has thickened and cleared (if cooked too long, sauce will thin out). Serve with lobster meat or shrimp simmered in the sauce until just cooked. May be served over rice or Chinese noodles. May be prepared a day ahead and reheated. Serves 6.

4 Poultry

Poultry

Southern Chicken with Rice and Gravy

1 cup raw, long grain rice
4 to 4½ cups chicken broth
3 tablespoons oil
2 tablespoons butter
2 onions, diced
8 pieces chicken (breasts, legs, thighs)
1½ tablespoons flour
salt and pepper, to taste

Kathryn Silber
Wife of
Dr. John R. Silber
President of
Boston University

Preheat oven to 350°. In a saucepan, cook rice in 2 cups chicken broth until liquid is absorbed. Meanwhile, in a skillet, heat oil and butter, add onions and chicken and cook until chicken is brown on both sides. Put rice in a 9x11 casserole dish and place chicken and onions on top. Salt and pepper, to taste. Pour on ½ cup chicken broth to moisten. Cover with foil and bake 30 minutes. Pour off all but 1½ tablespoons fat from skillet. Stir in flour and cook over low heat. Add remaining chicken broth and cook, stirring until thickened and smooth. Serve chicken with gravy on side. Serves 8.

Garlic Roast Chicken

Natalie McCracken
*Assistant to the Dean
College of Liberal Arts*

1	*5 lb. roasting chicken*
6	*tablespoons butter*
	salt, to taste
1	*large head garlic, peeled*
2 to 3	*sprigs parsley*
1	*cup chicken stock*
4 to 6	*potatoes, boiled*

Preheat oven to 325°. Rub chicken inside and out with 3 tablespoons butter and 1 tablespoon salt. Stuff with all garlic cloves and parsley sprigs. Truss. Place chicken, back up, on a rack in a shallow roasting pan. Roast 20 minutes, baste with butter, turn to 1 side. Roast 20 minutes, baste with butter. Turn to the other side, baste with juices. Roast 20 minutes. Finally turn, breast up, and roast 20 minutes. Chicken should be cooked through and easily browned. To test: Tilt chicken so juices run from tail vent. They should run clear or test with meat thermometer for 165°. Remove from oven and pan. Let rest on warm platter uncovered in a warm area of kitchen. Remove trussing and discard parsley. Pour off most of fat from pan. Add stock and simmer, scraping up browned bits until reduced by half. Stir in 1 tablespoon of butter. Correct seasoning with salt and pepper. Serve with potatoes, giving each guest 2 to 3 cloves garlic to mash in. Serve sauce with chicken. Best if served within 40 minutes after removing chicken from the oven. Serves 4 to 6.

Chicken-Artichoke Kabobs

There is definitely a gourmet flavor to this dish. The combination of tarragon and vermouth add a unique touch.

Claire Shapiro Soja
CLA '68
*Cookbook Committee
Harvard, Massachusetts*

¾	*cup dry white vermouth*
¼	*cup olive oil*
1	*tablespoon dried tarragon*
1	*teaspoon salt*
¼	*teaspoon white pepper*
2	*chicken breasts, skinned, boned, cut into 1 inch cubes*
12 to 16	*fresh mushroom caps*
¼	*cup water*
1	*tablespoon butter*

| ¼ teaspoon salt |
| 8 canned artichoke hearts |

Preheat broiler. In a bowl, combine vermouth, olive oil, tarragon, salt and pepper. Add chicken and marinate 1 to 2 hours. Place mushroom caps in saucepan with water, butter and salt. Simmer 3 minutes. Drain. Arrange chicken, mushrooms and artichokes on skewers. Broil 5 inches from heat 10 minutes or until browned and cooked through, brushing with marinade. May be prepared for broiling the day before. Serves 4.

Country Captain Barbecue Chicken

| ½ cup butter |
| ½ cup vegetable oil |
| 1 onion, minced |
| 1 clove garlic, crushed |
| 2 tablespoons curry powder |
| ½ teaspoon thyme |
| ¼ teaspoon pepper |
| pinch of ground ginger |
| 9 chicken breasts or legs |
| ½ cup flour |
| 1 teaspoon salt |
| ½ teaspoon paprika |
| ½ teaspoon cayenne |

I first tasted this on a Canadian cruise around Halifax. It was so delicious that I asked for the recipe and now it's a family barbecue favorite.

Harry H. Crosby
Professor
Department of Science
College of Basic Studies

Place chicken in bowl. In a saucepan, combine butter and oil and sauté onion until soft. Stir in garlic, curry powder, thyme, pepper and ginger. Pour sauce over chicken and marinate 2 to 36 hours. When ready to broil, preheat grill or broiler. Drain chicken. Mix flour, salt, paprika and cayenne in a plate. Coat chicken pieces with flour mixture. Place chicken on grill. Broil 10 minutes, skin side down. Turn and broil 15 minutes longer or until cooked through, basting with marinade. Can be served cold. Serves 6.

When cold this Indian staple makes great sandwiches.

Leland C. Wyman
Professor Emeritus
College of Liberal Arts

Tandoori Chicken

2 2½ lb. broiler chickens
2 tablespoons lemon juice
3 teaspoons salt
1 teaspoon thread saffron
3 tablespoons boiling water
1 cup plain yogurt
3 or 4 cloves garlic, crushed
2 tablespoons minced gingerroot
2 teaspoons ground cumin
2 teaspoons ground coriander
1 teaspoon paprika
½ teaspoon cayenne
½ teaspoon red food coloring
¼ cup butter, melted
lemon slices, green pepper wedges, chutney, popadum

Skin chickens. Cut many deep slits in thighs, drumsticks, breasts and wings with a sharp knife. Combine lemon juice and salt and rub over chickens, pressing salt mixture into slits. Put chickens into deep pan. Pour boiling water over saffron and let stand 10 minutes. Drizzle saffron water over chickens and marinate for 30 minutes. Combine yogurt, garlic, gingerroot, cumin, coriander, paprika, cayenne and red food coloring. Mix well. Rub yogurt mixture over chickens, pressing mixture well into slits. Marinate in refrigerator for 24 hours. Preheat oven to 400°. Pour butter over chickens. Roast uncovered 15 minutes. Reduce heat to 350° and roast ¾ hour more. Garnish with lemon slices and green pepper wedges. Serve with chutney and popadum. Serves 4 to 8.

Low Calorie Broiled Chicken

1 tablespoon dry mustard
1/4 teaspoon sugar substitute
1/4 teaspoon minced garlic
1/2 teaspoon minced onion
1/4 teaspoon pepper
1/4 teaspoon salt
1 1/2 teaspoons paprika
1 broiler chicken, cut into pieces

Sally Kirshenbaum
SED '58/'60
Cranston, Rhode Island

Combine the mustard, sugar substitute, garlic powder, onion powder, salt, pepper and paprika. Rub into the chicken pieces. Broil until browned on both sides and cooked through. Serves 4 to 6.

Chicken Cordon Bleu

3 1 lb. chicken breasts
salt
3 large slices Swiss cheese, halved
3 large slices ham, halved
flour
1 egg, beaten with 2 tablespoons water
1/2 cup fine dry bread crumbs
oil

Barbara Tomashefsky
Abbott CLA '59
Cookbook Committee
Hudson, New Hampshire

Split, skin and bone breasts. Place between sheets of waxed paper and flatten carefully with mallet or rolling pin. Sprinkle with salt. Place a slice of cheese and ham at one end of cutlet and fold other end over. Press edges to seal. Dip in flour, egg and bread crumbs. Heat oil to 375°. Fry chicken until golden and cooked through, about 8 minutes. Serve at once. Serves 6.

Ken's North-South Fried Chicken

A. Kendall Holbrook
CLA '59
Reading, Massachusetts

1 to 1½ cups flour
1 teaspoon brown sugar
½ teaspoon paprika
½ teaspoon salt
¼ teaspoon chili powder
¼ teaspoon black pepper
⅛ teaspoon cinnamon
⅛ teaspoon nutmeg
⅛ teaspoon powdered sage
⅛ teaspoon powdered thyme
⅛ teaspoon marjoram
dash cayenne
2½ lb. chicken, cut up
2 eggs, beaten with 3 tablespoons milk
1 cup bread crumbs, unseasoned
oil

Preheat electric skillet to 380°. In plastic bag, combine flour, sugar, paprika, salt, chili powder, pepper, cinnamon, nutmeg, sage, marjoram and cayenne. Mix well. Coat chicken with flour. Dip into beaten egg and milk, then into bread crumbs. Fry in ¼ inch oil at 380°, 10 minutes on each side. Lower heat to 300°. Cover chicken and continue frying 15 minutes on each side. Remove cover and fry 5 minutes each side to firm. Can be served hot or cold. Serves 4.

Chicken Kiev

4 *chicken breasts, halved, skinned, boned*
12 *tablespoons unsalted butter, chilled*
salt and pepper, to taste
2 *eggs*
2 *cups flour*
2 *cups dry white bread crumbs*
oil

Dr. Matthew Witten
CLA '72
Cookbook Committee
Los Angeles, California

Place breasts smooth side down on cutting board. With a small, sharp knife and your fingers, remove the small fillet from each breast. Lay the breast and fillets, 1 pair at a time, on a sheet of wax paper. With the flat side of a cleaver or metal pounder, pound them to a thickness of ⅛ inch. If holes appear in the flesh, overlap the edges of the tear. Slightly cover the patch with wax paper and pound gently until meat joins together. Cut butter into 8 equal parts. Shape each piece of butter into a cylinder about ½ inch thick and 3 inches long. Wrap in wax paper and chill until firm. To assemble cutlets: Gently peel off wax paper and sprinkle chicken with salt and pepper. Wrap the chicken breasts and fillet around the butter fingers. Be sure no butter is exposed. Use small fillets on top of chicken to secure all butter. In a small bowl, beat eggs enough to combine them. Spread flour and bread crumbs on 2 separate strips of wax paper and 1 at a time, dip cutlets into flour, shake gently to remove excess, rolling it in your palms. Pat the cutlet into a long cylinder, tapering slightly at each end. Dip cutlets into eggs. Make sure entire surface is coated. Roll in bread crumbs and again make sure entire surface is coated. Place on platter and refrigerate for 1 hour to 2 days. Heat oil to 375° and fry to golden brown. Then, place cutlets in 200° oven that has been pre-heated for no longer than 10 minutes, or butter may escape. May be prepared ahead of time. If frozen, thaw in refrigerator before frying. Serves 8.

Chinese Red Stewed Chicken

Sterne E. Barnett CBA '35
Cookbook Committee
Chestnut Hill, Massachusetts

3½ lb. chicken, sectioned
3 tablespoons peanut oil
½ cup dark soy sauce
½ cup water
½ cup dry sherry or rice wine
2 cloves garlic
3 slices gingerroot, peeled, minced

In a wok or casserole dish, cook chicken in oil until well browned. Add soy sauce, water, wine, garlic and gingerroot. Simmer 1 hour. Serve hot with rice or cold (sauce will jell). Hard cooked and shelled eggs may be added to the sauce the last 15 minutes of cooking or eggs may be heated in any leftover sauce. Can be frozen or prepared and reheated. Serves 4 to 6.

Southern Fried Chicken with 'Erbal 'Ushpuppies

My dissatisfaction with 'the old family favorite' led to this creation.

Borden Deal
20th Century Archives
Mugar Library

1 2½ lb. chicken, cut up
1 clove garlic, crushed
9 tablespoons cornmeal
3 tablespoons flour
½ teaspoon salt
1 teaspoon chervil
1 teaspoon parsley
1 teaspoon tarragon
1 teaspoon paprika
corn oil
½ teaspoon baking powder
3 tablespoons milk

Rub the chicken parts with the garlic. Combine the corn-meal, flour, salt, chervil, parsley, tarragon and paprika. Mix well. Lightly coat chicken in cornmeal mixture and reserve excess. Heat ½ inch of corn oil in 2 skillets over medium heat. Add chicken; cover and cook 5 minutes. Turn over and cook covered 5 minutes longer. Uncover and cook until done, about 10 minutes longer on each side. Add baking powder to excess cornmeal mixture and stir in milk to make a batter of dropping consistency. Flour your hands. Make about 10 balls from the mixture. Drop in and around the chicken, along with the chicken liver and gizzards. Turn hush puppies occasionally so they rise and cook evenly until they are golden. Serve piping hot with Scottish bagpipers, if possible. Good served cold. Serves 4.

Simple Szechuan Chicken

2 whole chicken breasts, boned, cut into 1½ inch cubes
3 tablespoons cornstarch
1 tablespoon vegetable oil
3 cloves garlic, minced
5 tablespoons soy sauce
1½ tablespoons white wine vinegar
1 tablespoon sugar
¼ cup water
1 bunch scallions, 1 inch pieces
¼ teaspoon cayenne

Sandy Trainor
Friend of Boston University

Coat chicken with cornstarch. Heat oil in wok. Add chicken and garlic and stir fry until chicken is lightly browned. Add vinegar, soy sauce, sugar and water. Cook covered for 3 minutes. Uncover, add onions and pepper and cook for 2 minutes longer. Can be held about 30 minutes. Serves 4 to 6.

Chicken with Cashews in Hoisin Sauce

Dr. Linda Nelson CLA '74
Cookbook Committee
Lansdale, Pennsylvania

2 chicken breasts, boned, cut into ¾ inch slices
1 tablespoon sugar
1 tablespoon soy sauce
1 tablespoon cornstarch
¼ cup oil
½ teaspoon salt
¼ cup sliced water chestnuts
1 cup sliced mushrooms
1 large green pepper, cubed, or ¼ lb. snow peas
2 tablespoons hoisin sauce
¼ cup roasted cashews

Mix chicken with soy sauce, sugar and cornstarch. Set aside. Heat oil in wok. Add salt, water chestnuts, mushrooms, pepper or snow peas. Stir fry 2 minutes. Remove vegetables. Add chicken to the oil. Stir fry until no longer pink. Stir in hoisin sauce. Mix well. Add vegetables and cashews and reheat. Serves 6.

Low Fat, Low Calorie Hawaiian Chicken

Rebecca J. Gourley
SAR '74
Cookbook Committee
Medfield, Massachusetts
Cynthia Segal SFA '72
Brighton, Massachusetts

2 chicken legs, skinned
2 chicken breasts, skinned
salt and pepper, to taste
1 can unsweetened pineapple chunks
4 packages artificial sweetener
2 tablespoons cornstarch
1 tablespoon soy sauce
¾ cup cider vinegar
1 chicken bouillon cube
1 large green pepper, cut in circles

Preheat oven to 350°. Season chicken with salt and pepper. Bake 30 minutes. In a saucepan, combine pineapple juice to measure 1¼ cups. Add water, if necessary, sweetener, cornstarch, soy sauce, vinegar, bouillon cube. Boil 2 minutes, stirring until mixture thickens. Pour off accumulated fat from chicken. Sprinkle pineapple chunks over chicken and cover with sauce. Bake 45 minutes longer, or until done. Serve with rice. Can be reheated. Serves 4.

Chinese Chicken with Mushrooms

3 chicken breasts, boned, skinned
2 egg whites
3 tablespoons cornstarch
2 tablespoons dry sherry or rice wine
1 teaspoon sugar
½ teaspoon salt
¼ teaspoon ground white pepper
3 tablespoons flour
½ cup oil
½ lb. fresh mushrooms, sliced
1¼ cups chicken stock
6 oz. snow peas or 9 oz. package French style green beans, frozen
½ cup canned sliced water chestnuts

Susan Moger CLA '73
Cookbook Committee
Los Angeles, California

Partially freeze chicken. Slice lengthwise with the grain about ⅛ inch thick. In a small bowl, combine egg whites, 2 tablespoons of cornstarch, sherry, sugar, salt and white pepper. Dip chicken in flour and shake off excess. Dip chicken into egg white mixture. Heat oil in wok. Stir fry chicken a few pieces at a time, 3 minutes. Drain and set aside. Repeat with remaining chicken. Pour off all but 3 tablespoons of oil. Stir fry mushrooms. Mix ¼ cup stock with remaining tablespoon of cornstarch. Add to wok. Add 1 cup stock and bring to boil. Add snow peas or green beans, water chestnuts, reserved chicken and mushrooms. Heat and serve. Serves 6.

Chutney Chicken

Sharon Gamsin
DGE '69/SPC '71
Cookbook Committee
New York, New York

1 chicken, cut up
3 tablespoons butter
1 tart apple, chopped
1 large onion, chopped
1 stalk celery, chopped
2 tablespoons curry powder
1 tablespoon flour
1 cup orange juice
½ cup mango chutney

In a skillet, brown chicken in butter. Remove from pan. Sauté onion, apple and celery in a pan until soft. Sprinkle with curry and flour. Cook, stirring 1 minute. Add orange juice and chutney. Bring to boil. Add chicken. Cover and simmer 1 hour. Can be reheated. Serves 4.

Chicken Casserole

Edith Thompson Adams
SED '42
Marlboro, Massachusetts

3¼ to 4 lb. stewing chicken
1 cup chopped celery, cooked
1 cup chopped walnuts
1 cup cream of mushroom soup
1 cup mayonnaise
2 tablespoons minced onion
2 tablespoons lemon juice
¾ teaspoon salt
½ teaspoon pepper
½ cup bread crumbs, buttered

Boil chicken, remove meat and chop. Preheat oven to 350°. In a 2 quart casserole dish, combine chicken, celery, walnuts, soup, mayonnaise, onion, lemon juice, salt and pepper. Mix well and smooth the top. Sprinkle with bread crumbs. Bake for 20 minutes or until bubbly. May be prepared a day before. Serves 4.

Chicken à la King

2 tablespoons butter	
1 cup sliced mushrooms	
1 tablespoon flour	
2 cups milk	
2 cups diced chicken, cooked	
1 pimiento, thinly sliced	
1 teaspoon salt	
½ teaspoon pepper	
toast points or patty shells	

Gertrude E. McGuire
SED '42/'44
Portland, Connecticut

Sauté mushrooms in butter, 5 minutes. Sprinkle with flour. Cook, stirring for 2 minutes. Add milk. Cook until sauce thickens. Stir in chicken, pimiento, salt and pepper. Heat thoroughly. Serve on toast points or patty shells. Can be frozen. Serves 4 to 6.

Apricot Chicken

3 cups cooked rice
6 chicken breasts
¼ lb. butter
1 9 oz. jar apricot preserves
1 lemon, thinly sliced

This is a quick, easy dish to make for company. It's recommended for all those who work during the day.

Sylvia G. Brussel **GRS '74**
Professor
Graduate Psychiatric Nursing
School of Nursing

Preheat oven to 325°. Place cooked rice in greased baking pan. Place chicken on rice, skin side up. In a saucepan, combine butter and apricot preserves. Heat until butter is melted. Mix well and pour over chicken and rice. Place slices of lemon on each chicken breast. Bake 45 minutes or until chicken is cooked. If rice gets too brown at edges, lower heat. May be prepared for baking several hours ahead. Serves 6.

Chicken and Pork Adobo

A popular Filipino dish

Nannette Gonzalez
Kredlow SFA '79
Graphic Designer
Graphic Design Office

1 broiler chicken, cut into pieces
1 lb. pork shoulder, trimmed, cut into 1½ inch squares
⅓ cup wine vinegar
1 teaspoon black pepper
2 teaspoons salt
2 cloves garlic, crushed
1 bay leaf
½ cup water
4 tablespoons soy sauce
3 chicken livers
2 teaspoons water

Marinate chicken and pork in a saucepan with the vinegar, pepper, salt, garlic, bay leaf and ½ cup water. Let stand for about 1 hour. Remove chicken. Simmer pork in marinade for 30 minutes. Add the chicken and simmer for 30 minutes longer or until almost tender. Remove pork and chicken from the adobo sauce. Place in shallow pan and broil until brown. Add soy sauce and mash chicken livers mixed with 2 tablespoons water into the sauce. Simmer to thicken. Put back browned chicken and pork pieces. Simmer for 5 minutes. Reheating enhances flavor. Serve with boiled white rice. Serves 6.

Baked Glazed Chicken

Neila Straub SED '70
Beverly, Massachusetts

1 onion, sliced
2½ lb. chicken, cut up
salt and pepper, to taste
½ teaspoon minced garlic
½ cup currant jelly
1 teaspoon sherry

Preheat oven to 350°. Arrange onion slices in bottom of shallow baking pan. Top with chicken pieces. Sprinkle with salt, pepper and garlic. Combine jelly and sherry in small saucepan. Bring to a boil. Pour over chicken. Bake 30 minutes. Turn on broiler and broil until crispy, 10 minutes. May be prepared for baking several hours ahead. Good cold. Serves 4 to 6.

Chicken or Vegetable Briyani

3	*cups rice*
2	*large onions, minced*
1	*tablespoon butter*
1	*lb. chicken meat, boned or 12 oz. mixed vegetables*
1	*cup water*
3	*tablespoons tomato purée*
1	*tablespoon salt*
1	*teaspoon Tabasco sauce*
1	*teaspoon minced garlic*
½	*teaspoon curry powder*
½	*teaspoon ground ginger*
½	*teaspoon dry mustard*
½	*teaspoon crushed red pepper flakes*

Crushed potato chips can be used to garnish the top of this dish.

Dr. Prukash Lulla SGD '71
Cookbook Committee
Bombay, India

Cook rice in boiling salted water until half cooked; drain and set aside. In a casserole dish, sauté onion in butter until golden, stirring often. Add the meat or vegetables, water, tomato purée, salt, Tabasco, garlic, curry powder, ginger, mustard and pepper flakes. Simmer 15 minutes. Place ½ of rice in bottom of a baking dish. Spread over meat mixture. Completely cover meat with remaining rice. Place in a cold oven. Heat to 450°. Allow to cook 45 minutes. May be prepared for baking several hours ahead. Serves 4.

Curry Chicken

Francine Sabin SED '73
Brookline, Massachusetts

4 *tablespoons butter*
½ *cup honey*
¼ *cup prepared mustard*
1 *teaspoon salt*
1 *teaspoon curry*
6 *chicken breasts, skinned, boned*

Preheat oven to 350°. Melt butter in baking pan. Add the honey, mustard, salt and curry. Mix well. Roll chicken in mixture to coat evenly. Bake 30 minutes. Turn and bake 30 minutes longer. Serve hot or cold. Serves 6.

Chicken with Garlic

Forty cloves of garlic make this unique.

Gwendolen Rochester
Housing Office

3½ to 4 lb. *roasting chicken*
salt and pepper, to taste
bouquet garni of bay leaf, parsley, thyme, celery, rosemary, savory
¼ *cup olive oil*
40 *cloves garlic, unpeeled*
2 *tablespoons anisette liqueur*

Preheat oven to 350°. Rub chicken in salt and pepper. Stuff with bouquet garni and place in 3 quart casserole dish with tight fitting lid. Add the oil, garlic, anisette and salt and pepper to taste. Cover and bake 1 hour and 20 minutes. Serve 9 garlic cloves to spread on bread or potatoes. Can be reheated. Serves 4 to 5.

Chicken Dijon

4 *chicken breasts, skinned, boned*
3 *tablespoons butter*
2 *tablespoons flour*
1 *cup chicken broth*
½ *cup light cream*
2 *tablespoons Dijon mustard*

Sharon Gamsin
DGE '69/SPC '71
Cookbook Committee
New York, New York

In a skillet, sauté chicken in butter 20 minutes. Transfer to warm platter. Stir flour into pan. Add broth and cream. Stir until thick and bubbly. Stir in mustard. Return chicken to pan. Cover and simmer 10 minutes longer. Can be reheated. Serves 6 to 8.

Easy Chicken

¼ *lb. butter*
6 *chicken breasts*
salt and pepper, to taste
1 *lb. mushrooms, sliced*
½ *cup grated Parmesan cheese*

Janice Bernstein SED '75
Brighton, Massachusetts

Preheat oven to 350°. In a skillet, melt the butter. Turn the chicken over in the butter and place in a baking dish. Season with salt and pepper. Sauté mushrooms in skillet until tender. Pour over chicken. Sprinkle with cheese. Bake 1 hour. May be prepared for baking a day before. Keep refrigerated. Serves 6.

Chicken Ghana

My son brought this recipe back from Rhodesia. It was served to him by the wife of the principal of the Mount Silinda School.

Helen Crawford Bander
SED '31
Cookbook Committee
Paris, Arkansas

1 3 lb. chicken, cut up
salt
3 tablespoons vegetable oil
2 onions, chopped
2 green peppers, thinly sliced
½ teaspoon chili powder
½ teaspoon minced garlic
½ teaspoon crushed red pepper
½ cup peanut butter
½ cup cold water
2 teaspoons lime or lemon juice

Lightly salt chicken. In a skillet, sauté chicken in oil until browned. Set aside. Sauté onion in pan until golden. Stir in peppers, chili, garlic and pepper. Add the chicken. In a bowl, combine the peanut butter, water and lime juice. Pour over the chicken. Cover and simmer slowly for 50 minutes or until tender. Serve with rice. Can be reheated. Serves 4 to 6.

Lemon Yogurt Chicken

Lorraine Nelson Klein
GRS '76
Cookbook Committee
North Kingston,
Rhode Island

1 3 lb. chicken, cut up
½ cup lemon juice
½ onion, grated
½ cup yogurt or sour cream
1 cup bread crumbs, flavored or plain

Preheat oven to 400°. In a bowl, combine lemon juice and onion. Marinate chicken for 1 hour. Drain chicken and dip in yogurt; then coat in bread crumbs. Place on greased baking sheet and bake 30 minutes at 400°. Turn oven to 450° and bake 15 minutes. Good hot or cold. Can be frozen. Serves 4 to 6.

Irish Chicken Pie

1 1/4 cups cream of mushroom soup
5 to 6 potatoes, sliced
1 onion, sliced
1/2 lb. Cheddar cheese, grated
3 cups cooked chicken, diced
1 cup sautéed mushrooms
1 10 oz. package mixed vegetables, slightly thawed
juice of 1 lemon

Patricia A. Smith SAR '54
Vice President
General Alumni Association

Preheat oven to 350°. Place soup in bottom of 2 quart casserole dish. Layer potatoes on top of soup. Layer onion on top of potatoes. Place ¾ of the Cheddar over onion. Mix chicken, mushrooms and vegetables. Add to soup and sprinkle with lemon juice. Place remaining cheese on top. Cover and bake for 1½ hours. May be prepared two days ahead. Serves 4.

Lemon Chicken

1 3 lb. chicken, cut up
1/2 teaspoon salt
1/2 cup water
1/3 cup lemon peel
2 teaspoons lemon juice
1 teaspoon minced onion
1/2 teaspoon thyme
1/2 teaspoon marjoram
paprika
parsley

Peg Wallace LAW '76
Brookline, Massachusetts

Preheat oven to 400°. Sprinkle chicken with salt. Place skin side down in shallow baking pan. Combine water, lemon peel, lemon juice, onion, thyme and marjoram. Pour over chicken. Bake turning once and basting until crisp, about 45 minutes. Dust with paprika and add parsley. Serve with lemon quarters. Serves 4.

Mexican Chicken

Karen Stankiewicz
MET '78

1 2 lb. chicken, quartered

salt and pepper, to taste

dash paprika

½ cup butter, melted

½ to 1 bag taco chips, crumbled

½ cup chopped onions

1 cup grated Cheddar cheese

1 can enchilada sauce

Preheat oven to 350°. Place chicken in casserole dish and bake 30 minutes. Season with salt, pepper and paprika. Cover with melted butter and taco chips. Pour enchilada sauce over chicken. Cover with onions and cheese. Bake 15 minutes longer or until cheese melts. Can be reheated. Serves 4 to 6.

Chicken Paprikash

Cookbook Committee

1 large onion, chopped

½ cup olive oil

1½ teaspoon paprika

4 chicken breasts, thighs, legs

½ green pepper, sliced

2 teaspoons salt

¾ to 1 pint sour cream

In a large skillet, simmer onion in oil until soft but not brown. Add paprika; stir and add chicken. Add salt and pepper. Simmer 1 hour, stirring every 15 minutes. Remove from heat and cool slightly. Stir in sour cream and serve over wild rice or noodles. Can be reheated. Serves 6 to 8.

Chicken Parmigiana

4 chicken breasts, skinned, boned, halved
1 egg, lightly beaten
1 cup bread crumbs
salt and pepper, to taste
pinch of oregano
⅓ cup butter
2 cups tomato sauce
2 cloves garlic, crushed
½ teaspoon thyme
½ teaspoon oregano
grated Parmesan cheese

Nancy R. Seebert SON '68
Day's Creek, Oregon

Pound chicken breasts ¼ inch thick. Dip in egg and then in bread crumbs, seasoned with salt, pepper and oregano. In a skillet, sauté breasts 2 minutes on each side. Add tomato sauce, garlic, thyme and oregano. Simmer 20 minutes. Serve cheese separately. Serve with pasta. Can be frozen and reheated. Serves 4 to 6.

Chicken Piquant

¾ cup rosé wine
¼ cup soy sauce
¼ cup vegetable oil
2 tablespoons water
1 tablespoon brown sugar
1 teaspoon ginger
¼ teaspoon oregano
1 clove garlic, minced
3 whole chicken breasts, halved

Cheryl Germain CLA '74
Little Falls, New Jersey

In a bowl, combine the wine, soy sauce, oil, water, sugar, garlic, ginger and oregano. Marinate chicken 2 hours. Preheat oven to 375°. Place chicken in baking dish. Bake 1 hour. Serves 6.

Tipsy Chicken

Easy, foolproof and
delicious

Helen K. Hickey
SAR '50/SED '54
Associate Dean
Sargent College of
Allied Health Professions

3 to 4 lb. chicken, cut up

2 tablespoons butter

paprika, to taste

1 cup dry white wine

1 1/2 teaspoons tarragon

1/2 teaspoon pepper

1/2 teaspoon minced garlic

2 medium onions, thinly sliced

Preheat oven to 350°. Coat chicken with paprika. In a
skillet, brown chicken well in butter. Turn off heat and
pour wine over chicken. Add tarragon, pepper and
garlic. Transfer to a baking dish. Spread onion rings over
chicken. Bake 1 hour or until chicken is tender. Can be
reheated. Serves 4.

Chicken in Wine Sauce

Francine Sabin SED '73
Brookline, Massachusetts

8 chicken breasts, boned, skinned

2 cups bread crumbs

salt and pepper, to taste

6 tablespoons butter

1/2 lb. mushrooms, sliced

2 tablespoons flour

1 cup chicken stock

1 cup dry white wine

8 slices Monterey Jack cheese

Preheat oven to 350°. Coat chicken in bread crumbs,
season with salt and pepper and brown well in butter.
Remove to casserole dish. Sauté the mushrooms in pan
and transfer to casserole. Add 2 tablespoons flour to the
skillet. Cook, stirring in stock and wine. Put slices of
cheese on chicken. Pour wine sauce over chicken. Bake
uncovered for 20 minutes to 1/2 hour. Can be reheated.
Serves 6 to 8.

Chicken Fricassee with Dumplings

⅓ cup flour
1½ teaspoons salt
1 teaspoon marjoram
3 lbs. chicken pieces
¼ cup butter
1 cup chopped celery
2 onions, sliced
6 large carrots, pared, halved
1 bay leaf
4 whole cloves
9 whole black peppercorns
2½ cups chicken broth
1½ cups Bisquick
2 tablespoons chives
¼ cup milk
1 egg
½ cup light cream
chopped parsley

Nancy Seebert SON '68
Day's Creek, Oregon

Wash chicken and dry. Combine flour, salt and marjoram. Dredge chicken in mixture. Reserve left over flour. Put 2 tablespoons hot butter in a 6 quart Dutch oven. Sauté chicken, 4 pieces at a time, skin side down, until browned. Remove. To drippings, add celery, onions, carrots, bay leaf, cloves and peppercorns. Sauté 5 minutes. Stir in broth. Return chicken to Dutch oven. Simmer uncovered for 40 minutes. In a medium bowl, combine Bisquick and chives. With fork, blend in egg and milk. Drop batter by 6 rounded tablespoons, 2 to 3 inches apart onto chicken (not liquid). Cook uncovered over low heat 10 minutes. Cover tightly and cook 10 more minutes until dumplings are light and fluffy. Lift dumplings and keep warm. In a small bowl, combine reserved flour and cream, stirring until smooth. Stir into fricassee. Simmer 5 minutes until thickened. Replace dumplings and reheat. Sprinkle with chives or parsley. Can be reheated. Serves 4 to 6.

Coq au Vin

Ellee Koss CLA '78
Auburndale, Massachusetts

1 *chicken, cut up*
4 *tablespoons butter*
1 *large onion, chopped*
1 *large clove garlic, minced*
1 *cup quartered mushrooms*
1 *tablespoon flour*
1 *cup red or white burgundy wine*

In a skillet, brown chicken in butter. Add onion and garlic. Cook 5 minutes. Add mushrooms and cook 5 more minutes. Stir in flour. Add wine, stirring. Bake 1 hour at 325° covered. Season with salt and pepper. Can be reheated. Serves 4.

Turkey Cacciatore

Rebecca J. Gourley
SAR '74
Cookbook Committee
Medfield, Massachusetts

12 oz. *cooked turkey, sliced*
½ *cup olive oil*
1 *green pepper, minced*
1 *medium onion, minced*
1 *clove garlic, minced*
3 *cups tomato sauce*
½ *cup red wine*
1 *teaspoon basil*

Sauté turkey in oil until browned. Remove turkey and drain off excess oil. Sauté onions, pepper and garlic. Add sauce, wine and basil. Add turkey and simmer for 15 to 20 minutes. Can be reheated. Serves 4.

Turkey Breast Italian

3 to 4 lb. turkey breast
1 clove garlic, split
salt and pepper, to taste
1 lb. fresh mushrooms, sliced
2 cups Italian tomato sauce
½ cup red wine
½ bay leaf

Preheat oven to 350°. Place turkey breast in a baking dish. Rub with garlic, salt and pepper. Pour on mushrooms, tomato sauce and red wine. Bake 1½ hours, basting often. Can be reheated. Serves 6.

This is for people who hate to cook a whole turkey. Serve it with spaghetti.

Susan Freedman Mandel
SED '70
Cookbook Committee
Oakland, New Jersey

Molé

1 5 lb. chicken or turkey, poached
1 16 oz. can whole tomatoes, chopped
1 large onion, chopped
2 cloves garlic, crushed
2 squares baking chocolate, melted
4 tablespoons chili powder
½ teaspoon anise seed, crushed
1 teaspoon cinnamon
1 teaspoon coriander
1 teaspoon black pepper
1 teaspoon salt
½ teaspoon ground cloves
½ teaspoon ground cumin
chicken broth

Libby Cohen SED '77
Cape Elizabeth, Maine

Preheat oven to 350°. Cut chicken or turkey into bite size pieces, discarding skin and bones. Place in a casserole dish. Add tomatoes, onion, garlic, chocolate, chili, anise, cinnamon, coriander, pepper, salt, cloves and cumin. Pour over enough chicken broth (preferably from poaching chicken) to cover. Bake 30 minutes. Can be reheated. Serves 6 to 8.

"You Won't Believe It's a Stuffing" Stuffing

I could never stand plain old bread or cornmeal stuffings.

Dr. Matthew Witten
CLA '72
Cookbook Committee
Los Angeles, California

chopped chicken giblets
1 onion, diced
½ cup chopped scallion with greens
2 cloves garlic, minced
1 cup chopped celery
4 tablespoons butter
2½ lbs. wild rice, cooked, rinsed, drained
3 cups diced apples, preferably sweet
1 oz. Cointreau or Grand Marnier
1 cup raisins
3 tablespoons orange peel, shredded
2 cups chicken stock
3 pieces bread, soaked, squeezed dry
salt and pepper, to taste

In 4 tablespoons of butter, sauté giblets, onions, scallion, garlic and celery until tender. Add rice, apples, Grand Marnier, raisins and orange peel. Add stock. Simmer 40 minutes or until liquid is absorbed. Add bread and salt and pepper to taste. Makes enough to stuff a 6 to 8 lb. bird.

5 Meats

Meats

5

Cold Sliced Tenderloin of Beef

5	lb. tenderloin of beef, whole, fat trimmed
2	teaspoons butter
2	teaspoons flour
1	teaspoon butter

Marinade

½	cup soy sauce
½	cup peanut oil
4 to 5	cloves garlic
	grated rind of 1 orange
½	cup Madeira wine
1	tablespoon black pepper

Mary Ross Finn
The late wife of
Daniel J. Finn
Vice President for
University Relations

Marinate the tenderloin for 12 to 24 hours turning several times. Preheat oven to 500°. Place fillet on a rack in a roasting pan and reduce oven to 350°. Bake for 18 to 30 minutes. A fillet is usually cooked rare when the internal temperature reaches 120°. Boil the marinade and stir in a mixture of 2 teaspoons butter and 2 teaspoons of flour to thicken the sauce. Add another teaspoon of butter. Slice the tenderloin into 1 inch or thicker slices and spoon some of the sauce over them. The remainder of the sauce can be served separately hot or at room temperature. Serves 12 to 15 people.

Chateaubriand

Hans Bucher
Executive Chef
Hyatt Regency
Cambridge, Massachusetts

2 lbs. tenderloin of beef

1 cup peanut oil

2 tablespoons cognac

1 tablespoon Worcestershire sauce

1 clove garlic, crushed

dash ginger

½ onion, minced

pepper, to taste

Have a butcher remove all fat and "silverskin" from beef. Place in a bowl. Add the oil, cognac, Worcestershire, garlic, ginger, onion and pepper. Turn to coat. Marinate for 12 to 24 hours. Drain dry with toweling. Preheat broiler. Broil for 10 to 20 minutes until meat is done as desired. Good cold. Serves 4.

Boeuf en Brochette

The marinade really makes this dish. It's great cooked on the grill for summer cookouts or under the broiler during the winter.

Leah F. Gould PAL '37
Cookbook Committee
Elberon, New Jersey

2 cups salad oil

¼ cup vinegar

1 tablespoon minced onion

2½ teaspoons salt

1 teaspoon basil

1 teaspoon oregano

¼ teaspoon ground black pepper

¼ teaspoon minced garlic

2½ lbs. sirloin steak, cut into 1 inch squares

16 tiny white onions, parboiled

2 large green peppers, 1 inch squares

8 large mushrooms

4 medium tomatoes, quartered

Combine oil, vinegar, onion, salt, basil, oregano, pepper and garlic. Pour over beef. Cover and let marinate 3 to 4 hours at room temperature or overnight in refrigerator. Preheat broiler. Alternate cubes of beef, onions, green peppers, mushrooms and tomatoes on 8 skewers. Brush with marinade and broil until meat is done as desired. Brush with marinade during cooking. Serve immediately. Serves 8.

Bul-Kogi

¼	cup minced scallion
2	tablespoons peanut oil
2	tablespoons crushed sesame seeds
2	tablespoons granulated sugar
1	tablespoon white vinegar
1	teaspoon minced garlic
¼	teaspoon ground ginger
2	lbs. flank steak

Korean Flank Steak—this is particularly good at a picnic or for an appetizer.

Judith Walker Tait
SPC '62
Rockville, Maryland

In a glass or enamel baking dish (do not use aluminum), combine the scallion, oil, sesame seeds, sugar, vinegar, garlic and ginger. Add steak and turn over in the marinade rubbing it with your hands. Marinate covered for 6 to 24 hours. Add soy sauce and rub in well. Preheat broiler. Broil 3 to 6 minutes on each side. Slice diagonally into thin slices. Serve hot or cold. Serves 4.

Beef Stroganoff

12	½ inch thick tenderloin of beef slices
¼	cup unsalted butter
4	teaspoons paprika
2	cups beef stock
4	teaspoons lemon juice
½	cup dry sherry
½	cup cognac
1	lb. mushrooms, thinly sliced
¼	cup unsalted butter
1	cup sour cream
	salt, to taste

Claudia Duff
Alumni House

Melt ¼ cup butter and sauté mushrooms until lightly browned; set aside. Put fillet slices and butter into a cold pan and bring to high heat to brown the beef fast. Add paprika and salt to taste. Remove from heat and turn the meat to coat it. Return to heat and add beef stock, lemon juice, sherry and cognac. Remove the meat and keep warm. Reduce the sauce to about 1½ cups; remove the pan from heat and add sour cream. Stir well. Reheat a little, but not too much or the sauce will curdle. Turn meat and mushrooms in the sauce and serve immediately. Serve with rice or noodles. Serves 6.

Bistecca Pizzaiola

This makes a delicious meal when served with baked artichokes, potatoes and tossed salad.

Filomena Sinclitico
Costello CBA '48
Chelmsford, Massachusetts

2	*tablespoons olive oil*
1	*2 lb. sirloin steak, 1½ inch thick*
1	*clove garlic, crushed*
3	*cups (1 can) Italian tomatoes*
½	*teaspoon crushed oregano*
½	*teaspoon crushed basil*
	salt and pepper, to taste

Heat olive oil in a heavy skillet and brown meat on both sides with garlic. Remove and set aside. Add tomatoes and simmer 10 minutes. Return steak to pan. Add basil and oregano. Correct seasoning with salt and pepper. Simmer 20 minutes. Remove from heat. Can be reheated. Serves 3 to 4.

Stir-Fried String Beans with Sliced Meat

Sterne E. Barnett CBA '35
Cookbook Committee
Chestnut Hill, Massachusetts

3	*tablespoons dark soy sauce*
1	*tablespoon sugar*
1	*tablespoon sherry*
1	*tablespoon cornstarch*
2	*tablespoons water*
1	*lb. sirloin or pork, cut into 1 inch squares, ¹/₁₆ inch thick*
2	*tablespoons peanut oil*
½	*cup beef or chicken stock, boiled*
1	*lb. string beans, ½ inch diagonal slices*

Combine soy sauce, sugar, sherry, cornstarch and water. Blend ½ mixture with cut up meat and let marinate 10 to 15 minutes. Heat 1 tablespoon oil in heavy skillet or wok. Add string beans and stir fry for 1 minute. Boil remaining marinade, add to wok and cover. Cook 3 minutes. Remove cover. Cook 5 minutes more, stirring constantly. Remove beans from pan and set aside. Add remaining tablespoon oil to wok. Add meat mixture and fry for 2 minutes. Add string beans and juices and cook together for 1 minute more. Serve with steamed rice. Serve immediately. Serves 6.

Beef with Oyster Sauce

½ lb. sirloin, cut into 1½ inch slices, ¼ inch thick
¼ cup white wine or dry sherry
1 tablespoon cornstarch
1 tablespoon soy sauce
3 tablespoons peanut oil
1 tablespoon sugar
ground black pepper, to taste
1 scallion, chopped
1 tablespoon oyster sauce (from Chinese grocery stores)
½ lb. mushrooms, sliced
1 teaspoon cornstarch mixed with ¼ cup water

In traditional Chinese cooking, you serve one pork, one shrimp, one chicken and one beef dish. This is a common Chinese beef dish, but is sufficient in itself served with rice.

Dr. Lily Lee Salcedo
Professor
Department of Biochemistry
School of Medicine

Marinate beef in mixture of wine, cornstarch, soy sauce, 1 tablespoon oil, sugar and pepper, 20 minutes. Stir fry beef in 2 tablespoons of hot peanut oil for 1 minute. Remove beef. Add scallion, marinade, oyster sauce and mushrooms. When cooked, return beef to pan. Add cornstarch mixture and cook until sauce thickens and clears. Serve immediately. Serves 4.

Boston Sukiyaki

This can be assembled at the table for guests.

Mary Shroeder CLA '41
Brookline, Massachusetts

2	lbs. top round or London broil 2 inch strips, thinly sliced
4	tablespoons vegetable oil
½	cup stock
¾	cup Japanese soy sauce
⅓	cup sugar
3	onions, finely sliced
1	cup sliced celery
1	cup sliced canned bamboo shoots
1	lb. mushrooms, thinly sliced
4	scallions, sliced

In a large skillet, heat 2 tablespoons oil and brown meat. Combine the stock, soy sauce and sugar in a bowl. Add ½ mixture to the meat. In a separate pan, sauté the onions and celery in 2 tablespoons oil for 3 minutes. Add mushrooms and bamboo shoots, cook 3 minutes longer. Add scallions, cook 1 minute. Add remaining stock mixture. Combine vegetables with meat, heat together 1 minute. Serve hot over rice. Can be reheated.

Variation: Before serving toss in 10 oz. fresh cleaned spinach and cook until wilted.

Beef Provençale

This is a truly international dish—I copied it from a friend in England who copied it from a friend in France.

Sandra J. Levine SED '59
Cookbook Committee
Newtonville, Massachusetts

1	lb. beef, cut into 1 inch cubes
2	tablespoons oil
1	slice bacon, diced
2	tablespoons butter
1½	onions, sliced
¼	red or green pepper, diced
1	large tomato, diced
1	large carrot, diced
4	small mushrooms
1½	cups water

4 tablespoons red wine

1 tablespoon tomato paste

2 teaspoons salt

1 teaspoon oregano

1 teaspoon thyme

$\frac{1}{8}$ teaspoon pepper

Preheat oven to 325°. In a skillet, brown meat in oil.
Place in 2 quart casserole dish. Sauté bacon, onion, pepper, tomato, carrots and mushrooms in butter. When
soft, add to meat. Combine water, wine, tomato paste,
salt, thyme and pepper. Bring to a boil on top of the
stove and add to casserole. Bake 1½ to 2 hours or until
tender. Correct seasoning with salt and pepper. Can be
frozen. Serves 4.

Hungarian Beef Goulash with Caraway Noodles

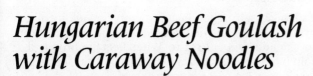

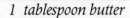

1 tablespoon butter

1 lb. lean beef, cut into 1½ inch cubes

1 medium onion, chopped

1 teaspoon salt

1 teaspoon thyme, parsley, bay leaf

$\frac{1}{8}$ teaspoon pepper

1 tablespoon paprika

1 cup water

$\frac{1}{4}$ cup tomato paste

4 oz. medium egg noodles

caraway seeds

Barbara G. Papesch
CLA '62
Boston, Massachusetts

In a large skillet, sear beef cubes on all sides in butter.
Add onions and cook until lightly brown. Stir in water,
tomato paste, paprika, salt, herbs and pepper. Cover and
simmer gently for 2½ hours. Cook egg noodles. Serve
goulash on noodles, sprinkled lightly with caraway
seeds. Can be reheated. Serves 2 to 3.

Beef Ragoût

Phyllis Ratcliffe Hamilton
CLA '62
Libertytown, Maryland

cooking oil
2½ lbs. lean beef, cut into 1½ inch cubes
salt and pepper, to taste
2½ cups beef broth
¾ cup dry red wine
2 large cloves garlic, minced
1 large bay leaf
10 small white onions
2 lbs. baby carrots
2 lbs. small whole potatoes
½ lb. sliced mushrooms
2 tablespoons flour

In a large cast iron pot, heat just enough cooking oil to cover the bottom. When hot, put in beef cubes, seasoning, salt and pepper to taste. When beef has browned, drain off excess fat. Add wine, garlic and bay leaf. Cover and simmer 1½ to 2 hours until beef is tender. Add vegetables, simmer ½ hour. Blend ¼ cup of water with flour. Put meat and vegetables aside and stir mixture slowly into sauce. Cook and stir until thickened. Can be reheated. Serves 6.

Italian Beef Stew

A variation of Spezzatino di Vitello, a veal stew, using stew beef or boneless chuck instead of veal.

Yole Ames CLA '51
Past Vice-President
General Alumni Association
National Alumni Council

4 onions, thinly sliced
4 large green and/or red peppers, sliced lengthwise
3 tablespoons butter
3 tablespoons oil
½ lb. mushrooms, sliced
4 lbs. boneless beef, cut into 2 inch chunks
⅓ to ½ cup semi-dry sherry
salt and pepper, to taste
2 to 3 cups cut up tomatoes or canned whole or sliced tomatoes with juice
10 oz. package frozen peas, thawed

In a skillet, sauté onion and peppers in butter and oil until tender crisp. Remove. Add mushrooms to pepper and onion and toss well. Set aside. Brown the meat in the pan. Pour off excess oil. Add sherry, stirring up brown bits, salt and pepper and tomatoes. Simmer 1½ hours or until tender. Add onion mixture and peas. Heat 10 minutes. Freezes well. Serves 8.

Sweet and Sour Short Ribs

3 lbs. short ribs	
3 tablespoons vegetable oil	
¾ cup water	
¼ cup brown sugar	
2 tablespoons cornstarch	
1 teaspoon salt	
⅓ cup vinegar	
1 tablespoon soy sauce	
1 (No. 2) can pineapple chunks	
½ cup thinly sliced green pepper	
¼ cup thinly sliced onion	

Camille Anthony
William Anthony
Director
Sargent Rehabilitation Counseling
Sargent College of Allied Health Professions

In a skillet, brown the short ribs in oil, add water to cover and simmer for 1½ to 2 hours or until tender. Add more water, if required. In a small saucepan, combine the sugar, cornstarch, salt, vinegar and soy sauce. Drain syrup from pineapple. Add water to make 1 cup, if necessary. Add to sauce and cook, stirring until thick and clear. Pour over meat and simmer 10 minutes. Stir in pineapple, peppers and onions. Simmer 5 minutes. Serve with rice. Can be reheated. Serves 4 to 6.

Italian Braciole

Filomena Sinclitico
Costello CBA '48
Chelmsford, Massachusetts

4 *top round steaks, 6 inches in diameter,*
   ¼ inch thick

Italian bread crumbs

4 *tablespoons lard or bacon fat*

1 *(No. 2) can Italian plum tomatoes, drained*

6 *oz. can tomato paste*

½ *teaspoon crushed basil*

½ *teaspoon salt*

6 *oz. water*

Spread the steaks with 2 tablespoons lard or bacon fat. Do not use oil or butter. Spread the center of each steak with crumbs keeping 1 inch from edges. Pull firmly and truss. Melt remaining lard in kettle and brown meat rolls on all sides. Add tomatoes, tomato paste and 6 oz. of water. Stir to combine. Add basil and salt. Simmer very gently for 2 hours. Serve with pasta. Can be reheated. Serves 4 to 6.

Sauerbraten Cubes

Susan Moger CLA '73
Cookbook Committee
Los Angeles, California

¾ *cup water*

½ *cup dry red wine*

½ *cup wine vinegar*

½ *medium onion, sliced*

2 *tablespoons brown sugar*

1 *lb. beef round, cut into 1 inch cubes*

2 *tablespoons vegetable oil*

¼ *cup crushed gingersnap cookies*

In a bowl, combine water, wine, vinegar, sugar and onions. Stir in beef. Cover and marinate in refrigerator for 6 hours or overnight. Drain, reserving marinade. In medium skillet, brown meat in hot oil; drain off excess fat. Add reserved marinade and simmer meat covered for 45 minutes or until meat is tender. Add gingersnaps, cook and stir until mixture is thickened and bubbly. Serve over hot cooked noodles. Can be frozen and reheated. Serves 3 to 4.

Chulnt (Cholent)

1 lb. dried large lima beans
1 lb. dried chick peas
4 to 5 lbs. double brisket
8 carrots, cut in thirds
8 eggs, hard cooked, unpeeled
8 whole potatoes, peeled
salt and pepper, to taste
3 large onions, sliced
1 bunch celery, sliced

A traditional shabbat meal that must be made the day before and only served for the shabbat meal.

Shelley Tiber
Abe Tiber SMG '70
Cookbook Committee
Haifa, Israel

Two days before serving, soak beans overnight in water and cover. Brown the meat in a large skillet. Line the bottom of a large casserole dish or roasting pan with carrots. Drain beans and add with potatoes, meat and eggs to casserole. Season with salt and pepper. Add water to cover. Simmer on lowest heat overnight or crockpot set at 250°. The next morning add the onions and celery. Simmer until dinner. Can be reheated. Serves 8 to 10.

Italian Pot Roast

3 to 4 large onions, sliced
2 tablespoons butter
3 lb. pot roast
1½ cups plum tomatoes, drained
1 cup dry white wine
3 large carrots, sliced
3 stalks celery, sliced
2 teaspoons salt
½ teaspoon pepper
½ teaspoon basil

Dorothy Martin Apgar
SON '61
Flagler Beach, Florida

In a Dutch oven, sauté onions in butter until soft. Add meat, brown on all sides. Add tomatoes, carrots, celery, salt, pepper, wine and basil. Simmer 2½ hours or until tender. Slice meat and serve with sauce. Can be reheated. Serves 6.

Pot Roast with Potatoes

Ruth Albert
DGE '63/SED '65/'69
Brockton, Massachusetts

3 to 4 lbs. boneless beef, chuck or brisket
3 tablespoons vegetable oil
2 large onions, sliced
4 carrots, cut into chunks
1 stalk celery, thinly sliced
1 bay leaf
salt and pepper, to taste
1 cup apple juice
1 cup water
6 small potatotes, peeled
3 large sweet potatoes, peeled, halved
parsley

Preheat oven to 300°. Brown beef slowly on all sides in oil. Add onions, carrots, celery, bay leaf, salt, pepper, apple juice and water. Cover and place in oven for 1 hour. Discard bay leaf. Add potatoes and sweet potatoes. Cover and return to oven. Bake 1 more hour or until meat and potatoes are tender. Strain liquid that is left in pot. Remove any fat that rises to top. Serve liquid over potatoes and slices of meat. Garnish with parsley. Can be reheated. Serves 6 to 8.

Meat Loaf Pie

Denise Oberti SON '73
Danville, Pennsylvania

1 lb. ground beef
⅔ cup evaporated milk
½ cup fine bread crumbs
1 teaspoon minced garlic
⅓ cup tomato sauce
4 oz. mushrooms, sliced
1 cup shredded sharp Cheddar cheese
¼ teaspoon oregano
2 tablespoons grated Parmesan cheese

Preheat oven to 375°. In a bowl, combine beef, milk, crumbs and garlic. Pat into a 9 inch pie plate pulling up on sides of pan. Cover with tomato sauce and mushrooms. Top with Cheddar and sprinkle with oregano. Add Parmesan. Bake 25 minutes. Serve immediately. Serves 4 to 6.

Meat Loaf

1½ lbs. ground beef	**Family favorite**
½ lb. ground veal	
½ lb. ground pork	**Janet Asimov**
1 cup cracker crumbs	**Isaac Asimov**
2 eggs	*20th Century Archives*
1 large onion, minced	*Mugar Library*
1 clove garlic, crushed	
½ carrot, grated	
5 sage leaves, crumbled	
1 teaspoon freshly ground pepper	
2 cups milk, warmed	
2 strips bacon	

Preheat oven to 375°. In a very large bowl, mix meats, crumbs, eggs, onions, garlic, carrot, sage and pepper. Add warm milk, lifting lightly with a fork to mix. Put into a greased loaf pan gently. Do not press down. Top with strips of bacon. Bake uncovered for 1½ hours or until brown all around the sides. Can be served cold. Serves 6.

Meat Loaf in Pastry Crust

June Neves SMG '72
Fall River, Massachusetts

2 lbs. ground beef

1 lb. ground pork

1 onion, chopped

1 cup crushed Ritz crackers

3 eggs

1 tablespoon Dijon mustard

1 tablespoon salt

1 egg, lightly beaten

2 pie shells

8 oz. Port Salut cheese, sliced

Preheat oven to 350°. In a bowl, combine the beef, pork, onion, crackers, eggs, mustard and salt. Mix well. Pack into a loaf pan and bake 1 hour. Cool, drain off excess fat and chill. Preheat oven to 400°. Roll pie pastry into a rectangle large enough to wrap around meat. Place cheese slices on pastry and top with the meat loaf. Wrap pastry over meat loaf pinching edges to seal. Place on a baking sheet. Brush with egg. Bake 30 minutes or until golden. Serve hot or cold. Can be reheated. Serves 6.

Meat Loaf Supreme

Daphne S. Palmer
Friend of Boston University

2 lbs. lean ground beef

½ cup minced celery

1½ cups canned plum tomatoes

½ cup minced parsley

2 teaspoons grated onion

1 teaspoon salt

¼ teaspoon pepper

½ teaspoon oregano

2 teaspoons Worcestershire sauce

2 eggs, slightly beaten

1½ cups bread crumbs

Preheat oven to 350°. Grease a 9x5x3 inch loaf pan. In a bowl, combine the beef, celery, tomatoes, parsley, onion, Worcestershire, salt, oregano and pepper. Add bread crumbs and eggs. Mix well. Pack into the prepared pan. Bake for 1 hour. Serve hot or cold. Serves 6 to 8.

Stuffed Cabbage

2	lbs. ground beef
2	slices white bread, torn into pieces
1	egg
¼	cup tomato juice or water
1	teaspoon salt
½	onion, grated
1	large head cabbage
2	carrots, sliced diagonally
½	cup raisins (optional)
1	onion, sliced
1	large can tomatoes
1	tablespoon brown sugar
1	tablespoon lemon juice
1	tablespoon salt

This is even better the second day.

Sterne Barnett CBA '35
Cookbook Committee
Chestnut Hill, Massachusetts

In a bowl, combine the meat, bread, egg, onion, tomato juice and salt. Wilt cabbage by placing in boiling water and simmering for about 5 minutes. Peel the leaves off. Place a tablespoon of the meat mixture in the center of each leaf and close the leaf, envelope fashion. Place a layer of rolls, folded side down, in a large, heavy casserole dish or Dutch oven. Mix carrots, onion and raisins. Place on cabbage. Repeat and make layers. Use excess meat to make meat balls. Shred smaller leaves of cabbage and place on top. Add tomatoes, brown sugar, lemon juice and salt; pour over casserole. Cook covered on top of stove for 1 hour. Taste and correct seasoning. Preheat oven to 350°. Remove cover and bake 1 hour until juice is reduced and rolls are brown and glazed. Freezes beautifully. Serves 6.

Stuffed Whole Cabbage

This is a conversation piece.

Elaine Spivack Katz
SAR '76
Cookbook Committee
Oak Lawn, Illinois

1 *medium head cabbage*
½ *lb. lean ground beef*
½ *lb. mushrooms, sliced*
¼ *cup chopped celery*
¼ *cup chopped onion*
⅓ *cup rice, cooked*
2 *tablespoons tomato sauce*
2 *tablespoons grated carrot*
¼ *teaspoon minced garlic*
⅛ *teaspoon fresh ground pepper*
pinch of ground clove
1 *egg*
ketchup (optional)
cheesecloth
string

Preheat oven to 350°. Remove core from cabbage. Set aside. Hollow out cabbage from stem end, leaving ½ inch shell. In a skillet, cook beef, mushrooms, celery and onion on medium heat until meat is brown. Add rice, tomato sauce and carrot. Cook 3 minutes. Season with garlic, pepper and clove. While mixture is still hot, quickly stir in egg. Continue stirring until mixture is just warm to touch, about 5 minutes. Spoon filling into hollowed out cabbage until loosely packed; replace stem. Wrap cabbage in cheesecloth, tie tightly with string. Put cabbage in 9 inch square baking dish: pour in enough hot water to cover bottom of dish to ½ inch depth. Bake at 350° on lowest shelf of oven until cabbage is tender, about 45 to 60 minutes. Remove cheesecloth; transfer cabbage to heated serving platter. Cut into 4 to 6 wedges; open cabbage onto serving platter in decorative design. Can be reheated. Serves 4 to 6.

Hamburger Pie

1 9 inch pie shell
1 lb. ground beef
¼ teaspoon oregano
¼ teaspoon basil
1 small can tomato paste
½ pint sour cream
1 cup shredded mozzarella cheese
salt and pepper, to taste
½ teaspoon minced garlic

Neila Straub SED '70
Beverly, Massachusetts

Preheat oven to 350°. In a skillet, sauté ground beef, breaking it up until browned. Drain fat. Add garlic, oregano, basil, salt, pepper and tomato paste. Cook over low heat 5 minutes, stirring occasionally. Place beef mixture in crust. Carefully spread sour cream over top (do not mix in). Top with cheese. Bake 15 to 20 minutes or until crust is golden. Remove and let sit 10 minutes before cutting. Serves 6 to 8.

Sour Cream Beef Casserole

½ lb. broad noodles, cooked, drained
1 lb. lean ground beef
1 tablespoon butter
8 oz. can tomato sauce
1 teaspoon salt
¼ teaspoon minced garlic
⅛ teaspoon pepper
1 cup creamed cottage cheese
1 cup sour cream
6 onions, minced
¾ cup shredded mild Cheddar cheese

On clear nights, I often get a Baltimore radio program on my dial that spells out recipes for listeners. This is one of them.

Sandra J. Levine SED '59
Cookbook Committee
Newtonville, Massachusetts

Preheat oven to 350°. In a skillet, brown beef in butter. Add tomato sauce, salt, garlic and pepper. Simmer 5 minutes. Mix noodles, cottage cheese, sour cream and onions. Alternate layers of noodles and meat mixture in a greased 2 quart casserole. Begin with noodles and end with meat. Top with cheese. Bake 20 minutes until cheese bubbles and browns. Can be reheated. Serves 6.

Gourmet Casserole

This came from the dining room of Westminster College in Salt Lake City, Utah.

Helen Crawford Bander
SED '31
Cookbook Committee
Paris, Arkansas

7 lbs. ground beef
7 cups tomato sauce
4 lbs. cream cheese
4 lbs. cottage cheese
1 pint sour cream
2 lbs. scallions, minced
1¼ cups minced green pepper
1½ tablespoons salt
2 tablespoons pepper
4 lbs. egg noodles, cooked, drained

Preheat oven to 375°. In a large skillet, sauté the beef until browned. Add the tomato sauce and simmer 35 minutes. In a large bowl, beat the cream cheese until smooth. Fold in the cottage cheese, sour cream, scallions, peppers, salt and pepper. Spread ½ the noodles in a greased baking pan; add the cheese mixture to cover and top with remaining noodles. Pour sauce over the top. Cover with foil. Bake 45 minutes. Remove foil and bake 15 minutes longer. Can be made ahead and frozen. Serves 50.

Simple Moussaka

An easy way to make and enjoy an elegant international dish

Bert M. Hirshberg
Cookbook Coordinator

1 lb. ground beef
1 onion, chopped
salt and pepper, to taste
2 large eggplants, peeled, sliced
¼ lb. butter
2 eggs
¼ cup bread crumbs

Preheat oven to 350°. In a skillet, brown ground beef. Add onions and season with salt and pepper. Set aside. Brown eggplant slices in butter. Grease a 9x13 inch baking pan. Layer in eggplant and meat. Beat eggs and pour over the top. Sprinkle with bread crumbs. Bake 50 minutes. Can be reheated. Serves 6.

Moussaka

1½ lbs. ground beef
1 medium onion, minced
2 tablespoons butter
salt and pepper, to taste
1 teaspoon cinnamon
1 8 oz. can tomato paste
1 large eggplant, ½ inch slices, salted
½ cup grated Swiss cheese

Sauce

4 tablespoons butter
5 tablespoons flour
2 cups milk
salt and freshly ground pepper, to taste
1 egg
freshly grated Parmesan cheese

This is a real Greek recipe. It takes more trouble than most moussaka recipes to prepare, but what you lose in time you make up in flavor.

Claire Shapiro Soja
CLA '68
Cookbook Committee
Harvard, Massachusetts

Preheat oven to 350°. Brown meat and onion in butter. Season with salt, pepper and cinnamon. Dilute tomato paste with 2 cans of water and add to pan. Simmer 15 to 20 minutes. Salt eggplant. Let stand 20 minutes. Rinse and drain. Simmer in boiling water 10 minutes. Drain. Arrange a layer of eggplant pieces in a shallow casserole dish. Add a layer of meat sauce, sprinkle with cheese, add another layer of eggplant, then the rest of the meat mixture and cheese. Make sauce by melting butter, stirring in flour, and cooking for 3 minutes. Add milk, beating with a wire whisk until smooth and thickened. Correct seasoning with salt and pepper. Remove from heat, stir in egg and beat until well mixed. Pour ½ of sauce over moussaka. Bake for 10 to 15 minutes. Cook remaining sauce until it reaches a boil. Remove casserole from oven, add the rest of the sauce and sprinkle lavishly with grated Parmesan cheese. Bake 45 to 50 minutes or until golden brown. Allow more time if recipe is doubled. Cut into squares to serve. The meat and eggplant mixture may be made the day before and refrigerated, but make the egg sauce just before baking. Allow more time for baking if the dish is taken right from refrigerator. Serves 4 to 5.

Papas Rellenas

Ethel Chirinos SED '75
Cookbook Committee
Lima, Peru

2 tablespoons oil
1 onion, minced
½ lb. sirloin, diced, or ground beef
salt and pepper, to taste
½ cup seedless raisins
6 ripe olives, sliced
2 eggs, hard cooked, chopped
2 medium tomatoes, diced
12 medium white potatoes
1 egg
fat for deep frying

In a skillet, sauté the onion in oil until brown. Add the meat and cook until it loses its color. Add the tomatoes, salt and pepper and simmer 3 minutes. Add the raisins, olives and egg. Remove from heat and cool. Boil the potatoes in water covered until tender. Drain, peel and mash. While still warm, beat in the egg, salt and pepper. Knead well. Make balls about the size of a walnut. Dust fingers with flour to prevent sticking. Flatten dough, fill with a spoonful of filling and seal edges. Roll stuffed potatoes in flour. Heat fat to 375°. Fry until golden. Serves 6 to 8.

Texas Hash

Edith Thompson Adams
SED '42
Marlboro, Massachusetts

2 large onions, chopped
2 green peppers, finely sliced
3 tablespoons cooking oil
1½ lbs. ground beef
1 cup chopped celery (optional)
2 cups canned tomatoes
½ cup uncooked rice, scant
1 teaspoon pepper
¾ teaspoon chili powder (optional)

Preheat oven to 350°. Sweat onions and peppers slowly in oil until onions are yellow. Add beef and fry until mixture falls apart. Add celery, tomatoes, rice, salt, pepper and chili powder. Mix well. Put into large casserole dish. Cover and bake 45 minutes or until done. Can be reheated. Serves 6.

Quick Leftover Casserole

1¼ cups uncooked rice

3 to 4 medium carrots, 1 inch cubes

3 to 4 medium celery stalks, 1 inch cubes

1 large onion, thinly sliced

2¼ cups water

½ teaspoon salt

¼ teaspoon freshly ground pepper

¼ teaspoon curry (optional)

1 clove garlic, chopped

2 cups leftover meat or chicken,
   cut into 1 inch cubes

In large pot, combine rice, vegetables, water and seasonings. Bring water to a boil and simmer with pot tightly covered for 20 minutes. Stir meat into mixture and check seasonings. Simmer until all liquid is absorbed. Serve immediately. Serves 4 to 6.

Sharon Friedman
DGE '68/ SED '70
Sharon, Massachusetts

Potted Meatballs

1 lb. ground beef

2 tablespoons butter

¾ cup bread crumbs

1 egg

½ cup water

1 teaspoon salt

1 medium onion, sliced

8 oz. can tomato sauce with mushrooms

½ cup water

Mark Premack
DGE '73/CLA '75
Omaha, Nebraska

In a large skillet, brown onion in butter. Combine ground beef, bread crumbs, egg, salt and ½ cup water and form into meatballs. Put meatballs on top of onions. Add tomato mushroom sauce and ½ cup water. Simmer for 1 hour, stirring occasionally. Can be reheated. Serves 4.

Sweet and Sour Meatballs

Nancy R. Seebert SON '68
Day's Creek, Oregon
Pat Garrity CBS'81
Staff

1 *lb. lean ground beef*
½ *lb. ground pork*
1 *cup oatmeal or bread crumbs*
½ *cup chopped water chestnuts*
salt and pepper, to taste
¾ *cup vinegar*
½ *cup sugar*
½ *cup brown sugar*
½ *cup pineapple juice*
¼ *cup water*
¼ *cup ketchup*
½ *teaspoon paprika*

Combine the beef, pork, oatmeal, water chestnuts, salt and pepper. Mix well. Shape into 30, 1 inch balls. In a 2 quart saucepan, combine vinegar, sugars, pineapple juice, water, ketchup and paprika. Bring to boil. Add meatballs and simmer until cooked through. Serve over rice or as an hors d'oeuvre. Can be frozen. Serves 6.

Mushroom-Stuffed Meat Cakes with Cheese Sauce

Mark Premack
DGE '73/CLA '75
Omaha, Nebraska

½ *cup rice, cooked*
1 *tablespoon chopped scallion*
¼ *lb. mushrooms, sliced*
2 *tablespoons cornstarch*
2 *cups milk*
2 *tablespoons butter*
salt and pepper, to taste
1½ *cups shredded sharp Cheddar cheese*
1 *egg, beaten*
1 *cup soft bread crumbs*
1 *lb. ground beef*

Preheat oven to 350°. In a saucepan, mix cornstarch
with milk until smooth. Add butter, salt and pepper.
Bring to a boil over medium heat, stirring constantly;
boil 1 minute. Stir in cheese until melted and set aside.
Combine egg, ⅓ cup sauce and crumbs. Mix in meat.
Shape into 4, 6 inch patties. Mince ¼ cup of the mushrooms, mix with rice and scallion. Spoon 2 tablespoons
mixture onto each patty. Seal meat around stuffing.
Bake uncovered in 8x8x2 inch baking pan at 350° for
45 minutes. Combine remaining sauce and mushrooms;
heat. Serve over meat. Can be reheated. Serves 4.

Popover Pie

1 *small onion, thinly sliced*	
3 *tablespoons butter*	
¾ *lb. lean ground beef*	
½ *cup cooked vegetables*	
1 *cup gravy*	
¼ *teaspoon salt*	
⅛ *teaspoon pepper*	
2 *eggs*	
1 *cup milk*	
1 *cup sifted all-purpose flour*	
½ *teaspoon salt*	

This is an easy, economi-
cal main dish that is excit-
ing to serve because of the
puffy popover collar that
rings the meat and vegetable center.

Phyllis Young
Staff
School of Education

In a skillet, sauté onion in 1 tablespoon butter until
tender. Brown meat in onion and butter, breaking up
with spoon. Add vegetables. Stir ¼ cup of gravy into
meat mixture, blend well; add salt and pepper. Set
oven to 425°. In medium size bowl, mix together the
2 eggs, milk, flour and salt until batter is smooth. Melt
2 tablespoons of butter in the oven in a 10 inch pie plate
or quiche dish. When the butter is melted, remove pie
plate from the oven and pour in the popover batter.
Spread meat/vegetable filling evenly over the batter
within 1 inch of the edge. Bake for 30 minutes, or until
brown and puffy. Heat remaining gravy to serve with
pie. Serve immediately. Serves 4 to 6.
  Note: Any combination of leftover meat and vegetables may be used for pie filling.

Veal with Lemon and Wine

Many restaurants call this veal piccata. This is my variation after sampling the dish in several different restaurants.

Susan Freedman Mandel
SED '70
Cookbook Committee
Oakland, New Jersey
Susan Moger CLA '73
Cookbook Committee
Los Angeles, California

1	lb. veal cutlets
1	egg, beaten
1/2	cup bread crumbs
1/4	cup olive oil
1	clove garlic, peeled
2	lemons
1/2	cup white wine
1	bay leaf

Coat veal with egg then bread crumbs. In a skillet, brown veal in oil with garlic over medium heat. Squeeze juice of 1 lemon over veal. Add wine and crumbled bay leaf. Simmer 2 minutes. Slice other lemon thinly. Serve veal on a platter decorated with lemon slices. Pour sauce over all. Serve immediately. Serves 4.

Serve this Indonesian veal dish over saffron rice and decorate with sliced fried bananas.

Jane Meredith Lamson
CLA '68
Brooklyn, New York

Ihbwen'saut *(Indonesian Veal)*

10	veal cutlets, pounded thin, cut into julienne strips
1	package River Rice, steamed, fluffy
	butter
1	lb. mushrooms, cleaned, sliced
1	fresh pineapple, cut into small chunks
4	bananas, sliced lengthwise
1/2	lb. fresh cherries, pitted, cut up
1	tablespoon butter
1 to 2	tablespoons flour
4 1/2	pints heavy cream
1/4	cup wine
2	teaspoons salt
1/3	teaspoon pepper
1/2	teaspoon curry powder (or to taste)
1/4	teaspoon saffron

Sauté mushrooms in 2 tablespoons of butter. Remove to dish. Cook rice for 45 minutes to 1 hour, adding saffron when nearly done. In a saucepan sauté veal. Remove to dish. In saucepan, sauté pineapple chunks and cherries, adding additional butter. Remove to dish. To make white sauce: Stir in butter and flour. Add heavy cream and wine in saucepan over medium heat. Add veal, pineapple, cherries, mushrooms and seasoning to sauce. Heat and serve over saffron rice. Decorate with fried bananas. Serves 8 to 10.

Veal Sardon

1 cup raisins
1½ cups sweet vermouth
¼ lb. butter
1 large Bermuda onion, chopped
2 to 3 cloves garlic, minced
2 cups cooked rice
3 tablespoons fresh mint or 1 tablespoon dried mint
1 cup pignoli or chopped walnuts
1 breast of veal, cut with center pocket
salt, to taste
2 tablespoons soy sauce
paprika, to taste

A salad of Boston lettuce dressed with oil, lemon juice, salt and pepper nicely complements this dish and tangy lime or lemon sherbet caps it.

Francesca Zamcheck
Friend of Boston University
West Newton, Massachusetts

Preheat oven to 350°. Soak raisins in vermouth for 10 minutes. In a casserole dish, melt butter and brown onions. Add garlic. Drain raisins, reserving wine. Combine raisins, rice, ¾ cup vermouth, mint and nuts. Stir in butter and onions. Stuff veal with rice mixture. Sew up the opening. Place in casserole. Pour remaining wine over the top and season with salt. Pour on soy sauce and dust with paprika. Cover. Bake 1½ to 2 hours or until tender, basting several times. Bake 20 minutes uncovered. Can be reheated. Serves 6.

Veal Marengo

Richard Lucas
Executive Chef
Hotel Sonesta
Cambridge, Massachusetts

4 tablespoons butter

1 tablespoon flour

1 lb. veal leg, cut into julienne strips

6 mushrooms

1 small carrot, julienne

1 onion, diced

1 clove garlic

6 oz. fresh tomatoes, diced

¼ cup brandy

1 cup veal stock

¼ cup roux (2 tablespoons flour mixed with
2 tablespoons melted butter)

salt and pepper, to taste

In a skillet, melt butter. Add flour and veal and sauté in hot butter. Add carrots, onion, tomatoes, mushrooms and garlic. Add brandy and ignite. Add veal stock and bring to a boil. Add roux and cook for 5 minutes. Season to taste. Can be reheated. Serves 2.

Veal with Mushrooms

Phyllis Ratcliffe Hamilton
CLA '62
Libertytown, Maryland

2 lbs. veal cutlets

4 eggs, slightly beaten

2 cups seasoned bread crumbs

4 tablespoons olive oil

1 lb. mushrooms, thinly sliced

12 slices Muenster cheese

½ cup sherry

½ cup chicken stock

Preheat oven to 350°. Flatten cutlets and marinate in eggs for 1 hour. In a skillet, heat the oil, dip veal into crumbs and brown on each side. Place in baking dish. Top each cutlet with mushrooms and a slice of cheese. May be kept in refrigerator overnight. Combine sherry and bouillon and pour over cutlets. Bake for 25 minutes basting twice. Serves 6 to 8.

Poitrine de Veau Farcie aux Olives

(Stuffed Breast of Veal with Olives)

1 4 lb. boned breast of veal, reserve bones
2 cups dry bread crumbs, untoasted
½ lb. lean ground pork
⅓ cup milk
12 pitted black olives, chopped
6 sprigs parsley, minced
½ teaspoon basil
¼ teaspoon salt
¼ teaspoon black pepper
pinch of nutmeg
1 egg, lightly beaten
2 tablespoons olive oil
1 onion, sliced
2 tomatoes, skinned, chopped
1 cup white wine
1 cup chicken broth

Terence Janericco CLA '61
Cookbook Committee Editor
Boston, Massachusetts

Preheat oven to 325°. Combine bread crumbs, pork, milk, olives, parsley, garlic, basil, salt, pepper, nutmeg and egg. Mix well. Spread breast of veal flat. Spread the stuffing over the veal and roll up like a jelly roll or wrap the meat around a core of stuffing, overlapping the edges of the breast. Do not wrap the veal too tightly. Tie securely. To prevent the stuffing from coming out of the open end during cooking, tie a heel of bread to each end of the veal roll or a square of foil. Heat the olive oil in a skillet and sauté the onion until soft but not brown. Remove to a casserole dish. Brown the veal on all sides in the skillet. Place the stuffed veal in the casserole. Add the tomatoes and wine to the skillet and bring to a boil again, stirring up any brown bits. Pour the contents of the skillet over the veal and add as many of the reserved bones as will fit. Cover tightly and braise in the oven for 3 hours or until tender. To serve hot: Remove the veal and keep it hot. Reduce the liquid in the casserole by ⅓. Season to taste, remove any excess fat and serve separately. To serve cold: Allow the veal to chill in the casserole overnight. Remove the meat and cut into thin slices. Can be reheated. Serves 6 to 8.

Stuffed Breast of Veal

Helen Crawford Bander
SED '31
Cookbook Committee
Paris, Arkansas

½	cup butter
½	cup sliced onion
½	cup sliced celery
¼	cup dried green pepper
1	clove garlic, crushed
6	slices dry bread, toasted
	water
¼	cup pimiento
1	teaspoon salt
½	teaspoon sage
¼	teaspoon pepper
1	egg
1	large breast of veal
3	cups tomato juice

Preheat oven to 325°. In a skillet, melt the butter, add the onion, celery, pepper and garlic. Cover and simmer 15 minutes. Soak bread in water, squeeze dry. Pour onion mixture over bread. Add pimiento, salt, sage, pepper and egg. Mix lightly with 2 forks. Cut a pocket in veal and stuff with onion/bread mixture. Skewer opening closed. Roast for 2½ to 3 hours, basting often with tomato juice. Let rest 20 minutes before serving. Serves 6.

Veal Marsala

Be sure to buy excellent veal and this will always taste delicious.

Nina Freid
Friend of Boston University
Roslyn, New York

2	lbs. veal, thinly sliced
¼	lb. butter
	pepper, to taste
½	lb. fresh mushrooms, sliced
1	small whole onion, sliced
1	clove garlic, crushed
1	tablespoon tomato paste
¼	teaspoon oregano
1	teaspoon flour
1½	cups chicken stock
1	cup Marsala wine

Brown veal quickly on both sides in butter. Remove veal and place in baking dish. Place sliced mushrooms and onion in pan and sauté. Add chopped garlic, tomato paste, oregano, pepper and flour and mix well. Add chicken stock and wine. Simmer for 5 minutes. Pour mixture over veal and bake in oven to heat. To freeze: Cover dish with aluminum foil and when ready to bake put in 375° oven for 30 minutes and serve. Serves 4 to 6.

Ossobuco Milanese

3 *veal shanks, each cut into 3, 2 inch thick pieces*	
⅓ *cup flour*	
2 *teaspoons salt*	
½ *teaspoon freshly ground black pepper*	
3 *tablespoons olive oil*	
3 *tablespoons butter*	
½ *teaspoon ground sage*	
1 *teaspoon rosemary*	
1 *onion, minced*	
3 *cloves garlic*	
2 *small carrots, minced*	
1 *stalk celery, minced*	
1½ *cups dry white wine*	
1½ *cups chicken stock*	
2 *tablespoons tomato paste*	
1½ *tablespoons minced parsley*	
1 *tablespoon grated lemon peel*	

Risë Stevens
20th Century Archives
Mugar Library

Dredge the meat in flour that has been seasoned with 1 teaspoon of salt and pepper. Heat the oil and butter together in a large skillet. Over medium heat, cook the meat on all sides until golden brown. If necessary, add a little more oil or butter. Arrange the meat in a casserole dish, standing each piece on its side so the marrow in the bone does not fall out as the meat cooks. Sprinkle the veal with sage and rosemary. Add the onion, 1 garlic clove, minced, the carrots and celery. Sprinkle the vegetables with the remaining teaspoon of salt. Cover closely and braise 10 minutes. Remove the cover and add the wine, chicken stock and tomato paste. Cover and simmer on top of the stove for 2 hours or in a 325° oven. Mince the remaining 2 cloves of garlic and combine with the parsley and lemon peel. Sprinkle the mixture, called gremolata, over the veal and serve immediately. Can be reheated. Serves 6 to 8.

Herbed Roast Leg of Lamb, Greek Style

Pat Bjaaland
CLA '67/GRS '68
Cookbook Committee
Oslo, Norway

1 6 lb. leg of lamb
1 whole garlic, slivered
3 teaspoons oregano
1½ teaspoons salt
½ teaspoon ground black pepper
1 cup olive oil
2 tablespoons lemon juice

Preheat oven to 450°. Make 8 small slits at regular intervals in lamb. Insert 1 small garlic sliver into each slit. Mix together 1 teaspoon oregano, remaining garlic, 1 teaspoon salt and ¼ teaspoon black pepper and rub over the surface of the lamb. In a small saucepan mix ½ teaspoon salt, ¼ teaspoon black pepper, 2 teaspoons oregano, ½ cup olive oil, 2 tablespoons lemon juice and heat until warm. Using a pastry brush, brush the lamb with some of the olive oil mixture. Place the leg uncovered on a roasting rack in a large shallow baking pan. Turn several times coating with the hot olive oil dressing. Roast for 20 minutes. Lower heat to 350° and roast for 50 to 60 minutes turning several times. Baste with olive oil marinade. It should register 130° on a meat thermometer. Let rest out of oven for 20 minutes. Serves 6 to 8.

Evelyn's Lamb

Libby Cohen SED '77
Cape Elizabeth, Maine

1 leg of lamb, boned
⅓ cup lemon juice
4 tablespoons brown sugar
2 tablespoons Dijon mustard
2 tablespoons soy sauce
2 tablespoons olive oil
½ teaspoon salt
¼ teaspoon pepper
¼ clove garlic

Preheat oven to 400°. In a non-aluminum container, combine lemon juice, sugar, mustard, soy sauce, olive oil, salt, pepper and garlic. Pour over the lamb. Marinate in refrigerator for 12 to 24 hours. Roast lamb until done as desired. About 12 minutes per pound for medium. Can be served at room temperature. Serves 4 to 8.

Barbecued Breast of Lamb

3 lb. lamb breast, cut up
½ cup orange marmalade
2 tablespoons lemon juice
2 teaspoons brown sugar

Diana Lin SMG '72
New York, New York

Preheat oven to 375°. Marinate breast with marmalade, lemon juice and sugar overnight. Place lamb on a roasting rack and bake for 1 hour or until crisp. Serves 4 to 6.

Lamb in Yogurt Sauce

2 lb. lamb shoulder, cut into 1 inch strips
2 tablespoons salad oil
¼ cup finely chopped onion
¼ cup chopped green pepper
¼ cup flour, diluted in a little water
½ cup dry white wine
2 teaspoons salt
dash pepper
1 teaspoon dried, crushed tarragon
1 teaspoon dried, crushed thyme
1 cup natural whole-milk yogurt
1 8 oz. package medium width flat noodles, cooked

Ann Herzog SPC '61
Brookline, Massachusetts

In a large skillet, brown meat in oil. Add onions and green pepper and brown for 5 minutes. Add flour and wine and pour over meat. Stir until thickened. Add seasonings and cook over very low heat for approximately 30 minutes or until meat is tender. Blend in yogurt and heat thoroughly. Serve over hot buttered noodles. Serves 6.

Moussaka with Lamb

Gary S. Orgel
Professor
Department of Philosophy
College of Liberal Arts

5 medium eggplants, ½ inch thick slices
salt, to taste
olive oil
2 lbs. ground lamb
5 onions, diced
1 clove garlic, crushed
4 oz. tomato paste
¼ cup red wine
½ to 1 teaspoon cinnamon
8 tablespoons butter
6 tablespoons flour
1 quart milk
4 eggs, lightly beaten

Sprinkle eggplant with salt and let stand for ½ hour. Rinse under running water and squeeze moisture out of each piece. Dredge in flour. Sauté each piece in hot oil until golden, put aside. Sauté onions and garlic in oil until soft but not brown. Add lamb and continue cooking until meat loses its color. Add tomato paste, wine, cinnamon and salt to taste. Simmer for 45 minutes skimming oils as they rise to surface. This is crucial if the dish is to be light. In a 2 quart saucepan, melt butter. Stir in flour and cook stirring 6 minutes. Warm milk and add to roux. Cook until thick. Beat some white sauce into eggs and then add eggs to remaining white sauce. Cover with plastic wrap and set aside.

To Assemble: Preheat oven to 350°. Starting with eggplant, make a layer in a large 15x11x4 inch baking dish. Be sure to cover entire bottom using small pieces to fill holes. Spread about ½ the lamb over the eggplant. Continue making layers ending with eggplant. Spread sauce over top. Place in oven for approximately 30 minutes or until top is lightly browned. Can be reheated. Serves 6 to 8.

Lamb Moroccan

Denise Oberti SON '73
Danville, Pennsylvania

3 lb. lamb shoulder, cut into 2 inch cubes
4 tablespoons cooking oil
½ lb. mushrooms, sliced

1 onion, chopped

½ cup raisins

½ cup blanched almonds

3 tablespoons sugar

2 teaspoons cinnamon

2 teaspoons cloves

1 teaspoon salt

1 teaspoon allspice

1 lb. can tomatoes

4 cups rice, cooked

In a skillet, brown lamb in oil, remove from pan and drain off all but 2 tablespoons fat. Add mushrooms and onion. Cook until lightly browned. Stir in raisins, almonds, sugar, cinnamon, cloves, salt and allspice. Simmer 5 minutes. Add lamb and tomatoes. Simmer covered 1½ hours. Serve with rice. Can be reheated or frozen. Serves 4 to 6.

Braised Barbecued Lamb Riblets

1 breast of lamb, cut into riblets

flour

¼ cup vegetable oil

1 cup chili sauce

1 cup stock

1 onion, thinly sliced

2 tablespoons dry red wine

1 clove garlic, minced

1½ teaspoons salt

½ teaspoon pepper

½ teaspoon mint

8 small carrots, diced

This tastes best barbecued outside on the grill.

**Helen Crawford Bander
SED '31**
*Cookbook Committee
Paris, Arkansas*

Dredge lamb in flour. In a skillet, heat oil and brown lamb. Add the chili sauce, stock, onion, wine, garlic, salt, pepper and mint. Simmer 45 minutes, skimming any fat that comes to the surface. Add carrots. Simmer 30 minutes more. Serve over rice. Can be reheated. Serves 4.

Pork Tenderloin and Currant Sauce

MaryAnne Gannam
CLA '40/GRS '41
Nicholas Gannam
CLA '40/GRS '41
National Alumni Council
San Francisco, California

2	lb. pork tenderloin
1½	teaspoons salt
¼	teaspoon pepper
2	tablespoons vegetable oil
½	teaspoon rosemary
2	tablespoons butter
1	cup currant jelly
1	cup heavy cream
1	tablespoon flour

Season pork with salt and pepper and brown in a skillet in oil. Place in a casserole dish and sprinkle with rosemary. Spread the butter over the tenderloin and top with the currant jelly. Bake covered in a 350° oven for 1 hour. Blend flour and cream into the liquid. Bake 10 minutes. Can be reheated. Serves 4 to 6.

Normandy Loin of Pork in Cider

Cheryl Connery
John Connery CLA '69
National Alumni Council
Melrose, Massachusetts

6	lb. pork loin, boned, rolled, tied
2½	teaspoons salt
¾	teaspoon freshly ground black pepper
8	baking apples, cored
8	large onions, peeled, parboiled
8	medium potatoes, peeled, parboiled
1½	cups cider
2	tablespoons flour
¼	cup cognac

Preheat oven to 375°. Rub the pork with salt and pepper. Place in a roasting pan. Roast 1½ hours. Pour off the fat. Arrange the apples, onions and potatoes around the pork and add 1 cup cider. Reduce heat to 325° and roast 1¼ hours longer, basting frequently. Remove the strings from the pork. Let rest 20 minutes. Skim the fat from the pan. Place pan over low heat and stir in the flour. Gradually add the cognac and remaining cider, stirring constantly. Simmer 5 minutes. Arrange the pork, apples, onions and potatoes on a serving platter. Serve the sauce separately. Serves 8.

Shepherd's Pie

2 eggs, separated
2 cups mashed potatoes
pinch of salt
1 9 inch pastry shell, half baked
2 cups diced, cooked pork or other meat
2 tablespoons minced parsley
½ cup diced celery
½ cup gravy, tomato juice or ⅓ cup cream
salt, to taste
paprika, to taste
2 tablespoons butter
4 tablespoons grated Cheddar cheese

J. Kenneth Scott SFA '56
New York, New York

Preheat oven to 400°. Beat egg yolks into potatoes until very light. Beat whites until stiff with salt and fold into potatoes. Spread ½ of potato mixture in bottom of pastry shell. In a bowl, combine pork, parsley, celery, gravy, salt and paprika. Cover potatoes with meat mixture and dot with butter. Sprinkle with cheese. Bake until browned. Can be reheated. Serves 4 to 6.

Jambalaya

Susan Moger CLA '73
Cookbook Committee
Los Angeles, California

1	cup chopped onion
¾	cup chopped celery
1	medium green pepper, chopped
2	cloves garlic
4	tablespoons butter
1	cup cooked ham, cut into strips
2	lbs. tomatoes, peeled, chopped
1	8 oz. can tomato sauce
2	cups long-grained rice, uncooked
3	cups chicken or fish broth
1½	teaspoons salt
½	teaspoon thyme
2	tablespoons chopped parsley
¼	teaspoon freshly ground pepper
⅛	teaspoon cayenne
1½	lbs. shrimp, cooked, peeled, deveined

Preheat oven to 350°. Melt butter in a large skillet; sauté onion, celery, green pepper and garlic, stirring frequently until tender. Add ham strips and cook for a few minutes. Add tomatoes and tomato sauce and simmer 15 minutes to blend flavors. Add rice, broth and seasonings. Place mixture in large 4 quart casserole dish. Cover and bake approximately 50 minutes until rice is tender. During last 5 minutes of baking, add cooked shrimp. Best served immediately. Serves 8.

Ham and Corn Custard

Geraldine Hamlin
Friend of Boston University
Cambridge, Massachusetts

2	cups lean ham, diced
2	cups fresh corn kernels, uncooked
3	eggs, beaten
¼	cup flour
1	tablespoon brown sugar
¾	teaspoon salt
¼	teaspoon ground white pepper
¼	cup butter, melted

2 cups light cream

1 cup salted cracker crumbs

¾ teaspoon basil leaves

parsley sprigs

Preheat oven to 375°. Spread ham on bottom of a
12x8x2 inch baking dish. In a medium bowl, combine
corn with eggs. Stir in flour, sugar, salt and pepper. Add
2 tablespoons butter and cream. Mix well. Pour on top of
ham. Bake 35 minutes. Combine cracker crumbs with
basil and remaining butter. Sprinkle in an attractive pattern on custard. Bake 10 minutes longer or until custard
is set. Garnish with parsley sprigs. May be prepared for
baking several hours ahead. Serves 6 to 8.

Ham Loaf
with Mustard Sauce

1½ lbs. fresh pork

1½ lbs. smoked ham

1½ cups bread crumbs, moistened

1 cup milk

4 eggs, beaten

1½ cups brown sugar

½ cup vinegar

2 teaspoons dry mustard

⅓ cup vinegar

⅓ cup prepared mustard

⅓ cup sugar

⅓ cup butter

2 egg yolks, beaten

My late wife's grandfather
immigrated to Chicago
from Germany in 1870.
When he got enough
money together, he sent
for his wife, and she
brought the recipe
with her.

Harry Crosby
Professor
Department of Rhetoric
College of Basic Studies

Preheat oven to 350°. Grind pork and ham together. Stir
in crumbs, milk and eggs. Place in a 9x5x3 inch loaf pan.
Combine brown sugar, vinegar and mustard. Pour over
loaf. Bake 1¼ hours. In top of a double boiler, combine
vinegar, mustard, sugar, butter and egg yolks. Place over
simmering water and cook, stirring until thickened. Do
not let get too hot. Serve separately with ham loaf. Can
be reheated. Serves 6 to 8.

Sweet and Sour Ham Balls

Harry Crosby
Professor
Department of Rhetoric
College of Basic Studies

3 *cups ground cooked ham*
½ *cup fine dry bread crumbs*
1 *large egg*
¼ *cup vegetable oil*
1 *14 oz. can pineapple chunks in syrup*
2 *tablespoons soy sauce*
2 *tablespoons brown sugar*
2 *tablespoons cornstarch*
¼ *cup vinegar*
2 *green peppers, cut into strips*

Mix ham, crumbs and egg in large bowl; shape into 12 large balls. In a skillet, brown balls in oil. Remove. Drain syrup from pineapple into 1 quart measure. Add soy sauce, brown sugar and water to make 2 cups. Stir into drippings in pan. Place ham balls in sauce; simmer covered 15 minutes. Blend cornstarch and vinegar until smooth; stir into frying pan. Cook stirring until thickened and simmer 3 minutes. Stir in pineapple and peppers. Heat until bubbly. Serve over hot rice. Can be reheated. Serves 6.

Rabbit à la Moutarde

Accompany this dish with Irish potatoes or macaroni.

Deborah Cohen CLA '69
Cookbook Committee
Paris, France

3 *tablespoons Dijon mustard*
1 *tablespoon cooking oil*
½ *teaspoon thyme*
salt and pepper, to taste
1 *rabbit, cut into pieces*
1 *cup dry white wine*

Preheat oven to 350°. Combine mustard, oil, thyme, salt and pepper. Put rabbit into a baking dish and cover with mustard mixture. Bake 35 to 45 minutes. When cooked, place the rabbit onto a serving dish and add the wine to the baking dish to "deglaze" the sauce. Serve the rabbit with this sauce. Can be reheated. Serves 4.

Corned Beef or Tongue

⅓ cup (Kosher) salt
1 teaspoon saltpeter
1 heaping teaspoon pickling spice
1 large clove garlic, cut up
3½ lbs. double brisket or tongue

Marion Davidson
CLA '30/SFA '31
Newtonville, Massachusetts

Mix salt, saltpeter, pickling spice and garlic. Rub into meat with hands. Cover meat with water in crockpot or large dish (do not use aluminum). Refrigerate 12 days and turn every 4 days. Keeps in liquid for 1 month. To cook: Rinse off spices. Put in boiling water just to cover. Simmer 2½ to 3 hours until tender. Cool in liquid. Vegetables such as potatoes, carrots, cabbage or turnip may also be cooked in water. Can be reheated. Serves 6.

Calves' Liver with Onions and Sage

2 medium onions, thinly sliced
1 large clove garlic, minced
1 teaspoon dried ground sage
¼ cup olive oil
1 lb. calves' liver, cut into ¼ inch thick slices
salt and freshly ground black pepper, to taste
3 tablespoons minced parsley

Marilyn Wood
Staff

In a large skillet, sauté onion, garlic and sage in oil until onions are wilted and beginning to brown. Pat the liver dry and sprinkle lightly with salt and pepper. Add parsley to the skillet and sauté with the onion mixture for about 1 minute. Push onion mixture to the side of skillet and raise heat slightly. Sauté liver slices, without crowding in the pan, for about 30 seconds per side. When cooked, arrange on a warm platter and continue with remaining slices. Spread the oil/onion/herb mixture over the liver. Serve immediately. Serves 2 to 3.

English Kidneys

Dr. Alan A. Larocque
ENG '72/MED '80
Medford, Massachusetts

2 lbs. beef kidneys, cut into ¾ inch cubes

¼ cup minced beef suet

2 large onions, coarsely chopped

1 lb. mushrooms, quartered

½ teaspoon salt

½ teaspoon freshly ground black pepper

pinch of cayenne

1½ teaspoons Worcestershire sauce

1 cup rich beef stock (optional)

½ cup sour cream

minced parsley

Discard the central fatty portions of kidneys. Heat suet in a heavy kettle or Dutch oven until fat becomes liquid. Remove cracklings. Add the onion and sauté until transparent. Add the kidneys and cook, stirring almost constantly until thoroughly browned. Add the mushrooms, salt, pepper, cayenne and Worcestershire. Boil, stirring intermittently until the moisture from the mushrooms has evaporated. This sauce may be thinned with beef stock, if desired. Add the sour cream and serve with parsley. Can be reheated. Serves 4 to 6.

6 Vegetables

Vegetables

6

Molded Vegetable Casserole

2 *tablespoons butter*	
1 *cup unflavored bread crumbs*	
½ *cup minced parsley*	
4 *tomatoes, cut in wedges*	
½ *cup olive oil*	
3 *eggs, lightly beaten*	
salt and pepper, to taste	
¼ *lb. mozzarella, thinly sliced*	
2 *small zucchini, thinly sliced*	
1 *potato, thinly sliced*	
1 *eggplant, ½ inch slices*	

Jessica Haroian
Dr. Harry A. Haroian
SED '67/'73
Lincoln, Massachusetts

Preheat oven to 375°. Butter a 2 quart round casserole or soufflé dish. Sprinkle with crumbs and remove excess crumbs. Combine crumbs with parsley. Arrange tomato wedges on bottom of dish and drizzle with 2 tablespoons of oil, 2 tablespoons of egg and add salt and pepper. Cover with a layer of cheese. Sprinkle with parslied bread crumbs. Top with the zucchini, repeat oil, egg and cheese; then add a layer of potatoes, repeating oil, egg and cheese; then add a layer of eggplant. Sprinkle with parslied bread crumbs and drizzle on olive oil and remaining egg. Bake 45 minutes. Let rest 10 minutes before unmolding. Can be kept in refrigerator for 24 hours before baking. Serves 6 to 8.

Vegetables au Gratin

June Neves CBA'72
Fall River, Massachusetts

4 cups vegetables, cooked tender crisp

3 tablespoons butter

4 tablespoons flour

3 cups hot milk

salt, pepper and nutmeg

*¼ cup grated Parmesan cheese, or 1 cup grated
gruyère or Cheddar cheese*

Preheat oven to 325°. Place vegetables of your choice
in 9x13 inch oven-to-table baking dish. In a 1½ quart
saucepan, melt the butter, stir in the flour and cook until
the mixture is just starting to turn golden. Stir in the milk
and cook, stirring until thickened and smooth. Season to
taste with salt, pepper and nutmeg. Bake for 20 minutes
until bubbly. May be prepared for baking the day before.
Serves 6 to 8.

Brandayum *(Southern Vegetable Stew)*

Dr. Hélène R. Day
GRS'71
Co-chairwoman
Cookbook Committee
New England Consul
for Monaco

1 onion, minced

3 peppers, cut in strips

½ cup olive oil

4 eggplants, peeled, sliced

4 zucchini, peeled, sliced

2 tomatoes, peeled, quartered

salt, to taste

2 cloves garlic, minced

1 fresh bay leaf, minced

In a casserole, sauté onion and pepper in oil until soft.
Add eggplant, zucchini and tomatoes. Simmer until very
soft. Season with salt. Before serving, stir in garlic and
bay leaf. May be made ahead. Serve hot or at room temperature. Serves 6.

Vegetables en Croute

¼ cup warm milk (110°)
1 tablespoon yeast
1 tablespoon sugar
2 cups flour
½ cup butter
1 teaspoon salt
2 eggs, slightly beaten
4 cups broccoli, asparagus, cauliflower, mushrooms, etc.
4 tablespoons butter
salt and pepper, to taste
¼ cup grated Parmesan cheese
1 egg, beaten with ¼ teaspoon salt

Stewart Tabakin
*Boston University
Free School*

In a bowl, combine milk, yeast and sugar. Let sit until foamy, about 10 minutes. In a processor, place flour, butter and salt. Turn machine on and add yeast mixture. Pour in eggs and knead until smooth, about 2 minutes. Remove from machine to a buttered bowl. Turn dough over to coat surface. Let rise covered in a warm place until doubled in bulk, about 1½ to 2 hours. Punch down and place in refrigerator for 1 hour or freezer for 20 minutes, until well chilled. Meanwhile, cut vegetables into bite size pieces, slice mushrooms. Parboil vegetables until tender crisp; drain and toss with butter. Season with salt and pepper. Sauté mushrooms in butter until liquid has evaporated. Season to taste. Sprinkle with cheese. Roll the dough into a rectangle ¼ inch thick. Place vegetables down middle. Bring sides over top and pinch to seal. Place seam side down on buttered baking sheet. Cut a steam vent in top of dough and score with a knife in a decorative pattern. Let rise while oven is preheating to 350°. Brush top of pastry with egg and salt mixture. Bake 30 to 40 minutes until golden. Can be frozen and reheated. Serves 6.

Hot Bean Casserole

I'm one of those people who never liked chili. When we lived in Georgia, we hosted a lot of cookouts for students, so I came up with this dish to go with hamburgers.

Kathy Padulo
Louis Padulo
Dean, School of
Engineering

1 lb. can kidney or red beans, drained, rinsed
½ cup mayonnaise
⅓ cup chopped dill pickles
¼ lb. sharp Cheddar cheese, cubed
¼ cup thinly sliced scallions
½ teaspoon celery salt
16 salted crackers, crushed
2 strips bacon, cooked, crumbled

Preheat oven to 400°. In a soufflé dish, combine beans, mayonnaise, pickles, cheese, scallions and celery salt. Bake 10 minutes. Sprinkle with cracker crumbs. Bake 10 minutes longer. Garnish with crumbled bacon. Can be reheated. Serves 4.

Boston Baked Beans

Sterne Barnett CBA '35
Cookbook Committee
Chestnut Hill, Massachusetts

3 cups dried pea beans (or navy beans)
¼ cup unsulfured molasses
1 teaspoon dry mustard
1 small onion
salt and pepper, to taste
½ lb. salt pork, scalded, scored
water

Preheat oven to 250°. Pick over beans (discard broken or discolored). Wash thoroughly in cold water. Drain. Cover beans with water and soak overnight. Pour beans with water into a saucepan and bring to boil; simmer for 5 minutes. Place beans and water in crock or bean pot. Add molasses, mustard and seasoning. Stir. Push onion and pork half way down into pot and cover. Bake for 6 to 7 hours. Remove cover for the last hour, adding boiling water if necessary (beans should not be dry). Makes 12 to 14 half cup servings.

Haricots Verts au Lard

1 lb. snapped green beans, steamed

2 tablespoons butter

salt and pepper, to taste

nutmeg

8 slices bacon

Hans Bucher
Executive Chef
Hyatt Regency
Cambridge, Massachusetts

Preheat oven to 400°. Steam green beans in vegetable steamer until tender. In a bowl, toss beans with butter, salt, pepper and nutmeg. Group beans into single serving portions (9 to 10 beans per serving) and wrap tightly with bacon. Place on pan and bake in oven until bacon is browned. Serve immediately. Serves 8.

String Beans with Tomato

1 green pepper, minced

1 onion, minced

4 strips bacon, diced

2 cups chopped, drained tomatoes

2 cups string beans, cooked

1 teaspoon Worcestershire sauce

½ teaspoon salt

dash pepper and cayenne

¼ lb. sliced mushrooms

½ cup buttered bread crumbs

1 tablespoon butter

Edith Thompson Adams
SED '42
Marlboro, Massachusetts

Preheat oven to 350°. Sauté pepper, onion and bacon together for 5 to 8 minutes. Drain excess fat. Add drained tomatoes, mix well and simmer 5 minutes. Add beans, Worcestershire, salt, pepper and cayenne. Blend thoroughly. Add mushrooms. Place in greased quart casserole dish. Cover with bread crumbs, dot with butter, bake 20 minutes. May be prepared day before baking. Serves 6.

Texas Style Green Beans

Kathryn Silber
Wife of
Dr. John R. Silber
President of
Boston University

| 2 cans whole green beans |
| 1 clove garlic |
| 1 tablespoon bacon fat |

In a saucepan, combine beans, garlic and fat. Simmer 1 hour or longer, adding a little water if necessary. Discard garlic. Allow to cool. Reheat when ready to serve. Serves 6.

Broccoli-Macaroni Casserole

John B. Simpson
SED '50/'54
Director of Athletics
Marion Gorham
SON '52/'56
National Alumni Council
Holyoke, Massachusetts

| 12 oz. rigatoni, cooked · |
| 10 oz. package broccoli, cooked |
| ¾ lb. sliced mozzarella |
| 2 to 2½ cups tomato marinara sauce |

Preheat oven to 350°. In a 2 quart casserole dish, layer the rigatoni, broccoli, mozzarella and sauce. Bake 25 to 30 minutes. Let stand 10 minutes before serving. May be prepared for baking the day before. Serves 6 to 8.

Red Cabbage with Wine

Susan Freedman Mandel
SED '70
Cookbook Committee
Oakland, New Jersey

| 2 apples, cored, cut in ⅛ sections |
| 1 onion, sliced |
| 2 tablespoons butter |
| ½ cup red wine |
| 1 head red cabbage, shredded |
| 1½ tablespoons caraway seeds |

In a large casserole dish, sauté apples and onion in butter for 3 minutes. Stir in wine and bring to a boil. Add cabbage and caraway seeds. Simmer 45 minutes. Can be reheated. Serves 6.

Sweet and Sour Brussels Sprouts

2 *tablespoons butter*
¼ *cup minced onion*
⅛ *teaspoon ginger*
6 *tablespoons sugar*
2 *teaspoons cornstarch*
½ *cup cider vinegar*
½ *cup raisins*
2 *lbs. brussels sprouts, cooked*

Sharon Gamsin
DGE '69/SPC '71
Cookbook Committee
New York, New York

In a saucepan, melt butter; add onion and ginger and cook 1 minute. Combine sugar, cornstarch and vinegar; add to saucepan and simmer 5 minutes until almost thickened. Add raisins and simmer until the sauce is thick and raisins are plump. Pour over sprouts. Can be reheated. Serves 6.

Eggplant Casserole

3 *medium eggplants, peeled, cubed*
2½ *cups boiling water*
½ *cup minced onion*
2 *teaspoons salt*
4 *eggs, slightly beaten*
½ *cup grated Parmesan cheese*
4 *tablespoons butter*
4 *tablespoons heavy cream*
1 *cup buttered Italian style breadcrumbs*
½ *cup grated Cheddar cheese*

Kathy Padulo
Louis Padulo
Dean, School of
Engineering

Preheat oven to 350°. In a saucepan, simmer eggplant, water, onion and salt for 10 minutes. Drain. Put into a 2 quart baking dish. In a bowl, combine eggs, Cheddar, cream and butter. Pour over eggplant. Combine crumbs and Parmesan and sprinkle over the top. Bake 45 minutes. May be prepared for baking several hours ahead. Serves 6.

Carottes Glacées

Hans Bucher
Executive Chef
Hyatt Regency
Cambridge, Massachusetts

| 4 tablespoons butter |
| 2 tablespoons sugar |
| 5 large carrots, 1 inch sticks |
| juice of ½ lemon |
| dash salt |

In a saucepan, melt butter and add sugar and carrots. Stir until carrots are glazed. Add lemon juice and salt. Cover pan and cook on low heat approximately 15 minutes or until tender. Serves 4.

Stuffed Eggplant Sheikh

In Turkish, this dish is called Imam Bayildi which means "holy man fainted." According to the fable, when the holy man ate it, he either fainted because it was so good or because it cost so much to make.

Peg Mitchell CLA '67
Assistant Director
Reunions

| 2 medium eggplants |
| salt |
| 3 tablespoons olive oil |
| 1 medium onion, finely chopped |
| ¾ lb. ground beef or lamb |
| salt and black pepper |
| ¼ cup pine nuts, pignoli (optional) |
| 3 oz. can tomato sauce |
| 5 oz. can tomato paste |
| ¼ teaspoon allspice |
| 1 tablespoon lemon juice |

Preheat oven to 425°. Cut off stem of eggplant. Peel strips lengthwise, leaving alternate strips of flesh. Sprinkle salt on flesh; place in colander to drain 30 minutes to 1 hour; rinse well and pat dry. Make 1 lengthwise slit without cutting through. Heat 2 tablespoons olive oil in frying pan. Add onion and sauté until soft but not brown. Add meat and cook, stirring lightly until color changes. Season with salt and pepper. Add pine nuts, if desired, and cook 5 minutes. Mix tomato sauce and tomato paste in bowl. Add allspice. Use 1 tablespoon of oil to rub a baking dish large enough to hold eggplants comfortably. Stuff eggplants; place in baking dish and add tomato sauce. Bake for 10 minutes in hot oven (425°). Reduce heat to 325° and bake 45 minutes, or until tender. Serves 6.

Eggplant Calabrese

2 large eggplants
⅔ cup bread crumbs
⅓ cup grated Romano cheese
½ teaspoon salt
¼ teaspoon pepper
1 small clove garlic, minced
1 tablespoon minced parsley
8 oz. tomato sauce
3 tablespoons olive oil

The delicate flavor of the eggplant will be lost if not served with veal or lamb.

Filomena Sinclitico Costello
CBA '48
Chelmsford, Massachusetts

Preheat oven to 425°. Cut off stems of eggplant; cut in half and scoop out pulp leaving a ¼ inch shell. Cube pulp. Bring 4 quarts of water and 2 tablespoons salt to a boil; add eggplant shells and cubes. Cook shells 7 minutes until tender and drain. Cook pulp until soft; drain in colander. Combine bread crumbs, cheese, salt, pepper, garlic and parsley. Mash eggplant pulp with crumb mixture. Simmer in a skillet over medium heat with tomato sauce for 10 minutes. Place drained shells in a baking dish and fill with tomato mixture and drizzle with olive oil. Bake until bubbly. Before serving spread a tablespoon of hot sauce over the top. Can be reheated or served at room temperature. Serves 4 to 8.

Eggplant Parmigiana

1 medium sized eggplant, peeled ¼ inch slices
¾ cup olive oil
½ lb. mozzarella cheese, sliced thin
1½ cups tomato sauce
¼ cup grated Parmesan cheese

Lorraine Wysoskie Hurley
SED '67/'69
Chairwoman
Cookbook Committee
Newtown, Connecticut

Preheat oven to 400°. Brown eggplant in oil on both sides. Place a layer of eggplant slices in a baking dish. Top with mozzarella, tomato sauce and Parmesan. Continue alternating layers. Bake uncovered 15 to 20 minutes. Can be reheated. Serves 4.

Russian Tearoom Eggplant Oriental

I first tried this at the Russian Tea Room in New York City. It is a great side dish to any meal, especially Chicken Kiev.

Dr. Matthew Witten
CLA '72
Cookbook Committee
Los Angeles, California

3 large cans whole tomatoes

2 green peppers, diced

1 large onion, chopped

3 tablespoons vegetable oil

3 large eggplants, peeled, chopped

1 oz. tomato purée

1 oz. ketchup

1 oz. chili sauce

1 oz. tomato paste

1 clove garlic, chopped

pinch of red pepper

salt and pepper, to taste

Sauté green pepper, onion and tomatoes in vegetable oil; add eggplant and cook 20 minutes. Add tomato purée, ketchup, chili sauce, tomato paste, garlic, red pepper, salt and pepper and mix thoroughly. Simmer for 5 minutes more. Chill before serving. Keeps four days refrigerated. Serves 6 to 8.

Baked Onions

Mildred C. Makin
SON '48/SED '55
National Alumni Council
Waltham, Massachusetts

8 large onions, halved horizontally

1 tablespoon butter

2 tablespoons tomato juice

2 tablespoons maple syrup

1 teaspoon salt

1/3 teaspoon pepper

Preheat oven to 350°. Put onions in greased casserole dish. Combine tomato juice, syrup, butter, salt and pepper. Pour over onions. Bake in covered casserole for 1 hour or until done. Can be reheated. Serves 8.

Oriental Mushrooms for Fish

¼ cup butter
¼ cup chopped onion
1 lb. mushrooms, thinly sliced
2 tablespoons flour
½ cup beef stock
1 tablespoon soy sauce
¼ cup toasted slivered almonds

Dr. Linda Nelson CLA '74
Cookbook Committee
Lansdale, Pennsylvania

In a large skillet, sauté onions in butter until soft but not brown. Stir in mushrooms and cook until tender. Sprinkle flour over mixture and combine. Mix in stock. Cook, stirring until thickened. Stir in soy sauce and almonds. Good over cooked flaked fish. Can be reheated. Serves 4.

Sausage Stuffed Peppers

6 green peppers, seeded, steamed
6 hot Italian sausages
1 onion, minced
1 clove garlic, minced
2 cups beef stock
1 tablespoon ketchup
¼ teaspoon salt
¼ teaspoon pepper
1 cup uncooked rice
½ cup minced parsley
¼ cup Parmesan cheese
6 oz. diced mozzarella cheese (optional)

A great recipe for working people. I just make double batches each time and freeze one.

Carla Kindt   SED'75
Development Office
Bill Beckett
SED'76/SSW '78

Preheat oven to 350°. Cook peppers in boiling salted water for 4 minutes. Drain and cool. Remove casings from sausage. In a skillet, sauté sausage meat until brown. Drain off ½ the fat. Add onions and garlic; cook 5 minutes. Stir in stock, ketchup, salt and pepper. Add rice. Mix; simmer 25 minutes. Add parsley, Parmesan and ½ of the mozzarella and mix. Stuff mixture into peppers and top with remaining cheese. Place peppers in baking dish. Add ½ inch of water. Bake 35 minutes. Freezes well. Serves 4.

Gnocchi Verdi *(Spinach Dumplings)*

These are often called Ravioli Verdi.

My husband and I are semi-vegetarians and this makes a great main dish. Actually, it's quite versatile and, depending on your preference, it can be used as an appetizer, side or main dish.

Claire Shapiro Soja
CLA '68
Cookbook Committee
Harvard, Massachusetts

6 tablespoons butter
1 tablespoon minced onion
3 10 oz. packages chopped spinach, thawed, drained
1 cup ricotta cheese
¾ cup flour
½ cup grated Parmesan cheese
¾ teaspoon salt
¼ teaspoon garlic powder
½ teaspoon pepper
¼ teaspoon ground nutmeg or mace
2 tablespoons minced parsley
2 eggs, slightly beaten
flour
12 cups water or chicken stock
¼ cup butter, melted
½ cup grated Parmesan cheese

Melt butter in large skillet. Stir onion in butter until tender. Add spinach; cook over medium heat until spinach is quite dry. Mix in ricotta cheese; cook and stir 3 minutes. Transfer to large bowl. Mix in flour, ½ cup Parmesan , salt, pepper, nutmeg and parsley. Cool mixture 5 minutes. Stir in eggs. Drop spinach mixture 1 tablespoon at a time, into small bowl of flour; roll to coat with flour. Shape into balls. May be refrigerated in 1 layer overnight, if desired. Heat water or broth to boiling. Poach uncovered until gnocchi are quite firm and rise to the top of broth, about 10 minutes.

Avoid overcrowding. Remove gnocchi with slotted spoon. Place in oven-proof serving dish; drizzle with ¼ cup butter. Sprinkle ½ cup Parmesan on gnocchi. Serve with additional grated Parmesan. Can be reheated one to two hours later in 350° oven until hot. Serves 6.

Onion Pie

6 *large onions, thinly sliced*
3 *tablespoons butter*
1 *egg, lightly beaten*
½ *cup milk*
½ *cup shredded Swiss cheese*

Preheat oven to 350°. In a skillet, sauté onions in butter until soft but not brown. Line pie plate with onions. In a bowl, beat egg and milk together. Pour over onions. Sprinkle cheese on top. Bake 20 minutes. Cut into quarters. May be prepared for baking several hours ahead. Serves 4.

Rebecca J. Gourley
SAR '74
Cookbook Committee
Medfield, Massachusetts

Herb Spinach Bake

1 *package chopped spinach, cooked, drained*
1 *cup rice, cooked*
1 *cup shredded cheese*
2 *eggs, slightly beaten*
2 *tablespoons butter*
⅓ *cup milk*
2 *tablespoons chopped onion*
½ *teaspoon Worcestershire sauce*
1 *teaspoon salt*
¼ *teaspoon thyme or rosemary*

Preheat oven to 350°. In a shallow casserole, combine spinach, rice, cheese, eggs, butter, milk, onion, salt, Worcestershire and thyme. Bake 25 to 30 minutes until a knife comes out clean. May be prepared hours before baking. Serves 6.

Ruth Benner Danis
Development Office

Spinach Pie

This is a very easy and foolproof recipe. It always cuts beautiful wedges.

Barbara Lanciani SED '66
Cookbook Committee
Leominster, Massachusetts

2 *packages frozen chopped spinach*
8 *oz. cream cheese*
½ *cup butter*
½ *teaspoon minced garlic*
salt, to taste
½ *cup Italian bread crumbs*

In a bowl, combine spinach, cheese, butter, garlic and salt. Mix well. Pour into 10 inch pie plate and top with Italian bread crumbs. Bake 20 to 30 minutes. Can be reheated. Serves 6.

Spinach Puff Ring

Lorraine Nelson Klein
GRS '76
Cookbook Committee
North Kingston,
Rhode Island

1 *cup water*
½ *cup butter*
¼ *teaspoon salt*
1 *cup flour*
4 *eggs*
3 *packages frozen chopped spinach, cooked*
4 *oz. cream cheese*
2 *eggs*
2 *teaspoons Tamari sauce*
salt, pepper and nutmeg, to taste

Preheat oven to 450°. In a saucepan, bring water, butter and salt to a boil. Immediately remove and add the flour all at once. Stir vigorously until the mixture leaves the sides of the pan and forms a ball. Cool slightly. Beat in the eggs, 1 at a time, until smooth and glossy. Spread mixture around the sides of a pie plate to form a circle. Bake 15 minutes at 450°; then reduce heat to 350° and bake 20 to 30 minutes longer or until golden brown and the shell is rigid. Cool. Cook the spinach as per package directions. Drain spinach and return to pan; add cheese; cover and leave on lowest heat until cheese melts. Add the 2 eggs, Tamari, salt, pepper and nutmeg. Slice off the top of the ring, using a sharp knife. Fill with spinach mixture and replace top. Bake another 15 to 20 minutes at 350° or until the spinach mixture is set. Serve immediately. Serves 4 to 8.

Spinach and Muenster Cheese Pie

2 10 oz. packages chopped frozen spinach, cooked
8 oz. cottage cheese
12 oz. muenster cheese, thinly sliced
nutmeg, to taste

Carol Lowe
Philip L. Lowe
Former Member
Board of Visitors
School of Management

Preheat oven to 350°. Drain spinach, pressing out all the water. Line a 9 inch pie plate with ½ muenster cheese. In a bowl, combine spinach and cottage cheese. Season with nutmeg. Place mixture on top of muenster in pie plate and top with remaining muenster. Bake 20 to 30 minutes or until brown and bubbly. May be prepared for baking the day before. Serves 6.

Spinach Cheese Bake

10 oz. frozen spinach
16 oz. cottage cheese
8 oz. sharp Cheddar cheese
3 eggs, beaten
3 tablespoons flour
½ teaspoon pepper
⅛ teaspoon garlic
½ cup sliced almonds

Helena Kelley
Staff
School of Nursing

Preheat oven to 375°. In a bowl, combine cottage cheese, Cheddar, spinach, eggs, flour, garlic and pepper. Pour into greased 8x8 inch pan. Sprinkle almonds over top. Bake 45 minutes. Cool 10 minutes. Cut into squares and serve immediately. Serves 6.

Spinach Cheese Pie

Prepare the eggs and
cheese in a blender, and
the pie will come out very
fluffy.

Janet Oppenheimer
Alumni Representative

9 inch pie shell

6 eggs

3 oz. softened cream cheese

¼ cup grated Cheddar cheese

10 oz. chopped spinach

2 tablespoons scallions

2 tablespoons parsley

½ teaspoon salt

pepper, to taste

2 tablespoons Parmesan cheese

Preheat oven to 425°. Cook pie shell for 5 minutes just before putting in filling. Blend eggs with cream cheese and Cheddar in electric blender for 1 to 2 minutes. In a large bowl, combine spinach, scallions, parsley, salt and pepper with the egg mixture. Place into shell. Sprinkle with Parmesan. Bake 15 minutes. Lower heat to 350° and bake 20 to 30 minutes longer until set. Can be reheated. Serves 6.

Spinach Phyllo Pie

For those who like thick
crust, just add a little extra
phyllo dough to the top
and bottom layers for
extra body.

Claire Shapiro Soja
CLA '68
Cookbook Committee
Harvard, Massachusetts

½ cup sliced scallion

½ teaspoon dried dill

1 tablespoon cooking oil

1 10 oz. package frozen chopped spinach, thawed

4 tablespoons butter

¼ cup flour

½ teaspoon salt

1½ cups milk

2 beaten eggs

1 cup cream style cottage cheese

2 oz. feta cheese, crumbled

¼ teaspoon baking powder

2 16x16 inch sheets phyllo dough

2 tablespoons melted butter

Preheat oven to 325°. In skillet, cook onion and dill in oil until tender. Squeeze excess water from spinach; add to skillet. Cook until hot; keep warm. In large saucepan, melt 4 tablespoons butter; blend in flour and salt. Stir in milk all at once. Cook, stirring until mixture is thickened. Cook 1 minute more. Add a moderate amount of hot mixture to beaten eggs. (This is done to keep mixture from curdling.) Return to saucepan. Stir in cheeses, spinach mixture and baking powder. Brush half of 1 sheet of phyllo dough with butter; fold in half. Butter half of dough rectangle and fold again, forming an 8x8 inch square. Place in 8x8x2 inch baking pan. Pour in spinach mixture. Fold and butter the second sheet of phyllo dough. Place on top of the spinach mixture and tuck in edges. Bake for 35 to 40 minutes until set and browned. Let stand 10 minutes before serving. Can be served hot or at room temperature. Serves 8.

Stuffed Yellow Squash

3	*summer squash*
3	*tablespoons butter*
2	*tablespoons flour*
½	*teaspoon salt*
1	*cup milk*
2	*10 oz. packages frozen chopped spinach, cooked, drained*
4	*teaspoons lemon juice*
½	*teaspoon ground nutmeg*

Susan K. Moger CLA '73
Cookbook Committee
Los Angeles, California

Trim ¼ inch slice from bottom end of each squash; cut off neck; cut each bottom section in half lengthwise and scoop out pulp and seeds to make 6 boats. Parboil 3 minutes in boiling, salted water; drain. Melt butter over low heat. Stir in flour and salt; add milk; cook, stirring until thick and smooth. Stir spinach, lemon juice and nutmeg into sauce. Place squash boats in oven-to-table serving dish. Fill with spinach mixture. Can be reheated in 350° oven. Serves 6.

Acorn Squash with Applesauce

June Neves CBA '72
Fall River, Massachusetts

3 small acorn squash, split
6 tablespoons butter
6 teaspoons brown sugar
¾ cup applesauce

Preheat oven to 350°. Remove seeds from squash and bake on a baking sheet 35 minutes or until tender. Place 1 tablespoon butter, 1 tablespoon of sugar and enough applesauce to fill the cavity of each squash. Bake until applesauce is bubbling. May be prepared for baking the day before. Serves 6.

Lois' Low Cal Zucchini Lasagna

My mother, Lois, developed this recipe. The difference between using cottage cheese instead of ricotta is considerable.

Dr. Jane Norton
SED '70/'74
President
Women Graduates' Club

½ lb. ground beef
1 qt. tomato sauce
12 oz. low fat cottage cheese
4 oz. shredded mozzarella cheese
1 egg
2 tablespoons flour
¼ cup grated sharp cheese
2 lb. zucchini, ¼ slices lengthwise
¼ cup romano cheese

Preheat oven to 350°. In a skillet, brown meat; drain well. Add sauce and simmer for 20 minutes. Parboil the sliced zucchini 1 minute. Combine cottage cheese, sharp cheese, mozzarella, egg and flour. Into an 8x12 inch glass pan, put ½ cup of meat sauce, a layer of zucchini and a layer of cheese mixtures. Continue layering; end with sauce on top; sprinkle with romano. Bake for 40 to 45 minutes. Let stand for 20 minutes before serving. Can be reheated. Serves 6.

Zucchini Italienne

4 cups zucchini, ½ inch slices
¾ cup Italian tomato sauce
½ cup grated mozzarella cheese

Ruth Albert
DGE '63/SED '65/'69
Brockton, Massachusetts

Preheat oven to 350°. Put zucchini in greased baking dish. Pour on sauce. Bake for 50 minutes. Sprinkle with cheese; bake until cheese is melted. Can be reheated. Serves 4 to 6.

Zucchini Casserole

2 to 3 small zucchini, peeled, diced
1 lb. sausage meat
¼ cup chopped onion
2 tablespoons minced green pepper
2 tablespoons minced pimiento
1 cup shredded Cheddar cheese
2 eggs, beaten
½ cup cracker crumbs
¼ teaspoon minced garlic
¼ teaspoon salt
¼ teaspoon oregano
dash pepper
½ cup grated Parmesan cheese

Phyllis Cook PAL '47
Union, Iowa

Preheat oven to 350°. In a skillet, combine zucchini, sausage, onion, green pepper and pimiento and cook until sausage loses its color. Drain off fat. In a bowl, combine cheese, cracker crumbs, eggs, garlic, salt, oregano and pepper. Stir in sausage combination. Place in greased 2 quart casserole dish. Sprinkle with Parmesan. Bake 1 to 1½ hours, or until zucchini is tender. Can be frozen and reheated. Serves 6.

Zucchini Custard Casserole

One summer, when we lived in New Hampshire, the only thing that grew was the zucchini. I had to hunt around for different variations, and this particular one became a great favorite with the five Chapin children.

Zara O. Chapin
Assistant Director
University Professors Program

3 medium zucchini, ¼ inch thick slices
1 large onion, sliced
½ green pepper, sliced
½ teaspoon minced garlic
¼ cup olive oil
3 eggs, lightly beaten
⅔ cup light cream or evaporated milk
1½ cups grated cheese (Parmesan or gruyère)
½ teaspoon salt
¼ teaspoon nutmeg
pepper, to taste

Preheat oven to 375°. Sauté zucchini, onion, pepper and garlic in oil until just cooked. Combine the eggs, cream, cheese, salt, nutmeg and pepper. Put the vegetables in a 1½ quart greased casserole dish; pour the cheese and egg mixture on top and bake 45 minutes in water bath. Bake until puffed and golden brown. Serve as soon as possible. Can be reheated. Serves 6.

Bulgur (cracked wheat) may be found in Middle Eastern markets, health food stores and specialty stores.

Suzanne Pachter Wallach
SON'69
Cookbook Committee
Miami, Florida

Tabbouleh *(Bulgur Salad)*

½ cup bulgur
3 medium tomatoes, chopped
1 bunch scallions, minced
½ cup minced fresh mint
½ cup olive oil
3 cups minced fresh parsley
4 to 6 tablespoons lemon juice
salt, pepper and cinnamon, to taste

Soak bulgur in hot water for 30 minutes. Drain and squeeze dry. In a bowl, combine bulgur, tomatoes, scallions, mint, olive oil, parsley and lemon juice. Mix well. Correct seasoning with salt, pepper and nutmeg. Serve as a salad. Makes about 4 cups.

Agro Dolcie (Sweet and Sour Zucchini)

1 medium onion, diced
1 cup chopped celery
1 cup diced mushrooms
¼ cup olive oil
15 oz. can tomato sauce
¼ cup water
¼ cup cider vinegar
3 tablespoons sugar
½ teaspoon thyme
salt and pepper, to taste
5 to 6 zucchini, sliced
1 green pepper, diced
1 red pepper, diced
1 tablespoon chopped parsley

Sharon Friedman
DGE'68/SED'70
Sharon, Massachusetts

In large skillet, sauté onions, celery and mushrooms in oil until tender. Add sauce, water, vinegar, sugar, thyme, salt and pepper. Simmer 5 minutes. Add zucchini and peppers; cover and cook 15 minutes or until vegetables are tender crisp. Sprinkle with parsley. Serve hot or cold. Can be reheated. Serves 6 to 8.

Potatoes Joseph

6 medium potatoes, peeled
vegetable oil
salt

Preheat oven to 350°. Parboil potatoes 2 minutes. Cut in ¼ inch slices. Cover baking sheets with oil and place slices on sheets in 1 layer. Sprinkle with salt. Bake 15 to 20 minutes until tops crinkle. Turn each slice over and bake until crisp and brown on the top. Serve immediately. Serves 6.

Joseph is a friend of mine and this is his family recipe. Be sure the grease is extremely hot so that the potatoes won't absorb too much of it.

James Dutton
Staff
Department of History
College of Liberal Arts

Potato Latkes

Cookbook Committee

6 medium potatoes, grated
1 onion, grated
2 eggs, lightly beaten
1 teaspoon salt
pepper, to taste
3 tablespoons flour
¼ teaspoon baking powder
vegetable oil

In a bowl, combine the potatoes, onion, eggs, salt, pepper, flour and baking powder. Mix well. Pour off any accumulated liquid and use the batter immediately, otherwise the potatoes will darken. To fry, heat a ¼ inch layer of oil in a skillet and drop in the mixture by the spoonful to make pancakes about 2½ inches across. Sauté until golden on one side, turn and brown on the second side. Drain. Serve with applesauce or sour cream on the side. Can be made small and served as an appetizer. Can be frozen and reheated. Makes about 30.

Dutch Greens and Potatoes

Anthony P. Vogelpoel
ENG '64
Manlius, New York

3 lbs. potatoes, boiled, peeled
3 cups shredded lettuce, romaine or spinach
¼ lb. bacon, fried
6 eggs
¼ lb. grated Edam or Gouda
pepper, to taste

Preheat oven to 350°. Mash potatoes and lettuce together. Stir in cooked bacon. Put in baking dish. Fry eggs in bacon fat. Place on top of potatoes; sprinkle cheese over eggs. If necessary, reheat in oven until hot. Serve immediately. Mix all ingredients together and let each guest add pepper. Serves 6.

Candied Sweet Potatoes

6 sweet potatoes, peeled, cooked
1 cup brown sugar, firmly packed
¼ cup butter
¼ cup water
½ teaspoon salt
2 whole cloves (optional)

Preheat oven to 375°. Cut potatoes in half lengthwise. Arrange in a baking dish. In a saucepan, simmer sugar, butter, water, salt and cloves 5 minutes. Pour over potatoes. Bake for 45 minutes, basting occasionally. Serves 6.

Denise Oberti SON '73
Danville, Pennsylvania

Fried Rice

1 onion, minced
1 clove garlic, crushed
3 tablespoons oil
1 egg
1⅓ cups cooked rice
1 tablespoon soy sauce
1 teaspoon brown gravy sauce

In a skillet, sauté onion and garlic in oil until soft, but not brown. Add egg, stirring until it shreds. Stir in rice, soy sauce and brown gravy sauce. Mix well. Can be reheated. Serves 4.

Laurie Carmusin
Development Office

Spinaci con Riso

2 onions, minced
¼ cup olive oil
1 lb. spinach, washed, drained, chopped
2 cups chicken broth
1 cup raw rice, washed
salt and pepper, to taste

Sauté onions in 2 tablespoons olive oil in a 1½ quart saucepan. Add spinach and broth with remaining olive oil and bring to a boil. Add rice; stir; add salt and pepper to taste. Simmer 25 minutes or until rice has absorbed broth. Can be reheated in 200° oven. Serves 4 to 6.

Velia Tosi
Vice President
Friends of the Libraries

Green Rice Casserole

Judith Walker Tait
SPC '62
Rockville, Maryland

3 cups cooked rice
1 cup milk
1 cup grated Cheddar cheese
½ cup butter, melted
3 scallions, minced
1 teaspoon minced parsley
1 egg, slightly beaten
salt and pepper, to taste

Preheat oven to 350°. Grease a 1 quart casserole dish. In a bowl, combine rice, milk, cheese, butter, scallions, parsley, egg, salt and pepper. Add to casserole. Bake 30 to 45 minutes or until all milk is absorbed. Can be reheated. Serves 6.

Orange Rice Pilaf

Phyllis Forman SFA '66
New York, New York

1 cup minced onion
¼ cup minced green pepper
2 tablespoons butter
1 cup long grain rice
1 cup orange juice
1 cup buttermilk
¼ teaspoon dried crushed oregano
½ teaspoon salt
2 oranges, peeled, cut into small pieces
3 tablespoons toasted slivered almonds

In a 10 to 12 inch skillet over medium heat, sauté onion and green pepper in butter until soft but not brown. Add rice and brown lightly, stirring constantly. Add the orange juice, buttermilk, oregano and salt. Stir and bring to a boil over high heat. Cover. Simmer 25 minutes or until the liquid is absorbed. Stir in orange pieces and almonds. Heat through. Spoon the rice into a serving bowl and serve hot with veal, poultry or lamb. Serve immediately or can be held in 250° oven for 45 minutes. Serves 6.

7 Pasta, etc.

Pasta, etc.

7

Spaghetti Carbonara

4 *slices bacon, cut into 1 inch pieces*
3 *oz. prosciutto, cut into julienne strips*
1 *medium onion, sliced*
¼ *cup cream sherry*
½ *cup butter*
1 *lb. spaghetti, cooked*
3 *eggs, beaten*
salt and pepper, to taste
1 *cup Parmesan cheese*

Jane C. Craven SED '73
Santa Barbara, California

In a skillet, sauté bacon until almost crisp. Add pro-sciutto and brown slightly. Drain on paper towel. Sauté onion in skillet until soft. Return bacon and prosciutto to pan. Stir in sherry. Simmer 2 minutes. Take from heat. Add pieces of butter and cooked spaghetti. Return to heat and toss. Remove from heat, add eggs, salt, pepper and Parmesan. Toss and serve immediately. Serves 4 to 6.

Pasta de Casamicciola

You may vary this tomato salad for pasta in many ways. Add 1 small, sweet red pepper, diced or slivered and about ½ cup of cubed mozzarella. Black olives are an excellent addition as well. A few anchovy fillets add even more taste.

Terence Janericco CLA '61
Cookbook Committee Editor
Boston, Massachusetts

1 lb. tomatoes, peeled, seeded, chopped
½ cup olive oil
1 tablespoon fresh basil
lemon juice
salt and pepper, to taste
1 lb. small pasta (shells, cavatelli, rigatoni)

In a bowl, combine the tomatoes with olive oil, basil and enough lemon juice to make a pleasant flavor. Add salt and pepper. Refrigerate 30 minutes before using. Boil pasta al dente, drain and add to the bowl with the tomatoes. Toss and serve immediately. Serves 4 to 6.
Note: Grated cheese is not served with this dish.

Manicotti

Loosely translated from Italian, manicotti means macaroni muff or package.

1 cup olive oil
4 cloves garlic, sliced
2 (No. 2½) cans tomato purée
2½ teaspoons salt
2 teaspoons dried, crushed oregano
½ teaspoon minced parsley
¼ teaspoon pepper

Alice Hazlehurst Barreca
SAR '53
National Alumni Council
Weston, Connecticut

In a Dutch oven, heat olive oil. Sauté garlic until lightly browned. Discard garlic. Add tomatoes, salt, oregano, parsley and pepper, stirring constantly. Cook rapidly uncovered, about 15 minutes or until thickened. Stir occasionally. Can be frozen. Makes 7 cups.

Manicotti Pancakes

1¼ cups flour
½ cup water
½ cup milk
2 tablespoons olive oil
1 teaspoon salt
6 eggs

Place flour in a mixing bowl. Combine water, milk, oil and salt. Gradually add liquid to flour, beating after each addition until smooth. Add eggs, 1 at a time, beating well after each. Heat a 6 inch iron skillet over medium flame and grease lightly with an oil-soaked paper towel. Add 2 to 3 tablespoons batter into skillet, rolling evenly around pan and cook about 1 minute. Flip over and allow to remain in pan 30 seconds off the heat. Remove pancake to a paper towel. Transfer to a sheet of waxed paper. Repeat, placing a layer of waxed paper between each pancake. Can be frozen. Makes about 48.

The Filling

2	lbs. ricotta cheese
1	cup grated Romano cheese
1	tablespoon minced parsley
1	teaspoon dry crumbled basil
1	tablespoon sugar
4	eggs
48	cubes mozzarella cheese

In a bowl combine ricotta, Romano, parsley, basil, sugar, and eggs. Mix well.

To Assemble

Preheat oven to 350°. Spread about 1 cup sauce on the bottom of greased 9x13x2 inch baking dish. Place 1 tablespoon of filling in center of each pancake. Place a cube of mozzarella into center. Fold sides over, then fold opposite sides over to enclose filling, envelope fashion. Place, folded side down, in baking dish. Repeat until all crêpes and cheese mixture are used. Cover generously with tomato sauce. Bake uncovered until piping hot and bubbling, about 30 minutes. The manicotti will swell. Serve with grated Parmesan and extra sauce. Can be frozen and thawed completely before baking. Serves 12.

Canneloni

Dorothy Martin Apgar
SON '61
Flagler Beach, Florida

1 *lb. ground beef*
2 *onions, minced*
1 *lb. ricotta cheese*
1 *cup bread crumbs*
1 *egg, slightly beaten*
10 *oz. package frozen chopped spinach, thawed, drained*
1 *teaspoon oregano*
1 *teaspoon salt*
¼ *teaspoon pepper*
3 *cups spaghetti sauce*
9 *lasagna noodles, cooked, drained*
1 *cup shredded mozzarella cheese*
1 *cup grated Parmesan cheese*

Preheat oven to 350°. In a skillet, sauté beef and onion until meat loses its color. Pour off fat. In a bowl, combine beef mixture, crumbs, eggs, spinach, oregano, salt and pepper. Mix well. Spread a layer of sauce in the bottom of a 13x9x2 inch pan. Cut noodles in half across the width. Place 2 tablespoons of mixture on each noodle half. Roll and place seam side down in the baking dish. Sprinkle rolls with mozzarella and Parmesan. Cover with foil and bake 10 minutes. Remove foil and bake 20 minutes longer. Can be frozen. Serves 6 to 8.

Salsa al Gorgonzola

This works well with long pastas such as spaghetti, linguine and vermicelli because it clings to the pasta. Fettucine (or egg noodles) and green or spinach fettucine are particularly pleasant.

4 *oz. gorgonzola cheese*
⅓ *cup milk*
3 *tablespoons butter*
salt
¼ *cup heavy cream*
⅓ *cup grated Parmesan cheese*
1 *lb. pasta*

Place a large shallow serving dish over low heat. Put the gorgonzola, milk, butter and 2 teaspoons of salt into the dish. Mash the gorgonzola with a spoon and stir to incorporate it into the milk and butter. Cook for 2 to 3 minutes, or until the sauce has a dense, creamy consistency. Remove from heat. When pasta is almost cooked, return to low heat and stir in the heavy cream. Drain pasta and add to sauce. Toss until well coated, then sprinkle on grated cheese. Serve immediately. Additional grated cheese is served with this pasta. Serves 4 to 6.

Terence Janericco CLA '61
Cookbook Committee Editor
Boston, Massachusetts

Ligurian Pesto and Vegetables

Pesto Sauce

2	*cups fresh basil leaves*
2½	*cloves garlic, crushed*
¼	*cup grated imported Parmesan cheese*
2	*tablespoons pignoli or walnuts*
⅔ to 1	*cup olive oil*
	salt and pepper, to taste

In a blender, combine basil, garlic, cheese, nuts and olive oil to make a creamy thick sauce. Season with salt and pepper. Set aside. Can be frozen. Serves 6.

	6 to 8 oz. green beans
	6 to 8 oz. asparagus, cut in half
1½	*large potatoes, ¾ cooked, peeled, cubed*
3 to 5	*tablespoons butter*
1	*lb. Italian imported bucazini or linguini, cooked al dente.*
	grated Parmesan or Romano cheese

In a skillet, sauté beans and potatoes until tender. Toss with linguini and pesto. Serve immediately with grated cheese on the side. Serves 6.
   Variations: You can use broccoli or add mushrooms. Add ½ cup ricotta for a creamy effect.

Serve with chilled glass of wine.

Carine Ravosa CLA '82
Boston, Massachusetts

Matthew's Best Lasagna

I used to call this 'Second Day Lasagna' because it develops an extra scrumptious flavor after the second day.

Dr. Matthew Witten
CLA '72
Cookbook Committee
Los Angeles, California

1 cup diced celery
2 large onions, diced
4 large cloves garlic, chopped
2 tablespoons olive oil
3½ cups stewed tomatoes
2 6 oz. cans tomato paste
2 cups white wine
1 to 2 cups fresh mushrooms, sliced
2 lbs. lean ground beef
2 bay leaves
2 tablespoons sugar
1 tablespoon oregano
1 teaspoon salt
½ teaspoon pepper
1 lb. lasagna noodles, cooked, drained
15 oz. ricotta cheese
8 to 10 oz. mozzarella cheese
grated Parmesan cheese

In a large skillet, sauté celery, onions and garlic in oil for 5 minutes. Add tomatoes and tomato paste. Simmer 5 minutes, add wine and cover skillet. In another skillet, brown meat until crumbly, drain off fat and add to sauce. Add mushrooms, bay leaves, sugar, oregano, salt and pepper. Mix well. Simmer covered 30 minutes. In a baking dish, place a layer of noodles, covering the bottom with a layer of meat sauce. Place ½ of ricotta and mozzarella on top, cover with noodles. Repeat the process, making 3 layers of noodles. Cover the top layer with some of the sauce (without the meat) and sprinkle with Parmesan. Bake in oven preheated to 350° for approximately 30 minutes. Serve remaining sauce separately. Can be frozen. Serves 6.

Gloria's Spinach Lasagna

28 oz. can crushed tomatoes

2 tablespoons minced onion

1 clove garlic, minced

1 teaspoon oregano

1 teaspoon basil

1 teaspoon parsley

1 teaspoon salt

1 lb. ricotta cheese

10 oz. frozen chopped spinach

½ cup Parmesan cheese

½ cup water

½ lb. lasagna noodles, uncooked

8 oz. mozzarella cheese, sliced

Cookbook Committee

Preheat oven to 375°. In a bowl, combine tomatoes, onions, garlic, oregano, basil, parsley and salt. In another bowl, combine ricotta, spinach and Parmesan. In a 7x11 inch baking dish, place water, 3 tablespoons tomato mixture and ½ of uncooked lasagna noodles. Top with ⅓ of sauce and ½ of spinach. Add remaining lasagna, ⅓ of sauce, remaining spinach, remaining sauce and mozzarella slices. Cover and bake 45 minutes. Remove cover and bake 20 minutes longer. Can be frozen. Serves 6.

Spinach Noodles with Cream Cheese

¼ lb. sweet butter, melted

1 lb. softened cream cheese

1 lb. spinach noodles, cooked, drained

grated pepper, to taste

grated Parmesan cheese

Dr. Peter Cohen SED '65
National Alumni Council
Wellesley, Massachusetts

Melt butter and add softened cream cheese. When well blended, pour over cooked pasta and mix. Grind fresh pepper over, top with freshly grated Parmesan cheese. Must be prepared and eaten immediately. Serve hot. Serves 4 to 6.

Pizza Rustica
(Italian Meat and Custard Pie)

In certain provinces of
Italy, this recipe was
considered a traditional
Easter dish.

14 large eggs
2 lbs. ricotta cheese
½ lb. mozzarella, diced
½ lb. prosciutto, finely chopped
½ lb. Genoa salami, finely chopped
1 lb. provolone cheese, diced
½ cup grated Parmesan cheese
½ cup pignoli
freshly grated pepper

Yole Ames CLA '51
Former Vice President
General Alumni Association
Arlington, Massachusetts

Preheat oven to 375°. Line an 11x14x4 inch pan with
½ of the pie crust. In a large bowl, beat the eggs and the
ricotta until smooth. Cut the mozzarella into very small
cubes, about ⅛ inch. Add mozzarella, prosciutto, salami,
provolone, grated cheese and the pignoli to the eggs and
ricotta. Add freshly grated pepper and blend well. Pour
into crust lined pan. Cover with crust, make vents all
over top crust with a fork. Bake at 375° for 45 minutes to
1 hour or until knife comes out dry. Serve warm or at
room temperature.

Apple Kugel

Marriette Ostrovsky
Staff
Development Office

12 oz. medium noodles
1 can apple pie filling
4 eggs
½ cup sugar
½ cup butter
½ cup orange juice
½ cup raisins (optional)
½ teaspoon salt
½ cup cornflakes
3 tablespoons sugar
½ teaspoon cinnamon
juice of ½ lemon

Preheat oven to 350°. Grease a 9x13 inch baking dish. In
a bowl, combine noodles, apple filling, eggs, sugar, but-

ter, orange juice, raisins and salt. Mix well. Pour into prepared dish. Combine cornflakes, sugar and cinnamon. Sprinkle over top. Sprinkle on lemon juice. Bake 1 hour. Can be made ahead and reheated. Serves 6.

Noodle Pudding

1 lb. broad noodles, cooked, drained
4 eggs
1 pint sour cream
1 pint creamed cottage cheese
12 oz. apricot preserves
¼ lb. butter, melted

Lenore Ryan
Staff
School for the Arts

Preheat oven to 350°. Place noodles in a large bowl. Beat in eggs 1 at a time. Add sour cream, cottage cheese, preserves and butter. Pour into a 9x11 inch baking dish. Will keep two hours before baking. Bake 1½ hours or until browned. Can be frozen.

Noodle Charlotte

1 lb. cottage or pot cheese
3 oz. softened cream cheese
8 oz. sour cream
4 tablespoons butter
½ cup sugar
2 eggs, well beaten
1½ teaspoons vanilla
11 oz. package egg noodles, ¼ inch wide, cooked
½ teaspoon cinnamon

Anna E. Bessette
SON '63/'65
Attleboro, Massachusetts

Preheat oven to 350°. Grease an 8x11 inch Pyrex baking dish. In a bowl, combine cheeses, sour cream, butter, sugar, eggs, vanilla. Mix noodles in gently. Turn into long, prepared baking dish. Sprinkle cinnamon on top. Bake uncovered for ½ hour. Serve hot or cold. Makes 8 to 10 servings.

Noodle Pudding

Sharon Gamsin
DGE '69/SPC '71
Cookbook Committee
New York, New York

8 oz. cream cheese

1 pint sour cream

6 eggs

1 cup sugar

½ lb. butter

1 teaspoon vanilla

½ teaspoon cinnamon

½ teaspoon lemon juice

1 lb. wide egg noodles, cooked, drained

1 cup raisins

cornflake crumbs

3 tablespoons butter

Preheat oven to 350°. In a bowl, beat cream cheese, sour cream, eggs, sugar and butter together. Add vanilla, cinnamon and lemon juice. Mix in noodles and raisins. Put in 8x8 inch baking pan. Top with crumbs and small dabs of butter. Bake for 1 hour. Serve hot or cold. Can be made ahead and frozen. Serves 6.

Fruit Kugel

Libby Cohen SED '77
Cape Elizabeth, Maine

8 matzos

1 cup butter, melted

8 eggs

6 tablespoons strawberry or cherry preserves

4 apples, peeled, sliced

¼ cup raisins

2 teaspoons sugar

1½ teaspoons cinnamon

1 teaspoon salt

Preheat oven to 400°. Cover matzos with warm water. Let sit until soft. Drain well in a colander. Squeeze out excess water. In a bowl, mix butter, eggs, preserves, apples, raisins, sugar, cinnamon and salt. Pour over matzos into a greased 9x12 inch pan. Bake ½ hour. Reduce heat to 375°, bake 10 to 20 minutes longer. Keeps two days refrigerated. Best served warm. Makes 24, 2 inch squares.

Apple Orange Noodle Pudding

2 tablespoons butter or margarine, melted
½ lb. broad noodles, cooked, drained
3 eggs, beaten
1 teaspoon vanilla
1 teaspoon lemon juice
pinch salt
2 tart apples, sliced thin
¼ cup raisins
1 small can mandarin oranges, drained
½ cup sugar
cinnamon

Preheat oven to 350°. Pour butter into 1½ quart baking dish. Set aside. Rinse noodles and drain again. In a bowl, combine eggs, vanilla, lemon juice and salt. Stir into noodles with apples, raisins, oranges and sugar. Pour into casserole dish. Sprinkle with cinnamon. Bake 1 hour. Can be reheated. Serves 6.

This is a traditional Jewish holiday side dish.

Susan Freedman Mandel
Cookbook Committee
Oakland, New Jersey

Rice Kugel

1 cup rice
4 cups water
¾ cup butter, melted
3 eggs
½ cup sugar
½ cup golden raisins
1 apple, peeled, diced
1 cup cornflakes
cinnamon, to taste

Preheat oven to 375°. Boil the rice in water until tender, 20 minutes. Place butter in 1 quart casserole dish. In a bowl, beat the eggs with the sugar and raisins, stir in rice and pour into the baking dish. Sprinkle on cornflakes and cinnamon. Bake 35 minutes or until set. Can be reheated. Serves 6.

Gail Ucko CLA '78
Fort Lauderdale, Florida

Laura's Asparagus Quiche

Martha Blaustein
Ernest Blaustein
Assistant Dean
College of Liberal Arts

13 oz. evaporated milk
4 eggs
⅔ cup shredded Swiss cheese
¼ cup sour cream
2 teaspoons Worcestershire sauce
½ teaspoon dry mustard
½ teaspoon salt
dash pepper, cayenne, nutmeg
10 asparagus spears, steamed
1 cup mushrooms, sautéed in butter
1 unbaked pie shell

Preheat oven to 400°. In a bowl, combine milk, eggs, cheese, sour cream, Worcestershire, salt, nutmeg, cayenne and pepper. Arrange asparagus and mushrooms in pie shell. Pour on egg mixture. Bake for 10 minutes. Reduce heat to 350°, bake 40 minutes. Serve hot or cold. Serves 6.

Norma's Quiche

Norma Oliver MET '78
Women's Guild

1 cup whole wheat pastry flour
6 tablespoons butter, cut into bite size pieces
½ teaspoon salt
cold water, to roll
1 cup minced onion
1 tablespoon butter
2 tablespoons crumbled bacon bits
3 eggs, lightly beaten with 1 teaspoon salt
2 cups plain yogurt
¼ teaspoon nutmeg
⅛ teaspoon cayenne
½ lb. grated Swiss or gruyère cheese

Preheat oven to 450°. Place flour in a bowl, work in butter with finger tips until it looks like coarse meal. Add
water, a tablespoon at a time, until it forms a dough. Roll
out and fill a 9 inch pie plate and set aside. In a skillet,
sauté onion in butter until soft. Stir in bacon, eggs,
yogurt, nutmeg and cayenne. Mix well. Fold in cheese.
Pour into shell. Bake 10 minutes. Lower heat and bake
25 minutes or until firm. Let rest 10 minutes before serving. Serves 6.

Mushroom, Sausage and Onion Quiche

1	lb. onions, thinly sliced
1	tablespoon bacon fat
2	eggs
2	egg yolks
2	teaspoons Dijon mustard
½	cup Parmesan cheese
½	lb. mushrooms, sliced
2	tablespoons butter
1	tablespoon lemon juice
½	lb. pork sausage meat, cooked, crumbled
1¼	cups light cream, scalded
½	teaspoon salt
¼	teaspoon pepper
1	10 inch pie shell, half-baked

This is great as a main
dish with salad, a loaf of
bread and a good bottle of
wine.

Katherine A. Judge
Staff
School of Management

Preheat oven to 350°. Sauté the onions in bacon fat until
soft but not brown. Sauté mushrooms in butter in a separate pan. In a bowl, beat eggs, egg yolks, mustard and
cheese. Add lemon juice, drained sausage meat, mushrooms, cream and onions to eggs. Pour into the pie shell.
Bake 20 to 25 minutes or until knife inserted in center
comes out clean. Can be made ahead and reheated.
Serves 6 to 8.

Corn Quiche

This is just so good, I love it. You can vary the ingredients slightly or use a whole wheat crust for variety.

Claire Shapiro Soja
CLA '68
Cookbook Committee
Harvard, Massachusetts

4 leeks, thinly sliced

10 oz. frozen corn, thawed

¼ cup butter

¼ cup dry white wine

4 oz. emmenthaler cheese, diced

10 inch pastry shell, baked

½ cup finely diced ham or chicken

4 eggs, beaten

2 cups heavy cream

½ teaspoon salt

⅛ teaspoon pepper

Preheat oven to 350°. In covered medium skillet, cook leeks and corn in butter until tender but not brown. Remove from heat; stir in wine and set aside. Sprinkle cheese over bottom of baked pastry shell. Top with cooked leek mixture, ham or chicken. In a bowl, combine eggs, cream, salt and pepper. Pour into shell. Bake 40 to 45 minutes or until almost set in center. Let stand 5 minutes before serving. Can be reheated. Serves 8.

Quiche Raphel

Dorothea Raphel
Staff
School of
Public Communication

12 slices crisp bacon, crumbled

1 cup shredded Swiss cheese

2 cups milk

4 eggs

⅓ cup finely chopped onion

½ cup Bisquick baking mix

¼ teaspoon salt

⅛ teaspoon pepper

Preheat oven to 350°. Lightly grease a 9 or 10 inch pie plate. Sprinkle bacon and cheese evenly over the bottom of the pie plate. Place milk, eggs, onion, Bisquick, salt and pepper in a blender. Blend on high speed for 1 minute. Pour into pie plate. Bake 50 to 55 minutes until golden brown and a knife inserted in center comes out clean. Let stand 5 minutes before cutting. Refrigerate any leftovers. Serves 6.

Seafood Quiche

3 tablespoons butter	
1 small onion, minced	
1 cup crab, shrimp or lobster	
½ teaspoon salt	
pepper, to taste	
2 tablespoons dry white vermouth	
3 eggs	
1 cup heavy cream	
1 tablespoon tomato paste	
1 8 inch pie shell, half-baked	
¼ cup grated Swiss cheese	

June Neves CBA '72
Fall River, Massachusetts

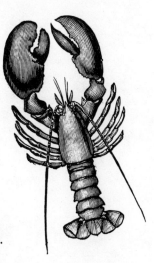

Preheat oven to 375°. Sauté onions in butter, add crab, salt, pepper and vermouth; remove from heat. Pour mixture into pie shell, top with ¼ cup grated Swiss cheese, bake at 375° for 30 minutes. In a bowl, combine eggs, cream and tomato paste. Stir in crab mixture. Pour into pie shell and sprinkle with cheese. Bake 30 minutes. Can be served hot or at room temperature. Serves 4 to 6.

Tuna Quiche

6½ oz. tuna, crumbled
9 inch pie shell, half-baked
1½ cups grated Swiss cheese
½ cup chopped onion
2 eggs, beaten
1 cup evaporated milk or medium cream
1 tablespoon lemon juice
¼ teaspoon crushed garlic
½ teaspoon salt
⅛ teaspoon pepper

Mark Premack
DGE '73/CLA '75
Omaha, Nebraska

Preheat oven to 450°. Distribute tuna over bottom of pie shell. Sprinkle cheese and onion over tuna. Beat eggs, milk, lemon juice, garlic, salt and pepper. Pour over tuna. Bake 15 minutes. Reduce oven to 350°, bake 12 to 15 minutes or longer until top is golden brown. Can be reheated. Serves 4 to 6.

Crustless Vegetable Quiche

Beatrice Trum Hunter
20th Century Archives
Mugar Library

¼ cup peeled, cubed eggplant

1 onion, chopped

4 raw mushrooms, sliced (optional)

3 eggs

3 tablespoons sunflower or sesame seeds

1 cup low fat milk

1 teaspoon paprika

½ cup sharp Cheddar chunks

1 tablespoon vegetable oil

herbs of choice

Preheat oven to 300°. Butter a 9 inch pie plate. In a bowl, combine the eggplant, onion and mushrooms. Put into pie plate. In a blender or processor, purée eggs, milk, cheese, oil and herbs. Pour over eggplant. Sprinkle with seeds and paprika. Bake 1¼ to 1½ hours or until firm. Serve hot or cold. Serves 6.

Variation: Add diced green pepper, celery or fresh peas.

Cheese Soufflé

Lorraine Nelson Klein
GRS '76
Cookbook Committee
North Kingston,
Rhode Island

¼ cup butter

¼ cup flour

1½ cups milk, scalded

salt, to taste

Worcestershire sauce

cayenne, to taste

½ lb. Cheddar cheese, grated

4 eggs, separated

Preheat oven to 375°. Butter a 1 quart soufflé dish and set aside. In a 1 quart saucepan, melt butter, stir in flour and cook until bubbly. Stir in milk vigorously and continue stirring until thickened and smooth. Stir in salt, Worcestershire and cayenne. Cool 3 minutes. Stir in cheese until it melts. Stir in egg yolks 1 at a time. Cool slightly. Beat egg whites until stiff but not dry. Fold into the cheese mixture. Pour into the soufflé dish. Bake 45 minutes. Serve immediately. Serves 4 to 6.

Super Spinach Crêpes

4 10 oz. packages frozen chopped spinach, thawed
1 lb. feta cheese
8 oz. cream cheese
½ cup grated Romano or Parmesan cheese
4 eggs
1 small onion, minced
3 tablespoons olive oil
1 teaspoon chopped dill (optional)
1 teaspoon salt
¼ teaspoon pepper
18 crêpes

Paula K. Peterson SPC '80
Minneapolis, Minnesota

Preheat oven to 300°. Squeeze excess moisture from spinach and place in bowl. Add the feta, cream cheese, Romano, eggs, onion, olive oil, dill, salt and pepper. Mix well. Place 2 to 3 tablespoons on a crêpe and roll. Place in a baking dish. Bake until heated throughout. May be prepared a day ahead. Makes 18.

The Crêpe

4 eggs
1 cup milk
1 cup water
2 cups whole wheat flour
1 teaspoon salt
3 tablespoons butter or oil, melted

In a blender, combine eggs, milk, water, flour and salt. Blend until smooth. Add the oil and blend again. Let rest overnight in the refrigerator. Wipe a hot, heavy-bottomed skillet with oil. Pour about ¼ cup batter into pan while tilting the pan in a big arc to distribute the batter thinly. Makes 7 inch crêpes. Cook about 45 seconds, until the edges dry and begin to shrink up from the pan. Can be stacked or refrigerated. For freezing put wax paper between each crêpe.

Cream Cheese Soufflé

This is a very versatile meal. You can use it for breakfast or brunch.

Shirley Coyne
Woburn, Massachusetts

4 eggs
4 oz. Cheddar or Swiss cheese, cubed
3 oz. cream cheese, cubed
¼ cup grated Parmesan cheese
½ tablespoon minced onion
¼ cup milk

Preheat oven to 350°. Grease a 1 quart soufflé dish. Dust with Parmesan. In a processor or blender, combine eggs, cheeses, onion and milk. Blend until smooth. Pour into prepared dish and bake 40 to 45 minutes. Serve immediately. Serves 4.

Baked Cheese Puff

Easy recipe that never fails

Sandy Raphaelson
Parent
Bal Harbour, Florida

10 slices white bread, crusts removed
4 oz. Cheddar cheese, grated
½ cup butter
6 eggs
2 cups milk
1 teaspoon salt
pepper, to taste

Butter an 8 inch soufflé dish with ¼ cup butter. Layer bread and cheese and dot with remaining butter. Continue layering ending with butter. In a bowl, combine the eggs, milk, salt and pepper. Pour over the bread-cheese mixture. Refrigerate 24 hours. Preheat oven to 350°. Place 1 inch hot water in a baking pan; set soufflé dish in pan of water and bake 1 hour. May be prepared 24 hours ahead. Serves 6.

Baked Cheese Fondue

David K. Farnsworth
SED '40

1 cup milk, scalded
1 cup soft bread crumbs
½ lb. gruyère or Cheddar cheese
1 tablespoon butter
½ teaspoon salt
3 eggs, separated

Preheat oven to 350°. In a bowl, combine milk, crumbs, cheese, butter and salt. Beat egg yolks until lemon colored. Fold in. Beat egg whites until stiff, but not dry and fold into mixture. Pour into greased 9x13 inch baking dish and bake 30 minutes. Serve immediately. Serves 6.

Baked Cheese Pudding

4 *slices day old bread, cubed*	
1 *cup, Cheddar, Edam or Boursin cheese, cubed*	
2 *cups milk*	
2 *eggs*	
salt and pepper, to taste	

Excellent luncheon or supper dish. Serve with salad. Wonderful après ski.

Elizabeth Yates
20th Century Archives
Mugar Library

Preheat oven to 350°. Butter a 9 inch baking dish. Make a layer of bread crumbs and top with cheese. In a bowl, beat milk and eggs together and pour over the bread-cheese mixture. Season with salt and pepper. Let stand at room temperature for 30 minutes. Bake 30 minutes until crusty and brown. Best served at once. Can be allowed to sit overnight before baking. Serves 3 to 4.

Chile Rellenos Casserole

1 *cup grated Cheddar cheese*
1 *cup grated Monterey Jack cheese*
1 *small can green chilies*
4 *eggs, separated*
13 *oz. can evaporated milk*
3 *tablespoons flour*
1 *teaspoon salt*
1 *cup enchilada sauce*

Marilyn Peters SAR '76
Grosse Point Shores, Michigan

Preheat oven to 325°. Layer Cheddar, Monterey Jack and chilies in casserole dish. Beat egg yolks then add evaporated milk, flour and salt. Beat egg whites until stiff and fold into yolk mixture. Pour the egg mixture over the chilies and the cheese. Bake 45 minutes. Pour on the enchilada sauce. Bake 20 minutes more. Serve immediately. Serves 4 to 6.

Enchiladas Suisas

Libby Cohen SED '77
Cape Elizabeth, Maine

3 chili peppers, sliced

3 green peppers, sliced

2 cups heavy cream

2 tomatoes, sliced

salt and pepper, to taste

2 chickens, cooked, diced

18 tortillas

16 slices American or Monterey Jack cheese

Preheat oven to 300°. Purée peppers, cream, tomatoes, salt and pepper in blender or processor until smooth. Roll a tortilla around 2 to 3 tablespoons of cut up chicken. Place rolled tortillas in a casserole dish. Place slices of cheese on top of tortillas. Cover with sauce. Bake 30 minutes or until bubbly. May be prepared for baking two to three hours ahead. Serves 6.

Howell's Texas Chili

Feeds 20 New Englanders or 10 Texans

Dr. James M. Howell
Trustee
Boston, Massachusetts

3 lbs. ground chuck

3 medium onions, chopped

2 green peppers, chopped

3 stalks celery, chopped

3 tablespoons chopped parsley

1 15 oz. can tomato sauce

1 15 oz. can whole tomatoes, broken up

1 can tomato paste

1 bottle Lone Star beer

4 tablespoons chili powder

2 tablespoons salt

black pepper, to taste

1 teaspoon crushed garlic

dash nutmeg

3 lbs. canned ranch-style beans

Brown meat, onion, peppers, celery and parsley. Add tomato sauce, tomatoes, tomato paste, beer, chili powder, garlic, pepper and nutmeg. Cover and simmer for 1½ to 2 hours. Add beans and heat thoroughly. May be reheated.

Chili

3	lbs. ground chuck
1	lb. lean bacon, cooked crisp
2	large onions, chopped
2	1 lb. 12 oz. cans tomatoes, undrained
2	15 oz. cans tomato sauce
5	tablespoons chili powder
1	can red enchilada sauce
1	cup water
2	cans whole green chili peppers
5	cloves garlic, minced
3	tablespoons powdered cumin
2	tablespoons sugar
1	tablespoon salt
2	teaspoons black pepper
2	teaspoons dry mustard
½	teaspoon cayenne
4	cans kidney beans
	taco chips
	ground hot red pepper
	Tabasco sauce

Chili must never be spooned into your mouth. That's obscene. The only way to eat chili is to plop spoonfuls onto sturdy chips and gulp them down.

Bob Montgomery
Professor
Department of
Communication
School of
Public Communication

In a large deep skillet, sauté the meat until it loses its color. Add the bacon, onions, tomatoes, tomato sauce, enchilada sauce, chili powder, water, green chili peppers, garlic, cumin, sugar, salt, pepper, mustard and cayenne and simmer for 2 to 3 hours or all day. A half hour before serving add the kidney beans. Serve with taco chips and ground red hot pepper and Tabasco for those who like more fire. Keeps one week refrigerated. Serves 8.

New England French Toast

The trick is to cut your bread extra thick and punch holes to soak up the batter. Of course, the finishing touch is real Vermont maple syrup.

Dr. Jane S. Norton
SED '70/'74
President
Women Graduates' Club

2 1½ to 2 inch thick slices French or Italian bread
2 eggs
¼ cup milk
½ teaspoon rum
¼ teaspoon orange liqueur
   butter
   maple syrup

Place bread slices in pie plate. In a bowl, beat eggs, milk, rum and orange liqueur. Pour over bread. Poking holes into bread to help it absorb the liquid, heat butter in skillet or on a grill. Sauté bread slices until golden on both sides. Serve immediately with syrup and butter. Serves 2.

Blintz Soufflé

Sue Lavien
David Lavien
LAW '29/SMG '30
Former Trustee
Boston, Massachusetts

12 cheese blintzes
¼ cup butter, melted
6 eggs
2 cups sour cream
1 teaspoon vanilla
¼ cup orange juice
¼ cup sugar
1½ teaspoons salt

Preheat oven to 350°. Arrange blintzes on bottom of a 2 quart oven-to-table casserole. Pour on melted butter. In a bowl, beat eggs, sour cream, vanilla, orange juice, sugar and salt until smooth. Pour over blintzes. Bake 1 hour. Serve with fruit or sour cream. Can be frozen. Serves 6.

Blintzes

½ cup flour
pinch of salt
3 eggs
½ cup milk
½ cup water
butter

Sterne Barnett CBA '35
Cookbook Committee
Chestnut Hill, Massachusetts

Place flour and salt in a bowl. Beat in the eggs to make a paste. Combine the milk and water. Gradually stir in the milk mixture to make a smooth batter the consistency of heavy cream. Let rest 30 minutes. Heat a 7 inch crêpe pan over medium heat, butter lightly. Pour 1 tablespoon of batter into the pan, twisting and turning the pan to cover the bottom with batter. Cook until the edges are dry. Turn over onto a sheet of waxed paper, uncooked side down. Repeat with the remaining batter. Put a generous tablespoon of filling on the cooked side of the blintz. Fold in the 2 sides then roll as a jellyroll. Sauté in butter until golden.

Filling

½ lb. farmer cheese
½ lb. cream cheese
½ lb. cottage cheese
2 egg yolks
almond or vanilla extract, or grated orange peel, to taste
sugar, to taste

In a bowl, combine the cheeses and the egg yolks. Add the flavoring of your choice and sugar. Serve the blintzes with sour cream, cinnamon, sugar, jam or applesauce, if desired. Blueberries, peaches or thinly sliced apples may be added to the cheese mixture or used in place of it. Can be frozen. Makes 24.

Blintzes

Pancake

Carol Ekster SED '73
Andover, Massachusetts

4 eggs

4 tablespoons butter, melted

2½ cups milk

3 cups sifted flour

6 tablespoons sugar

1 teaspoon salt

½ cup water

Beat eggs until thick and combine with melted butter and milk. Sift together flour, sugar and salt. Beat into eggs, adding water to make a smooth batter. In a small round greased or Teflon pan, make thin pancakes like crêpes. Cook just on 1 side over low flame.

Cheese Filling

2 lbs. cottage cheese, farmer cheese or combination

6 oz. cream cheese

6 tablespoons sugar

1 teaspoon vanilla

2 egg yolks

In a bowl, combine the cheeses, sugar, vanilla and egg yolks. Flavor with sugar and vanilla to taste. Put filling in center of pancake and roll up. Brown in butter in skillet to serve. Freezes well. Makes 20 cheese blintzes with batter left for about 10.

8 Salads & Sauces

Salads & Sauces

8

Margaret's Cabbage Salad

1	head cabbage, shredded
1	onion, thinly sliced
1	green pepper, thinly sliced
1	teaspoon celery seed
2	tablespoons salt
1½	cups sugar
¾	cup vinegar
¾	cup corn oil

In a non-aluminum bowl, combine cabbage, onion, pepper, celery seed and salt. In a saucepan, combine sugar, vinegar and oil. Bring to a rolling boil and pour over vegetables at once. Stir. Refrigerate 12 hours, at least, stirring occasionally. Drain just before serving. Keeps a week. Serves 6.

Margaret was the cook in our family for 27 years. This particular recipe of hers is great for picnics, because it can be made up to a week ahead of time.

Natalie McCracken
Assistant to the Dean
College of Liberal Arts

Tangy Cole Slaw

Susan Freedman Mandel
SED '70
Cookbook Committee
Oakland, New Jersey

¾ *cup mayonnaise*

2 *tablespoons chili sauce*

2 *tablespoons vinegar*

¼ *teaspoon celery seed*

⅛ *tablespoon Worcestershire sauce*

salt and pepper, to taste

½ *head cabbage, coarsely shredded*

1 *carrot, thinly sliced*

1 *green pepper, diced*

In a bowl, combine mayonnaise, chili sauce, vinegar, celery seed, Worcestershire, salt and pepper. Stir in cabbage, carrot and pepper. Mix well. Keeps two days refrigerated. Serves 4 to 6.

Cole Slaw and Capers

Carla Marcus Schair
SED '70
Scarborough, Maine

1 *small head cabbage, shredded*

½ *onion, thinly sliced*

1 *to 1½ cups mayonnaise*

3 *tablespoons olive oil*

2 *tablespoons wine vinegar*

2 *tablespoons capers*

1 *teaspoon chopped basil*

1 *teaspoon thyme*

1 *teaspoon tarragon*

1 *teaspoon marjoram*

½ *teaspoon Tabasco*

salt and pepper, to taste

In a bowl, combine cabbage, onion, mayonnaise, olive oil, vinegar, capers, basil, thyme, tarragon, marjoram, Tabasco, salt and pepper. Mix well. Chill. Keeps three days refrigerated. Serves 6.

Mother's Best Cole Slaw

1 head cabbage, shredded
1 teaspoon salt
2 celery stalks, minced
1 green pepper, minced
1 carrot, grated

Dressing

¾ cup mayonnaise
⅓ cup plus 1 tablespoon sugar
6 tablespoons cider vinegar
1 teaspoon salt (or to taste)
paprika

Soak cabbage in a bowl of ice water with 1 teaspoon salt for 1½ hours. Drain well. Mix with celery, green peppers and carrot. In a bowl, combine mayonnaise, sugar, vinegar and salt. Toss with cabbage. Macerate 4 hours refrigerated. Just before serving, toss lightly to coat with dressing and sprinkle with paprika. Serves 6.

My mother has made this coleslaw for as far back as I can remember. Of course, she never knew exactly how she made it. I had to watch and stop her at every step, in order to measure out her handfuls and dashes of ingredients.

Kathleen Ruskey Cole SPC '62
Cookbook Committee
Swansea, Massachusetts

Carrot Salad

1 lb. carrots, shredded
juice of 2 oranges
2 tablespoons sugar

Combine carrots, orange juice and sugar. Mix well. Keeps three days refrigerated. Serves 4 to 6.

Variation: Add ½ cup raisins and ¼ cup toasted almonds or ½ cup diced dates.

Shelley Tiber
Abraham Tiber SMG '70
Cookbook Committee
Haifa, Israel

Miriam Bar-Yam
Professor
Department of
Humanistic, Developmental
and Organizational Studies
School of Education

Eggplant Salad *(Israeli Style)*

1 medium eggplant
2 tablespoons fresh lemon juice
2 tablespoons finely chopped onion
2 tablespoons chopped parsley
1½ tablespoons mayonnaise
½ to 1 teaspoon garlic salt or mashed garlic clove
⅓ to ½ teaspoon salt
dash sugar
3 tomato wedges
18 black olives

Put eggplant in a pie pan on top of stove on medium heat. Roast on each side for about 15 to 20 minutes. Remove eggplant from stove and scoop out pulp into bowl. Mash thoroughly with a fork. Mix in lemon juice, onion, parsley, mayonnaise, garlic, salt and sugar. Serve on a central plate with sesame crackers or pita bread or on small plates with tomatoes. Keeps four days refrigerated. Serves 6 to 10.

Mystery Salad

Elsbeth Melville CLA '25
Dean of Women Emerita
National Alumni Council

1 head lettuce, shredded
1 cup chopped celery
1 small onion, thinly sliced, ringed
1 package frozen green peas, cooked 3 minutes, drained
2 tablespoons sugar
mayonnaise
¼ cup Parmesan cheese
¼ cup crumbled bacon

In a large bowl, layer lettuce, celery, onion rings, peas and sugar. Spread mayonnaise over top to cover. Cover tightly and refrigerate 24 hours. Top with Parmesan and bacon bits. Serves 6.

Salad Mediterranée Zobel

| 2 onions, sliced |
| 1 clove garlic, minced |
| ¼ cup olive oil |
| 2 zucchini, diced |
| 2 green peppers, diced |
| 1 medium eggplant, diced |
| ¼ cup minced parsley |
| 1½ teaspoons basil |
| 1 tablespoon salt |
| 2 large tomatoes, cut in wedges |

In a skillet over medium heat, sauté onion and garlic in oil until soft. Add zucchini, peppers, eggplant, ¼ cup parsley, basil and salt. Cover and simmer about 15 minutes or until tender crisp. Pour into a large bowl and gently toss in the tomatoes. Cover and refrigerate 4 hours before serving. Sprinkle on remaining parsley and serve. Keeps three days. Serves 6.

This salad is a Greek specialty that's delicious for outdoor occasions.

Dr. Matthew Witten
CLA '72
Cookbook Committee
Los Angeles, California

Tangy Spinach Bowl

| 2 tablespoons scallion, sliced |
| ¼ cup butter |
| 2 tablespoons flour |
| ¼ teaspoon salt |
| 1 cup water |
| 2 tablespoons lemon juice |
| 1 tablespoon prepared horseradish |
| ½ teaspoon Worcestershire sauce |
| 2 eggs, hard cooked |
| 1 lb. spinach, bite-size pieces |
| paprika |

In small saucepan, cook scallion in butter 1 minute; blend in flour and salt. Add water, lemon juice, horseradish and Worcestershire ; cook, stirring until it comes to a boil. Place spinach in a salad bowl. Pour on hot dressing; toss lightly. Slice eggs and arrange over salad. Sprinkle with paprika, if desired. Serve immediately. Serves 6 to 8.

Leah F. Gould PAL '37
Cookbook Committee
Elberon, New Jersey

Spinach Salad

Edith Thompson Adams
SED '42
Marlboro, Massachusetts

1 *lb. spinach, washed, stems removed*
2 *eggs, hard cooked, sliced*
4 *strips crisp bacon, crumbled*
1 *cup mayonnaise*
4 *tablespoons vinegar*
4 *tablespoons sugar*
croutons for garnish

In a bowl, combine spinach, eggs and bacon. In a small bowl, combine mayonnaise, vinegar and sugar. Toss with salad and sprinkle on croutons. Serve immediately. Serves 6.

Bob's Spinach Salad

Judy Banks CLA '82
Cambridge, Massachusetts

2 *lbs. spinach, washed, stems removed*
½ *lb. bacon, fried, crumbled*
3 *eggs, hard boiled, grated*
1 *avocado, peeled, sliced*
6 *large mushrooms, thinly sliced*
6 *tablespoons olive oil*
¼ *cup honey*
⅛ *cup wine vinegar*
1 *tablespoon white wine*
½ *tablespoon soy sauce*
½ *teaspoon paprika*
¼ *teaspoon dry mustard*
¼ *teaspoon minced garlic*
½ *teaspoon pepper*
red onion rings

In a bowl, combine spinach, bacon, eggs, avocado and mushrooms. In another bowl or jar, combine oil, vinegar, honey, wine, soy sauce, paprika, mustard, garlic and pepper. Mix well. Pour over greens and toss well. Garnish with onion rings. Serve immediately after adding dressing. Serves 4 to 6.

Potato Salad

3 cups cold potatoes, diced
½ cup celery, diced
½ cup onion, minced
1 teaspoon salt
1 cup mayonnaise
1 egg, hard cooked, sliced
6 radishes
1 cucumber, thinly sliced

Ida Disbrow SMG '54
Boston, Massachusetts

In a bowl, combine potatoes, celery, onion and salt. Add mayonnaise and mix well. Arrange on a platter. Garnish with eggs, radishes and cucumber. Keeps two days refrigerated. Serves 4 to 6.

Sour Cream Potato Salad

6 cups diced, cooked potatoes
½ cup diced cucumber
1 tablespoon minced onion
1 teaspoon celery seed
1½ teaspoons salt
½ teaspoon pepper
2 eggs, hard cooked
1 cup sour cream
1 teaspoon prepared mustard
½ cup mayonnaise
2 tablespoons vinegar

Mrs. John M. Sinclair
John M. Sinclair
SMG '62
Brookline, Massachusetts

Toss together lightly, potatoes, cucumber, onion, celery seed, salt and pepper. Separate yolks from whites of eggs. Chop whites and add to salad. Mash yolks and combine with sour cream, mustard, mayonnaise and vinegar. Add to potatoes and toss together lightly. Keeps two days refrigerated. Serves 6 to 8.

Cherry Tomato Salad

| 12 oz. cherry tomatoes, halved |
| 1 can artichoke hearts, drained |
| ½ lb. mushrooms, sliced |
| ½ cup minced parsley |
| juice of 2 limes |
| 1 clove garlic, minced |
| ½ teaspoon salt |
| ¼ teaspoon pepper |

Susan K. Moger CLA '73
Cookbook Committee
Los Angeles, California

In a bowl, combine tomatoes, artichokes, mushrooms and parsley. Add lime juice, garlic, salt and pepper. Mix well. Marinate in refrigerator 2 hours. Keeps 12 hours. Serves 6.

Vestkystsalat

(Norwegian West Coast Salad)

Pat Bjaaland
CLA '67/GRS '68
Cookbook Committee
Oslo, Norway

| ¼ lb. mushrooms, thinly sliced |
| ¾ cup oil and vinegar dressing |
| 1 quart steamed mussels, removed from shells |
| 10 oz. package frozen peas, thawed |
| ½ lb. cooked shrimp |
| 2 tomatoes, cut in wedges |
| ½ lb. asparagus, cooked, diced |
| lettuce |

In a bowl, combine mushrooms and ¼ cup of dressing. Marinate 2 hours. In a larger bowl, combine mussels, peas, shrimp, tomatoes and asparagus. Toss with enough dressing to coat evenly. Mix in mushrooms. Arrange lettuce leaves on a platter. Place salad on lettuce. May be made one day ahead. Serves 4.

Chicken Party Pie Salad

1½ cups cooked, diced chicken	
1 cup pineapple tidbits, drained	
1 cup chopped walnuts	
½ cup chopped celery	
1 cup sour cream	
⅔ cup mayonnaise	
1 baked 8 inch cheese pastry shell*	
2 to 3 tablespoons grated American or Cheddar cheese	

Marie D. Miller
President
Women's Council
Malloy Miller
Associate Dean
School for the Arts

* *Cheese pastry: Add ⅓ cup grated cheese to flour mixture in plain pastry recipe using 1½ cups flour.*

In a bowl, combine chicken, pineapple, nuts and celery. Mix sour cream with mayonnaise and add ⅔ cup to chicken mixture. Fill cheese pastry shell. Top with the remaining sour cream mixture. Chill. Sprinkle with grated cheese.

Chicken Jell-O Salad

1 cup diced chicken	
½ cup diced celery	
1 tablespoon vinegar	
6 oz. mayonnaise	
1 package lemon gelatin	
1 cup water, boiled	

Edith Thompson Adams
SED '42
Marlboro, Massachusetts

In a processor, place chicken, celery, vinegar and mayonnaise. Dissolve lemon gelatin. Add to processor and combine. Pour into 3 cup mold, chill until set. Keeps four days refrigerated. Serves 6 to 8.

Macaroni Salad

Susan Freedman Mandel
SED '70
Cookbook Committee
Oakland, New Jersey

½ lb. elbow macaroni, cooked

½ cup diced green pepper

1 carrot, shredded

1 teaspoon caraway seeds

¾ cup mayonnaise

salt and pepper, to taste

In a bowl, toss macaroni with pepper, carrot, mayonnaise, caraway, salt and pepper. Keeps two days refrigerated. Serves 4.

Ziti Salad

Sarah Brenner
Jeff Brenner CLA '75
Newton Centre, Massachusetts

1 lb. ziti, cooked, drained

¼ cup milk

1½ cups mayonnaise

½ cup sour cream

2 packets bouillon powder

3 grinds fresh pepper

1 tablespoon pickle juice

dash wine vinegar

6 sweet pickles, diced

2 tomatoes, diced

2 small green peppers, diced

1 red onion, diced

1 large shallot, minced

½ cup minced dill

Place cooked ziti in bowl. Add enough milk (about ¼ cup) to thoroughly moisten ziti. Toss. Beat the mayonnaise and sour cream together with a whisk until creamy and add the bouillon powder. Thin pickle juice and wine vinegar with milk if necessary. Pour over ziti. Add the pickles, tomatoes, green pepper, onion and shallot. Mix well. Garnish with dill. Serve chilled. Keeps 24 hours. Serves 6 to 8.

Apple Fruit Salad

2 medium size apples, sliced
3 stalks celery, diced
2 slices pineapple, diced
1 orange, peeled, sectioned
1 cup English walnuts, broken up
dash salt
1 cup mayonnaise
lettuce leaves

Ida Disbrow SMG '54
Boston, Massachusetts

In a bowl, combine apples, celery, pineapple, orange, walnuts and salt. Mix. Add mayonnaise and mix again. Arrange on lettuce leaves. Serves 4.

Cucumber Mousse

3 cucumbers, peeled, seeded, chopped
1 scallion, chopped
1/2 cup chopped celery
1/4 cup chopped parsley
1 1/2 cups chicken broth
1/2 cup cottage cheese
3/4 cup sour cream
1/4 cup mayonnaise
2 envelopes gelatin
1 tablespoon lemon juice

In a blender or processor, combine the cucumber, scallion, celery and parsley with 1 cup chicken broth. Soften the gelatin in the remaining chicken broth in a small saucepan and dissolve over low heat. Add to blender with the cottage cheese and blend until smooth. Fold in the sour cream, mayonnaise and lemon juice. Stir until smooth. Pour into a lightly oiled, 1 quart mold and chill until firm, about 4 hours. Keeps two days refrigerated. Serves 8.

Dorothy Snowman
University Editor

Cucumber Mousse

Leah F. Gould PAL '37
Elberon, New Jersey

1 package lime gelatin
¾ cup boiling water
¼ cup lemon juice
1 tablespoon grated onion
1 cup sour cream
1 cup cucumber, finely chopped

In a 1½ quart bowl, dissolve the gelatin in water. Stir in lemon juice and onion. Chill until almost set. (It will have the consistency of raw egg whites.) Stir in the sour cream and cucumber. Pour into an oiled mold and chill until firm. May be made up to two days ahead. Serves 6.

Tuna Mousse

Mary Ann Gannam
Nicholas Gannam
CLA '40/GRS '41
National Alumni Council
San Francisco, California

1 tablespoon gelatin
¼ cup cold water
2 6½ oz. cans tuna, drained, flaked
2 tablespoons lemon juice
½ cup mayonnaise
2 tablespoons minced onion
1 cup sour cream
2 tablespoons capers, drained
cucumbers, thinly sliced
cherry tomatoes

In a small saucepan, soften gelatin in cold water. Dissolve over low heat. In a mixer, combine tuna, lemon juice, mayonnaise and onion. Beat until smooth. Stir in gelatin, sour cream and capers. Spoon into 3 cup mold and chill 3 to 4 hours before serving. Unmold and garnish with thinly sliced cucumbers and cherry tomatoes. May be made two days before. Serves 6.

Bohemian Salad Dressing

1 cup olive oil
1/4 cup wine vinegar
1/2 lemon, discard seeds
1 clove garlic, pressed
1 teaspoon grated Parmesan cheese
1/4 teaspoon honey
1/2 teaspoon paprika
1/2 teaspoon Dijon mustard
1 teaspoon oregano
6 drops Tabasco
3 anchovies, mashed

Combine all ingredients in a large jar. Shake thoroughly. Keeps in refrigerator. Shake well before using.

Douglas Parker SFA '67
Senior Designer
University Relations

Dressing for Cold Sauerkraut

1/2 cup vegetable oil
1/2 cup sugar
1/2 cup ketchup
1/4 cup vinegar
1 teaspoon paprika
2 tablespoons minced onion
1 tablespoon minced green pepper
1 tablespoon celery
1 lb. sauerkraut, drained, chilled

Mix oil, sugar, ketchup, vinegar and paprika. Stir well to blend. Add onion, green pepper and celery. Pour over sauerkraut at serving time. Keeps 24 hours. Serves 6.

Mrs. John M. Sinclair
John M. Sinclair SMG '62
Brookline, Massachusetts

Blue Cheese Dressing

Mary Zoll GRS '79
Boston, Massachusetts

2 *cups mayonnaise*
6 *oz. imported Roquefort, crumbled*
2 *tablespoons lemon juice*

Combine mayonnaise, cheese and lemon juice, mixing well, leaving some of cheese in chunks. Thin with milk if needed. Keeps one week refrigerated. Serves 6 to 8.

French Dressing

Mrs. Justin Altshuler
Dr. Justin Altshuler
Faculty
Goldman School of
Graduate Dentistry

½ *cup oil*
¼ *cup cider vinegar*
1 *clove garlic*
½ *teaspoon salt*
½ *teaspoon sugar*
½ *teaspoon dry mustard*
½ *teaspoon Worcestershire sauce*
dash paprika

Place oil, vinegar, garlic, salt, sugar, mustard and Worcestershire in a jar. Shake well. Keeps four days refrigerated. Serves 6.

Herb-French Dressing

Lorraine Wysoskie Hurley
SED '67/'69
Chairwoman
Cookbook Committee
Newtown, Connecticut

¾ *cup corn oil*
¼ *cup wine vinegar*
1 *clove garlic, split*
1½ *tablespoons sugar*
1 *teaspoon salt*
1 *teaspoon paprika*
1 *teaspoon dry mustard*
½ *teaspoon tarragon*
½ *teaspoon thyme*
½ *teaspoon oregano*
¼ *teaspoon pepper*

Place corn oil, vinegar, garlic, sugar, salt, paprika, mustard, tarragon, thyme, oregano and pepper in a jar. Cover tightly. Shake well and refrigerate. Remove garlic before using. Serve on fresh crisp greens, cucumbers, tomatoes, radishes, red onion and croutons. Keeps one week refrigerated. Makes 1 cup.

Italian Dressing

1 cup oil
¼ cup cider vinegar
2 tablespoons lemon juice
1¼ teaspoons sugar
1 teaspoon salt
1 clove garlic, minced
1 bay leaf, crumbled
⅛ teaspoon cayenne pepper
pinch oregano
pinch basil

Claire Shapiro Soja
CLA '68
Cookbook Committee
Harvard, Massachusetts

In a jar, combine oil, vinegar, lemon juice, sugar, salt, garlic, bay leaf, cayenne, oregano and basil. Shake well. Keeps one week refrigerated. Makes 1½ cups.

Poppy Seed Dressing

¾ cup oil
⅓ cup honey
3 tablespoons poppy seeds
2 tablespoons vinegar
1 tablespoon prepared mustard
1 tablespoon minced onions
1 teaspoon salt

Gail Goodman Hamilton
SON '62
Cookbook Committee
Winston-Salem,
North Carolina

In a blender, mix oil, honey, poppy seeds, vinegar, mustard and onions until color changes. Serve over oranges and fruit salad. Keeps one week refrigerated. Serves 6.

Roquefort Dressing

Marie Tozzi Nelson
Friend of Boston University

1 cup mayonnaise

½ cup olive oil

¼ cup white wine vinegar

1 teaspoon sugar

 salt and pepper, to taste

4 oz. blue cheese, diced

In a blender, combine mayonnaise, oil, vinegar, sugar,
salt and pepper until smooth. Remove the mixture
to a bowl. Fold in the remaining cheese and store
covered for 2 days to develop flavor. Keeps one week.
Makes 2 cups.

Tomato Honey Salad Dressing

Dorothy Apgar SON '61
Flagler Beach, Florida

1 cup salad oil

½ cup ketchup

½ cup honey

⅓ cup vinegar

½ teaspoon paprika

½ teaspoon minced onion

¼ teaspoon celery seed

¼ teaspoon minced garlic

 salt and pepper, to taste

Combine salad oil, ketchup, honey, vinegar, paprika,
onion, celery seed, garlic, salt and pepper. Shake well.
Refrigerate for 2 days to combine flavors. Keeps one
week refrigerated. Serves 6 to 8.

Marinade for London Broil

3 tablespoons peanut oil
3 to 4 tablespoons hoisin sauce
3 tablespoons dry white wine
3 cloves garlic, crushed
1 teaspoon ginger
1½ teaspoons soy sauce

Suzanne Pachter Wallach
SON '69
Cookbook Committee
Miami, Florida

In a bowl, combine oil, hoisin sauce, wine, garlic, soy sauce and ginger. Use to marinate beef, lamb, pork or chicken 2 to 4 hours before broiling.

Beef Marinade

1 bottle dry white wine
1 teaspoon wine vinegar
2 large onions, minced
2 cups chopped mushrooms
2 cloves garlic, minced
1 green pepper, minced
1½ tablespoons Parmesan cheese
1 cup lemon juice
2 tablespoons minced parsley
1 tablespoon dill
1 tablespoon basil
1 tablespoon rosemary
2 teaspoons sugar
1½ teaspoons salt
1 teaspoon white pepper
½ teaspoon sage
½ teaspoon thyme
4 cubes chicken bouillon

Great for any cut of beef, if you like your meat spicy

Dr. Matthew Witten
CLA '72
Cookbook Committee
Los Angeles, California

In a bowl, combine the wine, onion, mushrooms, garlic, pepper, lemon juice, cheese, parsley, dill, basil, rosemary, sugar, salt, pepper, sage and thyme. Mix well. Stir in bouillon cubes. To use: Preheat oven to 325°. Marinate 4 lbs. of beef stew for 24 hours. Put everything into a casserole and bake 3 hours. Can be frozen and reheated. Serves 6.

Teriyaki Marinade

Rosemary Samuel
Friend of Boston University
Newton Centre,
Massachusetts

½ *cup soy sauce*

¼ *cup peanut oil*

2 *tablespoons vinegar*

2 *heaping tablespoons honey*

2 *to 3 cloves garlic*

2 *teaspoons ginger*

3 *to 4 lbs. flank steak,*
  London broil or chicken breasts

In a non-aluminum bowl, combine soy sauce, oil, vinegar, honey, garlic and ginger. Marinate meat for 24 hours. Preheat broiler. Broil to desired degree of doneness. May be served hot or cold. Serves 6 to 8.

Sweet and Sour Sauce

Lillian Regan Crapo
PAL '44/SED '50
Brookline, Massachusetts

¾ *cup water*

½ *cup sugar*

½ *cup white vinegar*

1 *tablespoon cornstarch*

1 *tablespoon soy sauce*

¼ *cup water*

In a small saucepan, bring water to a boil. Add sugar and cook 1 minute, stirring constantly. Add vinegar and cook for 1 minute, stirring constantly. In a small bowl, blend cornstarch, soy sauce and water to make a paste. Stir paste into the vinegar mixture until it thickens. Let cool (it thickens as it cools). To be used with chicken or fish. Keeps one week refrigerated. Heat before serving. Makes 1½ cups.

Barbecue Sauce

¼ cup vegetable oil
¾ cup finely chopped onion
¼ cup finely chopped green pepper
¼ cup thinly sliced celery
1 small clove garlic, minced
1¼ cups ketchup
½ cup tomato purée
½ cup vinegar
¼ cup grape jelly
¼ cup brown sugar
¼ cup chicken broth
1 tablespoon Worcestershire
½ teaspoon chili powder
½ teaspoon oregano leaves
½ teaspoon black pepper
¼ teaspoon salt
¼ teaspoon dry mustard
⅛ teaspoon Tabasco

Milan Bedrosian
Director
University Food Service

Heat oil in a skillet and sauté onion, pepper, celery and garlic until soft, but not brown. Add ketchup, tomato purée, vinegar, jelly, sugar, broth, Worcestershire, chili powder, oregano, pepper, salt, mustard and Tabasco. Simmer gently for 15 minutes. Cool and refrigerate. Brush on chicken or pork chops and grill. Keeps three weeks refrigerated. Makes 3 cups.

Tomato Marmalade

5 lbs. tomatoes, peeled, sliced
2 lemons, thinly sliced
2 teaspoons grated gingerroot
4 lbs. sugar

This might be made with tomatoes, but it tastes like strawberry jelly.

Dr. Matthew Witten
CLA '72
Cookbook Committee
Los Angeles, California

In a kettle, place tomatoes, lemons and ginger. Cook 1 hour over medium heat. Add sugar and cook until thick. Pour into sterilized jelly glasses. Seal. Keeps six months. Makes 8 cups.

Sweet Pickles

Cheryl Connery
John Connery CLA '69
Vice President
General Alumni Association
National Alumni Council

4 cups apple cider vinegar
4 cups sugar
½ cup coarse salt
1 teaspoon turmeric
1 teaspoon celery seed
1 teaspoon mustard seed
3 large onions, thinly sliced
4 clean quart jars
6 large cucumbers

In a large kettle, combine vinegar, sugar and salt until dissolved. Add turmeric, celery seed and mustard seed. Stir. Put cucumbers into jars. Distribute onions in jars evenly. Pour on brine, seal and refrigerate 1 week before serving. Keeps three months. Makes 4 quarts.

Pear Honey

Helen Crawford Bander
SED '31
Cookbook Committee
Paris, Arkansas

4 cups ground pear pulp
1 cup crushed pineapple
1 orange, ground whole, including skin
8 cups sugar

In a 4 quart casserole, combine pear, pineapple, orange and sugar. Boil 5 minutes. Add Certo or pectin and boil 5 minutes. Place in 10 sterilized glass jelly jars. Seal. Keeps one year. Makes 10 to 12 cups.

9 Desserts

Desserts

9

Grapefruit Mousse

2 3 oz. packages lemon gelatin	**Julie Conley**
1 cup water, boiled	*Staff*
2 tablespoons grapefruit juice	
1 cup sour cream	
8 oz. softened cream cheese	
1 cup milk	
1½ cups drained grapefruit sections	
¾ cup cubed, cooked seafood, turkey or ham	

Dissolve gelatin in boiling water. Add grapefruit juice. In
a bowl, beat sour cream into cream cheese, until smooth.
Beat in milk and dissolve gelatin. Chill until mixture
starts to thicken. Carefully fold in grapefruit sections,
juice and seafood, turkey or ham. Chill in mold. Serve
with raw vegetables. Keeps three days refrigerated.
Serves 4 to 6.

Almendrado (Mexican Dessert)

2 tablespoons unflavored gelatin

½ cup cold water

½ cup water, boiled

7 egg whites, room temperature

1½ cups sugar

1 teaspoon vanilla extract

½ cup chopped almonds (optional)

green and red food coloring

First invented to resemble the Mexican flag, it will get rave notices.

Alice Hazlehurst Barreca
SAR '53
National Alumni Council
Christopher A. Barreca
DGE '50/LAW '53
Trustee
Weston, Connecticut

Mix gelatin with cold water. Stir into boiling water until dissolved. Cool. Beat egg whites until stiff. Gradually add sugar and vanilla. Slowly beat in the gelatin. When mixture stands in peaks, divide into 3 equal parts in 3 bowls. To 1 part add the chopped almonds, to another red food coloring, and to the third, green food coloring. Spread mixtures in greased oblong or 9x9 inch baking dish with the white layer in the middle. Refrigerate for at least 4 hours. To serve, slice into 1 inch wide pieces, each with red, white and green strips. Top each slice with a dollop of custard sauce and a sprinkle of toasted slivered almonds.

Custard Sauce

7 eggs, beaten

1 pint half-and-half

½ cup sugar

½ teaspoon salt

½ teaspoon almond extract

toasted slivered almonds

In a saucepan over low heat, combine egg yolks, half-and-half, sugar, salt and almond extract. Cook, stirring constantly until it coats the body of a spoon (180° on a thermometer). Cool. May be made the day before. Serves 8.

The Cafe Budapest Apple Strudel

5 *green apples, peeled, shredded*
juice of ½ lemon
1 *lb. phyllo dough*
1 *lb. sweet butter, melted*
2 *cups sugar*
4 *cups coarsely ground almonds*
bread crumbs
raisins
cinnamon

The original recipe of
Elvira Slezak, pastry chef
at the Cafe Budapest

Elvira Slezak
Pastry Chef
Cafe Budapest
Boston, Massachusetts

Equipment: pastry brush, tablecloth, baking pan

Preheat oven to 350°. Toss apples in lemon juice; squeeze out excess juice. On work surface, spread tablecloth same width as phyllo dough. Sprinkle a little water on the cloth. Next, lay out 3 sheets of dough on the cloth in a row, overlapping the edges; brush the seams together with butter as if to seal. Dip the pastry brush in hot butter and splash onto the laid out dough. Be sure to splash the entire dough area. Next, sprinkle a layer of sugar and almonds on dough. Place 1 sheet of dough over the seam closest to you. Splash butter, sprinkle sugar and almonds as you did previously. Start from the bottom and place 1 piece of dough and then another in line upon it. Splash butter, sprinkle sugar and almonds again. On third layer, sprinkle a line of bread crumbs, then apples on the crumbs. Add raisins then sugar and cinnamon on the apples and finally more crumbs. Lift outside edges and overlap 2 inches along length of dough starting at edge where apples are. Roll as a jelly roll, using cloth to help lift the dough. Bake 15 minutes. Reduce temperature to 325° and bake 20 to 25 minutes or until golden. Remove from the oven. Cut portions with a serrated knife; sprinkle with powdered sugar and serve. Can be frozen. Serves 6.

Party Ambrosia

Lorraine Wysoskie Hurley
SED '67/'69
Chairwoman
Cookbook Committee
Newtown, Connecticut

1 cup sour cream

1 cup pineapple chunks, drained

1 cup mandarin oranges, drained

1 cup shredded coconut

1 cup mini marshmallows

In a bowl, combine cream, pineapple, oranges, coconut and marshmallows. Chill 4 hours or more. Keeps two days refrigerated. Serves 8 to 10.

Cottage Cheese and Apple Latkes

Sterne Barnett CBA '35
Cookbook Committee
Chestnut Hill, Massachusetts

½ cup matzoh meal

1 apple, coarsely grated

¼ cup cottage cheese

2 eggs, lightly beaten

1 tablespoon oil

1 tablespoon sugar

⅛ teaspoon cinnamon

oil

Combine matzoh meal and milk. Let soak for 10 minutes. Stir in the apple, cottage cheese, eggs, oil, sugar and cinnamon. In a frying pan, heat a thin layer of oil and sauté by the tablespoonful to make pancakes. Serve with cinnamon sugar or applesauce. May be made ahead and reheated in the oven. Makes 2 dozen 3 inch pancakes.

Apricot or Peach Mousse

1 lb. 14 oz. can apricots or peaches
1 package peach gelatin
3 tablespoons apricot brandy or Cointreau
1 teaspoon vanilla
1 cup heavy cream, whipped to soft peaks

Dr. Linda Nelson CLA '74
Cookbook Committee
Lansdale, Pennsylvania

Drain apricots, reserving liquid, and purée all but 6 apricots in blender. Boil reserved liquid plus enough water to measure 1¾ cups. Remove from heat and add gelatin, stirring until dissolved. Add puréed apricots, brandy and vanilla. Chill until it begins to thicken. Fold in whipped cream. Pour into serving bowls. Chill until set. Arrange reserved apricots on top. Keeps two days refrigerated. Serves 6.

Cranberries Jubilee

1 lb. fresh cranberries
½ cup sugar
2 oranges, rinds grated, juice retained
4 tablespoons cornstarch
2 tablespoons water
½ cup brandy
8 scoops vanilla ice cream

Richard Lucas
Executive Chef
Hotel Sonesta
Cambridge, Massachusetts

In a 2 quart saucepan, combine the cranberries, sugar, rinds and juice of oranges. Add 1½ cups water and simmer until cranberries are tender. Combine cornstarch and water. Add to cranberries. Cook until thickened and clear. Add ¼ cup of brandy and remove from heat. Place the cranberries and sauce in a chafing dish. Bring to a boil and add remaining ¼ cup brandy. Ignite. Pour over the scoops of ice cream in dishes while the cranberries are still flaming. Serve immediately. Serves 8.

Lemon Mousse

Joyce Mendillo GRS
Lexington, Massachusetts

1 tablespoon gelatin
2 tablespoons water
6 tablespoons lemon juice
3 eggs, separated
⅔ cup sugar
grated rind of 1½ lemons

In a small saucepan, soften 1 tablespoon gelatin in 2 tablespoons water. Add lemon juice and stir over low heat until gelatin dissolves. Beat egg yolks and ⅓ cup sugar until very light. Add the gelatin mixture. Beat egg whites until stiff, gradually adding ⅓ cup sugar. Fold beaten whites into yolk mixture and add rind. Turn mixture into mold and chill until firm. Serve with raspberry sauce or mandarin oranges. Keeps one day refrigerated. Serves 6.

Sweet or Sour Lemon Mousse

Deborah Cohen CLA '69
Cookbook Committee
Fort Lauderdale, Florida

3 eggs, separated
½ to 1 cup sugar (use smaller measure for sour mousse)
1 tablespoon cornstarch
1 cup water
2 lemons

In a small saucepan, beat egg yolks and sugar until they form a ribbon. Add cornstarch and water. Mix well. Add grated rind of 1 lemon and juice from both. Heat slowly, stirring constantly. When it starts to thicken, take off the heat and let cool. Beat egg whites stiff. Fold the cooked lemon mixture into the egg whites. Put into small dessert bowls and chill. Keeps two days refrigerated. Serves 4.

Frozen Lemon Rum Soufflé

1½ tablespoons unflavored gelatin
½ cup cold water
1 cup lemon juice
grated rind of 2 lemons
8 egg yolks
2 cups granulated sugar
⅔ cup Jamaica rum
2 cups heavy cream, whipped

Gail Ucko CLA '78
Fort Lauderdale, Florida

In a small saucepan, sprinkle gelatin over water. Stir to soften and put over low heat to dissolve. Combine lemon juice, rind and egg yolks and beat for 5 minutes. Add sugar to rum and beat until sugar is dissolved. Blend in gelatin mixture. Chill until consistency of egg whites. Fold in whipped cream. Pour into prepared 1 quart soufflé dish with paper collar extending 4 inches above rim all around. Freeze 3 hours. When set, peel off collar and serve. Keeps two weeks frozen. Serves 6.

Creamy Mango Sherbet

6 oz. pineapple juice
¾ cup sugar
1½ cups fresh mango pulp (4 to 6 mangoes)
½ cup milk or frozen coconut milk
½ cup heavy cream
1 teaspoon almond extract

Fresh peaches may be substituted, if mangoes are not available.

Clare Boothe Luce
HON '76
Honolulu, Hawaii

Beat pineapple juice and sugar together until sugar is dissolved, about 5 minutes. Add mango pulp, milk, cream and almond extract. Mix well and put in freezer tray. When slushy, put in bowl and beat until fluffy, then return to freezer. Freeze until firm. Keeps two weeks frozen. Serves 8.

Chocolate Orange Segments

Dr. Alan A. Larocque
ENG '72/MED '80
Medford, Massachusetts

2 *seedless oranges, peeled, segmented*
10 *oz. sweet or dark chocolate*

Place segments and a large, flat platter in the freezer to cool, do not freeze. Melt chocolate in a double boiler. Place the melted chocolate in refrigerator until it begins to thicken. Dip the chilled orange segments into the chocolate and place on the chilled dish. The chocolate may need to be reheated periodically in order to obtain a thin coating on the orange segments. Return segments to the refrigerator until ready to serve. Keeps 24 hours refrigerated. Makes about 20 pieces.

Delicious Jell-O Mold

Audrey Oshansky
Parent
Utica, New York
Lorraine Harris
Castle Manager

2 *3 oz. packages strawberry Jell-O*
1 *cup water, boiled*
2 *10 oz. packages frozen strawberries*
1 *(No. 1) can crushed pineapple*
3 *medium bananas, mashed*
1 *cup walnuts, broken*
1 *pint sour cream*

In a large bowl, dissolve Jell-O in boiling water. Fold in berries with juice and add pineapple, bananas and walnuts. Pour ½ mixture into 12x2x8 inch baking dish. Chill until firm. Spread on sour cream. Spoon on remaining strawberry mixture. Chill until set. Keeps two days. Serves 6 to 8.

L'Air du Fraise (Strawberry Mousse)

This is very light and airy.

Carolyn Goldstein
SMG '80
Roslyn Harbor, New York

1 *egg white*
1 *pint strawberries, thinly sliced*
½ *cup sugar*

In mixing bowl, beat egg white at high speed adding strawberries and sugar. Beat 3 minutes. Pour into a fluted gelatin mold. Freeze at least 5 hours. Unmold and garnish with fresh strawberries. Keeps frozen two weeks. Serves 4 to 6.

Cottage Cheese Pineapple Dessert

1 lb. 4 oz. can crushed pineapple, drained, juice reserved
1 6 oz. package lemon gelatin
3 cups cottage cheese, sieved
2 cups heavy cream, whipped
¼ cup butter, melted
¼ cup sugar
¼ cup finely chopped nuts
1 cup graham cracker crumbs
assorted fruits

Bring pineapple juice to boiling point. Pour over gelatin until dissolved. Stir in cottage cheese and pineapple. Fold in whipped cream and nuts. Put in lightly greased bundt pan. Combine sugar and butter with crumbs and press on top. Chill until set. Unmold onto a serving plate, crumb side down. Decorate with fruits. Keeps two days refrigerated. Serves 6.

Audrey Oshansky
Parent
Utica, New York

Instant Greek Cottage Cheese and Honey Pudding

1 lb. cottage cheese
½ cup sugar
2 teaspoons cinnamon
½ cup honey
4 eggs

Preheat oven to 325°. Lightly grease a shallow, wide casserole or pie plate. With an electric mixer, blend the cottage cheese, sugar and 1 teaspoon cinnamon. Blend in honey. Add eggs 1 at a time, beating well after each addition. Rub the mixture through a sieve into a second bowl or blend in an electric blender. Pour into baking dish and bake 45 minutes. Increase oven to 375° and bake 15 minutes more or until a knife inserted in the filling comes out clean. Sprinkle pudding with remaining cinnamon. Chill. Serve cold. Keeps four days refrigerated. Serves 4 to 8.

This is a quick version of an excellent recipe.

Barbara G. Papesch
CLA '62
Boston, Massachusetts

Winter Compote

Joan Fontaine
20th Century Archives
Mugar Library

1 cup dark cherries, pitted
1 cup sectioned tangerines
1 cup diced apples
1 tablespoon shredded fresh ginger
juice of ½ lemon
2 jiggers dark rum
sugar (optional)

In a bowl, combine cherries, tangerines, apples, ginger, lemon juice and rum. Add sugar, if desired. Let macerate 2 hours before serving. Keeps two days refrigerated. Serves 4 to 6.

Russian Cream with Melba Sauce

I actually saw this printed in *Gourmet* magazine, after I first made it. Someone requested the recipe after she sampled the dessert at a fancy New York restaurant.

Alvin C. Essig
Professor
Department of Physiology
School of Medicine

Russian Cream

1 tablespoon unflavored gelatin
¼ cup water
1½ cups heavy cream
½ cup sugar
1 cup sour cream
½ teaspoon vanilla

Sprinkle gelatin over water and soften for 10 minutes. In a saucepan, combine heavy cream, sugar and gelatin. Cook over moderate heat stirring until gelatin is dissolved, 5 minutes. Transfer to bowl and cool. Fold in sour cream and vanilla. Transfer to serving bowl. Chill at least 10 hours. Serve with Melba Sauce. Keeps two days refrigerated. Serves 6.

Melba Sauce

1 10 oz. package frozen peaches
1 10 oz. package frozen raspberries
1 tablespoon cornstarch, mixed with 1 tablespoon water
2 tablespoons Kirsch

Purée peaches and raspberries in blender. Transfer to pan and bring to a boil. Combine cornstarch with water. Stir into purée. Simmer mixture until thick and clear. Strain sauce into bowl. Stir in Kirsch. Chill and serve over Russian Cream, ice cream or other fruits. Keeps one week refrigerated. Makes 2 cups.

Macaroon Dessert

12 stale almond macaroons
½ cup raspberry or strawberry fruit juice
2 tablespoons gelatin
1 cup cold water
2 cups milk
4 eggs, separated
4 to 5 tablespoons sugar
whipped cream

Rosemary Samuel
Friend of Boston University
Newton Centre, Massachusetts

Soak macaroons in fruit juice. Soak gelatin in cold water 5 minutes. Add milk and stir until dissolved. Beat egg yolks and sugar until light. Pour gelatin mixture gradually into egg yolks. Cook in double boiler stirring constantly until thick and smooth. Cool. Pour into mold that has been lined with macaroons. Beat egg whites until stiff, fold into mold. Chill until firm. Serve topped with whipped cream. Keeps two days refrigerated. Serves 6.

Miss Salem's Chocolate Mousse

2 oz. semi-sweet chocolate
4 tablespoons warm water, coffee, rum or Grand Marnier
4 eggs, separated
2 tablespoons sugar
½ cup heavy cream, whipped, sweetened, flavored (optional)

Cookbook Committee

In a small saucepan set over boiling water, melt chocolate. Stir in water, coffee or liqueur until smooth. Stir in the egg yolks and mix well. Beat the egg whites until stiff but not dry, adding the sugar slowly after the eggs turn frothy. Fold into the chocolate mixture, pour into sherbet glasses and chill at least 1 hour. Serve topped with whipped cream. Keeps 24 hours. Makes 4 servings.

Tortoni

Great light dessert to serve
with Italian food

Barbara Goulson Arceneaux
PAL '54
Cookbook Committee
Jacksonville, Florida

1 egg white
⅛ teaspoon salt
1 tablespoon instant coffee
3 tablespoons confectioner's sugar
1 cup heavy cream
¼ cup confectioner's sugar
1 teaspoon vanilla
⅛ teaspoon almond extract
¼ cup finely chopped toasted almonds

Beat egg white and salt until soft peaks form. Blend in coffee and sugar and beat until stiff and satiny. Whip cream until stiff, adding ¼ cup sugar, vanilla and almond extract. Fold into egg white mixture with toasted almonds. Spoon into 8 2 oz. paper cups in muffin pan. Freeze until firm. Serve in paper cup frozen. Keeps three weeks in freezer. Serves 8.

Bitter Chocolate Mousse

A treat that is very rich,
but equally delicious.

Nancy Barton SED '77
Rehoboth Beach, Delaware

3 eggs separated
¾ cup superfine sugar
3 tablespoons brandy
1 teaspoon vanilla
5 oz. unsweetened chocolate, melted
4 tablespoons softened butter
3 tablespoons instant coffee
1 tablespoon superfine sugar
½ cup heavy cream, whipped

In top of double boiler, beat egg yolks with sugar, brandy and vanilla until mixture is thick and pale yellow. Place over barely simmering water and continue to heat until mixture is slightly foamy, about 5 minutes. Cool to room temperature. Stir butter into melted chocolate and add to egg yolk mixture. Stir in coffee. Beat egg whites until foamy. Sprinkle remaining sugar over them and continue beating until stiff peaks form. Stir part of this into chocolate mixture then fold the rest until no white streaks remain. Fold in whipped cream and pour into dessert dishes. Chill at least 4 hours before serving. Serve within 24 hours. Serves 6.

Chocolate Mousse

½ lb. sweet chocolate, grated
6 large eggs, separated
3 tablespoons water
¼ cup sweet liqueur (Amaretto, Grand Marnier, Mandarine, etc.)
2 cups heavy cream
6 tablespoons sugar
whipped cream
grated chocolate

Best of its genre

Sanford M. Reder, M.D.
Professor
Department of Medicine
School of Medicine

Place chocolate in saucepan over boiling water and cover. Let chocolate melt slowly. Put egg yolks in a heavy saucepan and add 3 tablespoons of water. Place saucepan over very low heat while beating vigorously and constantly with whisk. When yolks begin to thicken, add the liqueur, beating constantly. Cook until sauce achieves consistency of a hollandaise or sabayon sauce. Remove from heat. (Note: This step may be done over direct, low heat. Be careful not to scramble eggs.) Fold in the melted chocolate. Turn into mixing bowl. Beat the cream until stiff, adding 2 tablespoons of sugar toward the end. Fold this into the chocolate mixture. Beat egg whites until soft peaks start to form. Beat in the remaining 4 tablespoons of sugar and continue beating until stiff. Fold this into the mousse. Spoon the mousse into an appropriate serving bowl and chill until ready to serve. Garnish with whipped cream and/or grated chocolate. Keeps 24 hours refrigerated. Serves 12 or more.

Clever Judy

(Cake Filling or Fake Mousse)

1 cup confectioner's sugar
1 egg
¼ cup milk
1 teaspoon vanilla
3 squares baking chocolate, melted
1 teaspoon butter, melted

William Henneman
Professor
Department of Mathematics
College of Liberal Arts

In a bowl, combine sugar, egg, milk, vanilla, chocolate and butter. Set bowl in ice cubes. Beat until thick and glossy. Serves 6.

Chocolate Mousse Charlotte

Cookbook Committee

¾ lb. German sweet chocolate

6 eggs, separated

2 packages lady fingers

3 tablespoons confectioner's sugar

3 cups heavy cream, whipped

Melt chocolate in double boiler. Add 2¼ tablespoons water and blend well. Remove from heat. Add egg yolks, 1 at a time; add confectioner's sugar. Beat egg whites until stiff and fold into the chocolate mixture. Then fold ⅔ of cream into the mixture. Line 9 inch springform pan with lady fingers. Do not grease pan. Pour mousse into pan. Frost with remaining cream. Keep refrigerated. Can be frozen. Serves 8 to 12.

Patti's Delightful Chocolate Dessert

Serve this in small slices because it's incredibly rich. You can choose whether or not to whip the cream. It comes out delicious both ways.

Patti Marcus SAR '72
Cookbook Committee
Brighton, Massachusetts

1½ cups crushed chocolate wafers

⅓ cup butter, melted

8 oz. cream cheese

¼ cup sugar

1 teaspoon vanilla

2 eggs, separated

6 oz. semi-sweet chocolate, melted

¼ cup sugar

1 cup heavy cream

¾ cup chopped pecans

whipped cream

nuts

Preheat oven to 325°. In a bowl, combine crumbs and butter. Press into bottom of 9 inch springform pan. Bake 10 minutes. Cool. In another bowl, cream the cheese, sugar and vanilla. Beat in egg yolks and chocolate. Beat egg whites until stiff but not dry. Beat in sugar until stiff peaks form. Fold in cheese mixture with cream and pecans. Pour into pan. Chill until firm. Remove sides of pan and decorate with whipped cream and nuts. Keeps 4 days refrigerated. Serves 8 to 10.

Chocolate Chestnut Dessert

½ *lb. unsalted butter*
2 *15½ oz. cans chestnut purée*
12 *oz. semi-sweet chocolate chips, melted*
2 *tablespoons rum or orange liqueur (optional)*
2 *cups heavy cream, whipped*
red and green cherries or chocolate shavings

In a processor or mixer, cream butter. Add chestnuts, melted chocolate and rum or orange liqueur. Line a narrow high bowl or other mold with waxed paper or plastic wrap. Pack in dessert and chill at least 4 hours. Unmold, frost with whipped cream and decorate with cherries or chocolate shavings. May be made several days ahead and kept refrigerated. Serves 12.

Natalie McCracken's 'second best dessert.' Her favorite is her own cheesecake in winter and fresh raspberries in the summer.

Natalie McCracken
Assistant to the Dean
College of Liberal Arts

Steamed Carrot Pudding

1 *cup grated carrots*
1 *cup grated potatoes*
1 *cup chopped suet*
1 *cup sugar*
1 *cup raisins*
1 *cup flour*
1 *teaspoon soda*
1 *teaspoon salt*
1 *teaspoon nutmeg*
1 *teaspoon cinnamon*
1 *teaspoon clove*
¼ *teaspoon ginger*

This is better than plum pudding.

Jane G. Craven SED '73
Santa Barbara, California

Combine carrots, potatoes, suet, sugar, raisins, flour, soda, salt, nutmeg, cinnamon, clove and ginger. Pack into 1½ quart mold. Cover with a greased, floured cloth or foil. Secure in place. Place in a kettle of simmering water. Steam for 2½ hours. Serve hot with lemon sauce, hard sauce or custard sauce. Can be reheated. Serves 8 to 10.

Variation: Add 1 to 2 cups of figs, apricots, dates or prunes.

Pearl's Crispy Apple Pudding

Humanity who has so sur-
rounded me with love – my
cup runneth over – love
returned.   Pearl

Pearl Bailey
20th Century Archives
Mugar Library

6 *apples, peeled, sliced*

½ *cup brown sugar*

½ *cup flour*

4 *tablespoons butter*

½ *cup granulated sugar*

1 *teaspoon vanilla or lemon extract*

Preheat oven to 350°. In a baking dish, layer apples.
In a bowl, combine brown sugar, flour and butter until
crumbly. In another bowl, combine sugar and vanilla.
Sprinkle white sugar on apples and then some brown
sugar. Continue layering apples and sugar until you have
4 to 5 layers. Add enough water to barely cover, about
1 cup. Cover and bake 2 hours. Remove cover and bake
20 to 30 minutes longer.

Permission to reprint: Harcourt, Brace, Jovanovich, Inc., *Pearl's Kitchen*

Yummy Chocolate Soufflé

Nancy Barton SED '77
Rehoboth Beach, Delaware

3 *teaspoons butter*

⅓ *cup flour*

⅓ *cup sugar*

1 *cup medium cream*

3 *egg yolks, beaten*

3 *oz. unsweetened chocolate, melted*

1 *teaspoon vanilla*

4 *egg whites*

whipped cream

Preheat oven to 350°. Grease a 1½ quart soufflé dish and
coat with granulated sugar. Melt butter in a saucepan.
Blend in flour and sugar. Mix well. Add cream, cook and
stir over medium heat until thickened. Beat in egg yolks
and cook for 1 more minute. Cool slightly. Stir in melted
chocolate and vanilla. Beat egg whites stiff but not dry.
Fold into chocolate mixture. Spoon soufflé into prepared
soufflé dish. Set in pan of 1 inch water. Bake for 30 minutes until firm. Sprinkle with confectioner's sugar. Serve
at once with dollop of whipped cream. Serves 4 to 6.

Clafoutis

2	cups flour
2	cups milk
2 to 3	eggs
1	tablespoon sugar
pinch of salt	
vanilla or rum flavoring	
2	cups assorted fruit, cut up
granulated sugar	

A sort of flan traditionally made with sour cherries, but good with other fruits, especially a mixture of prunes, apricots and raisins.

Deborah Cohen CLA '69
Cookbook Committee
Paris, France

Preheat oven to 325°. Place flour in a bowl and gradually stir in milk, eggs, sugar, salt and flavoring. Let rest for 1 hour. In a greased shallow baking dish, scatter chunks of chosen fruit. Cover with batter. Bake for 45 minutes or until a knife inserted in the middle comes out dry. Sprinkle with sugar. Serve warm or cold. Serves 4 to 6.

Cranberry Crunch

1	cup sugar
¾	cup water
1½ to 2	cups fresh cranberries
4 to 5	sweet apples, peeled, cored, thinly sliced
4	tablespoons lemon juice
1½	cups rolled oats, uncooked
¾	cup firmly packed light brown sugar
½	cup butter, melted
1½	tablespoons all-purpose flour

This recipe may sound like a special treat for the holidays, but we have it year round with turkey and roast chicken.

Barbara Baumgardner
Jeffrey Baumgardner
Curator of Observatory

Preheat oven to 350°. In a medium saucepan, mix sugar and water and bring to boil over high heat. Boil 1 minute, then reduce heat slightly. Add cranberries and cook until berries pop, about 1 minute. Remove from heat. Toss apples in lemon juice and place in the bottom of a 9 inch square baking pan. Pour cranberry mixture over apples. In a medium bowl, mix oats, brown sugar, melted butter and flour. Sprinkle in a thin layer over fruit. Bake 35 to 40 minutes or until topping is lightly browned. Serve warm. Can be reheated. Makes 9 servings.

Coconut Pudding

You can serve this plain or
with a fruit purée sauce.

Patti A. Marcus SAR '72
Cookbook Committee
Brighton, Massachusetts

½ *cup water*
1 *cup sugar*
¼ *cup butter*
2 *cups grated fresh coconut*
5 *egg yolks, lightly beaten*
fresh strawberries
1 *cup strawberry purée*

Preheat oven to 350°. In a saucepan, combine water
and sugar. Cook over low heat, stirring until sugar is
dissolved. Wash down any sugar crystals on the side
of pan with a brush dipped in cold water. Increase heat
moderately and bring syrup to a boil. Boil until it spins a
thread (234°F.). Remove from heat and stir in butter. Let
mixture cool for 3 minutes and stir in coconut and egg
yolks. Pour into a greased 3 cup baking dish, set in baking pan and add enough water to reach halfway up side
of dish. Bake for 1½ hours. Check and cover with foil if
it browns too quickly. Let cool to room temperature.
Serve topped with strawberries and sauce. Keeps two
days refrigerated. Serves 6.

Grapenut Pudding

Judy Spellissey SFA '75
West Chelmsford,
Massachusetts

4 *eggs*
4 *cups milk, scalded*
1 *cup sugar*
1 *cup Grapenuts cereal*
1 *tablespoon cinnamon*
1 *teaspoon vanilla*
1 *tablespoon nutmeg*
1 *teaspoon salt*

Preheat oven to 350°. In a bowl, beat eggs, stir in milk
and sugar, mixing well. Blend in Grapenuts, nutmeg,
cinnamon, vanilla and salt. Pour into greased 9 inch baking dish. Set in water bath. Bake for 40 to 50 minutes or
until a knife inserted in the middle comes out clean.
Keeps two days refrigerated. Serves 6.

Governor Saltonstall's Favorite Indian Pudding

2	*cups milk, scalded*
¼	*cup cornmeal*
½	*cup molasses*
1	*teaspoon salt*
¼	*cup sugar*
½	*teaspoon cinnamon*
½	*teaspoon nutmeg*
½	*cup raisins*
¼	*cup butter*
2	*cups milk*
	heavy cream

Gertrude Gould
SMG '25/GRS '29
3rd Competition
Poetry Winner
Danvers, Massachusetts

Preheat oven to 225°. In a double boiler, pour milk over cornmeal and cook for 20 minutes. Stir in molasses, salt, sugar, cinnamon, nutmeg, raisins and butter. Pour into a greased 9 inch baking dish. Bake 3 to 6 hours. Serve hot with cream. Can be reheated. Serves 8.

Baked Pineapple

½	*cup butter*
¾	*cup sugar*
3	*eggs, beaten*
1	*(No. 2) can crushed pineapple, undrained*
5	*slices bread, cubed*
	dash salt
½	*cup crumbled Triscuits*

Elaine Hatch Laverty
CBA '72
Philadelphia, Pennsylvania

Preheat oven to 325°. Cream butter and beat in sugar until light and fluffy. Beat in eggs. Fold in pineapple, bread and salt. Pour into 1 ½ quart casserole dish. Top with Triscuit crumbs. Bake 40 to 50 minutes. Serve hot as a vegetable or cold as a dessert. Can be reheated.

Rice Kheer *(Indian Pudding)*

Dr. Prakash Lulla
SGD/MSD '71
Cookbook Committee
Bombay, India

2 cups instant rice

2 cups water

1 6 oz. can sweetened condensed milk

½ cup raisins

In a teflon saucepan, combine the rice, water and milk. Simmer 15 to 20 minutes, stirring and then boil 10 minutes, stirring. Cool. Mixture will become a thick paste. Pour into a serving dish. Sprinkle with raisins. Refrigerate for 30 minutes before serving. May be made two to three days ahead. Serves 4 to 6.

Snow Pudding

Mrs. Samuel Wexler
Friend of Boston University
Chestnut Hill, Massachusetts

1 envelope gelatin

¼ cup cold water

1 cup water, boiled

1 cup sugar

¼ cup strained lemon juice

1 teaspoon salt

3 egg whites

3 egg yolks

2 tablespoons sugar

1½ cups milk, boiled

vanilla

salt, to taste

In a saucepan, soften gelatin in cold water. Add boiling water. Stir until gelatin is dissolved. Stir in sugar, lemon juice and salt. Stir until sugar is dissolved. Cool until slightly thickened. Beat egg whites until stiff and fold into lemon mixture. Pour into a mold and chill.
Sauce: In top of double boiler, beat egg yolks and sugar until a ribbon forms. Stir in milk, vanilla and salt. Cook, stirring until thickened. Do not boil. Chill. Serve over pudding. Keeps two days refrigerated. Serves 3 to 6.

Chinese Pudding

1	cup rice, cooked
1	large can crushed pineapple
½	cup sugar
½	pint heavy cream

Combine rice, pineapple and sugar. Cool. Beat cream until soft peaks form. Fold into rice mixture just before serving. Serve immediately. Serves 6.

Edith Thompson Adams
SED '42
Marlboro, Massachusetts

Crêpes Suzette

1	cup sifted flour
2	tablespoons sugar
½	teaspoon salt
1¼	cups milk
3	eggs
	butter
½	lb. butter
½	cup confectioner's sugar
¼	cup orange juice
1	tablespoon lemon juice
1	tablespoon lemon rind
1	tablespoon orange rind
¼	cup Cointreau or Grand Marnier

Alice Hazlehurst Barreca
SAR '53
National Alumni Council
Christopher A. Barreca
CGE '50/LAW '53
Trustee
Weston, Connecticut

In a bowl, combine flour, sugar and salt. Gradually add milk and beat in eggs. Let rest 2 hours. Strain. Heat a crêpe pan, rub with butter and pour in 2 to 3 tablespoons batter turning pan to coat bottom. Cook until browned, turn and cook 30 seconds on second side. Turn out onto waxed paper. Continue with remaining batter. Can be frozen. Makes 20 to 24 crêpes. In a bowl, cream butter and sugar until light and fluffy. Add juices and rinds. Let stand covered until ready to finish dish. At serving time, melt butter in a chafing dish. Turn each pancake over in butter and fold in quarters. When all have been folded, heat butter until bubbly. Pour on liqueur and ignite. Serve immediately. Serves 6 to 8.

Teatime Waffles

Pat Bjaaland
CLA '67/GRS '68
Cookbook Committee
Oslo, Norway

| 4 eggs |
| 6 tablespoons sugar |
| 6 oz. butter, melted |
| 1¾ cups milk |
| 3 cups flour |
| 1 teaspoon cardamom |
| 1 teaspoon baking powder |
| ½ teaspoon salt |

In a bowl, beat ½ sugar and eggs until thick and golden. Add milk, flour, cardamom, baking powder and salt alternately. Let stand 1 hour. Bake in waffle iron. Batter keeps two days refrigerated. Makes 12 to 14 waffles.

Tomato Soup Cupcakes

Mary Ellen Cuenir
SED '73/SFA '78
Lynnfield, Massachusetts

| ½ cup butter |
| 1 cup sugar |
| 1¾ cups flour |
| 1 teaspoon cinnamon |
| 1 teaspoon nutmeg |
| 1 teaspoon cloves |
| ½ teaspoon salt |
| 1 rounded teaspoon baking soda |
| 1 can undiluted tomato soup |
| 1 cup raisins |
| 1 cup chopped walnuts |

Preheat oven to 350°. Cream shortening and sugar in a large bowl. In another bowl, sift flour, cinnamon, nutmeg, cloves and salt. In a small bowl, dissolve baking soda in soup. Add this alternately to the dry ingredients and then combine with the sugar mixture. Add the nuts and raisins. Pour into cupcake pans. Frost with a white butter cream frosting, if desired. Can be frozen. Makes 12 cupcakes.

Sour Cream Waffles

1 pint sour cream
1 cup milk
1 cup water
3 cups flour
4 to 5 tablespoons sugar
pinch of salt

In a bowl, combine the sour cream, milk, water, flour, sugar and salt until well blended. Heat a well greased waffle iron and cook as desired. Serve with sour cream and berries. Can be frozen. Makes 12 waffles.

Never a breakfast food and almost always heart-shaped, Norwegian *vafler* play an important role in the social and family life of the Norwegian household.

Pat Bjaaland
CLA '67/GRS '68
Cookbook Committee
Oslo, Norway

Chocolate Cream Cheese Cupcakes

1 lb. softened cream cheese
2 eggs
²/₃ cup sugar
¼ teaspoon salt
2 cups chocolate chips
1½ cups flour
1 cup sugar
¼ cup cocoa
1 teaspoon soda
½ teaspoon salt
1 cup water
⅓ cup oil
1 tablespoon vinegar
1 teaspoon vanilla
1 cup finely chopped nuts
½ cup sugar

Brian W. Foster CLA '68
National Alumni Council
University City, Missouri

Preheat oven to 350°. In a bowl, beat cream cheese, eggs, sugar and salt together. Stir in chocolate chips. Sift together flour, sugar, cocoa, soda and salt. Stir in water, oil, vinegar and vanilla. Beat until smooth. Fill paper cupcake liners ⅓ full of chocolate batter. Top with 1 heaping teaspoon of cream cheese mixture. Sprinkle with nuts and a little granulated sugar. Bake 30 to 35 minutes. Can be frozen. Makes about 60.

Sour Cream Latkes

Cookbook Committee

1 cup milk

1 cup sour cream

1 cup flour

½ teaspoon baking soda

¾ teaspoon salt

oil

In a bowl, combine the milk, sour cream, flour, baking soda and salt. Mix well. Lightly oil a skillet and place over heat. Drop tablespoons of the batter into the skillet and cook until browned, turn and brown the other side. Serve with confectioner's sugar, jam or syrup. Can be frozen. Makes about 50 small, thin pancakes.

Surprise Cakes

Good anytime and easy to make

Nancy Barton SED '77
Rehoboth Beach, Delaware

1½ cups cake flour

1 cup sugar

1 teaspoon soda

½ teaspoon salt

½ cup butter

2 oz. unsweetened chocolate

1 egg

milk

whipped cream

chocolate icing

Preheat oven to 350°. Sift flour, sugar, soda and salt into a bowl. Melt butter and chocolate. Set aside. Break egg, adding enough milk to make 1 cup. Stir into flour then stir in chocolate mixture. Fill greased cupcake tins ½ to ⅔ full. Bake 15 minutes or until a skewer comes out clean. Cool, slice in half and fill with cream. Reassemble, coat with your favorite chocolate icing or sprinkle sugar on top. Can be frozen. Makes 12.

Lemon Sponge Cups

2 *tablespoons butter*
1 *cup sugar*
4 *tablespoons flour*
pinch of salt
5 *tablespoons lemon juice*
rind of 1 lemon
3 *eggs, separated*
1½ *cups milk*

Cream butter, add sugar, flour, salt, lemon juice and rind. Stir in beaten egg yolks mixed with milk. Beat egg whites stiff and fold in. Pour into greased custard cups set in a pan of hot water and bake about 45 minutes. Can be frozen. Makes about 8.

Applesauce Cake

¼ *lb. butter or margarine*
1 *cup sugar*
1 *egg*
1½ *cups applesauce*
1 *cup flour*
1 *teaspoon vanilla*
½ *teaspoon cinnamon*
¼ *teaspoon clove*
¼ *teaspoon mace*
2 *teaspoons baking soda*
1 *cup raisins, nuts or currants*
½ *cup dates or apricots*

Grease a 9 inch tube pan. Preheat oven to 350°. Cream butter and sugar until light and fluffy. Beat in egg and applesauce. Stir in flour, soda, vanilla, cinnamon, clove and mace. Fold in raisins, nuts, dates or apricots. Pour into pan. Bake 45 to 60 minutes or until a skewer comes out dry. Cool. Can be frozen. Serves 8.

German Apple Cake

Sally Rege
Staff
Sargent College
of Allied Health Professions

2 large eggs

1 cup oil

2 cups brown sugar

1 teaspoon vanilla

2 cups sifted flour

2 teaspoons cinnamon

1 teaspoon baking soda

4 cups thinly sliced apples

1 cup chopped walnuts

6 oz. cream cheese

2 tablespoons butter, melted

2 teaspoons vanilla

2 to 3 cups powdered sugar

Grease a 9x13 inch pan. Preheat oven to 350°. In a large bowl, beat eggs and oil. Add sugar and vanilla and beat until foamy. In another bowl, sift together flour, cinnamon and soda. Add flour mixture in small amounts to egg mixture, beating well after each addition. Fold in apples and nuts. Mix well, breaking apples into smaller pieces. Bake 50 minutes to 1 hour. Cool. Cream cheese until smooth. Beat in butter and vanilla. Add sugar, beating until smooth. Spread on cake. Can be frozen. Makes approximately 18 pieces.

Apple Tea Cake

Carine Ravosa CLA '82
Boston, Massachusetts

3 cups flour

2 cups sugar

1 cup vegetable oil

4 eggs

1/4 cup orange juice

2 to 2 1/2 teaspoons vanilla

1 teaspoon baking powder

3 or 4 apples peeled, sliced

1/2 cup sugar

1/2 teaspoon cinnamon

Preheat oven to 350°. Grease a tube pan. Combine flour, sugar, oil, eggs, orange juice and vanilla. Mix until smooth. Spread ½ of batter on bottom of pan. Toss apples with sugar and cinnamon. Add layer of ⅔ apples. Cover with remaining batter. Sprinkle top with remaining apples. Bake 1 to 1¼ hours. Can be frozen. Serves 6 to 8.

Babe's Apple Cake

2 cups whole wheat flour
¼ cup toasted wheat germ
2 teaspoons baking soda
1 teaspoon cinnamon
1 teaspoon salt
½ teaspoon nutmeg
4 cups diced, peeled, tart, cooking apples
1 cup granulated sugar
1 cup packed brown sugar
1 cup chopped walnuts
½ cup oil
2 eggs, well beaten
1 teaspoon vanilla

Elaine Spivack Katz
SAR '76
Cookbook Committee
Oak Lawn, Illinois

Preheat oven to 350°. Grease 13x9x2 inch pan. In a bowl, combine flour, wheat germ, soda, cinnamon, salt and nutmeg. In another bowl, combine apples, sugar, brown sugar, walnuts, oil, eggs and vanilla. Mix well. Stir in flour and blend well. Pour into pan and bake 50 minutes or until cake pulls away from the sides. Cool in pan. Can be frozen. Makes 18 squares.

Blueberry Cake

Elizabeth Boldizar Poster
SON '68/'70
Jamaica Plain, Massachusetts
Denise Oberti SON '73
Danville, Pennsylvania

2	cups flour
1	cup sugar
2	teaspoons baking powder
½	teaspoon salt
½	cup milk
2	eggs
1	teaspoon vanilla
½	cup margarine, melted
½	cup flour
½	cup sugar
¼	cup butter
1	teaspoon cinnamon
1½	cups blueberries

Preheat oven to 350°. Grease and flour an angel cake pan. In a bowl, sift flour, sugar, baking powder and salt. In another bowl, beat milk, margarine, eggs and vanilla. Beat into flour mixture. Fold in blueberries and pour into pan. In a bowl, combine flour, sugar, butter and cinnamon. Sprinkle over the top. Bake 45 minutes. Cool. Can be frozen. Serves 16.

Blueberry Cake

A cake that melts in your mouth

Adele Melrose
Paul Melrose
Parents
Newton Centre,
Massachusetts
Elizabeth McIlwraith
PAL '26
Bridgewater, Massachusetts

1	cup butter
½	teaspoon salt
1½	cups sugar
4	eggs, separated
3	cups sifted flour
2	teaspoons baking powder
⅔	cup milk
2	teaspoons vanilla
3½	cups blueberries
½	cup sugar
½	teaspoon cinnamon

Preheat oven to 350°. Grease and flour a 9x13 inch pan. Cream butter, salt and 1 cup sugar. Beat well. Add yolks. Beat until very thick and creamy. Combine 2½ cups flour, baking powder, milk and vanilla, alternating flour mixture with milk. Beat egg whites until soft peaks form. Fold in ½ cup sugar until stiff. Fold egg whites into flour mixture. Mix blueberries with ½ cup flour. Fold into mixture. Pour into pan. Mix sugar and cinnamon, sprinkle on top. Bake 45 to 60 minutes. Cool in pan. Can be frozen. Makes 18 squares.

Butter Cake

6	cups sifted flour
4	teaspoons baking powder
1½	teaspoons salt
2	cups butter
3½	cups sugar
8	eggs
1½	cups milk
2	teaspoons orange or lemon extract
2	teaspoons vanilla extract
1	teaspoon butter flavoring
½	teaspoon cream of tartar

I ran a catering business in Florida at one time, and this was the recipe I used as my wedding cake. I just enlarged it quite a few times.

Margaret Wilkerson
Cookbook Committee

Preheat oven to 350°. Grease 2, 10 or 12 inch pans. Set aside. In a large mixing bowl, cream butter until very light, add 3 cups of sugar and beat well. Separate eggs and add egg yolks, reserving whites. Add extracts and butter flavoring. Beat well. Add dry ingredients, alternating with milk, beating only enough to blend. In another bowl, beat the reserved whites with cream of tartar until soft peaks form. Add the remaining ½ cup sugar and beat until stiff. Fold the whites into the batter gently. Fill pans. Bake 25 to 30 minutes. Cool. Frost, if desired. Can be frozen. Serves 12 to 14.

Kate Smith's Chocolate Cake

Frank Keville CLA '73
Charlestown, Massachusetts

1 cup sugar
½ cup mayonnaise
1 egg
1 teaspoon vanilla
1¾ cups flour
½ cup instant cocoa
½ teaspoon cinnamon
1 teaspoon baking soda
¾ cup lukewarm water

Preheat oven to 350°. Grease and flour a 5 inch loaf pan. Combine sugar, mayonnaise, egg and vanilla. Beat 1 minute. Sift flour, cocoa, cinnamon and soda. Add water all at once. Mix well. Bake 40 minutes. Cool. Frost as desired. Can be frozen. Serves 6 to 8.

My Wedding Cake
(Cherry and Nut Cake)

Claudia Duff
Alumni House

1½ cups pitted maraschino cherries, halved
1½ cups chopped walnuts
¼ cup kirsch
⅔ cup unsalted butter
1¾ cups sugar
2 eggs
1½ teaspoons vanilla
1½ teaspoons almond extract
3 cups flour
2½ teaspoons baking powder
1 teaspoon salt
1¼ cups milk

The day before preparing the cake, soak maraschino cherries and walnuts in kirsch.

Preheat oven to 350°. Grease and flour 2, 9 inch round layer pans. Cream butter and sugar until light. Beat in eggs, vanilla and almond extract until fluffy. Beat 5 minutes on high speed. Mix in flour, baking powder and salt alternately with the milk. Add approximately ⅛ cup flour to the cherry and nut mixture before folding them into the batter to prevent them from sinking to the bottom of the cake. Fold the nuts and cherries into the batter lightly until they are well coated. Divide the mixture evenly between pans. Bake for 30 to 35 minutes until a toothpick inserted in the center comes out clean. Frost with a butter/cream frosting. Can be frozen.

Fluffy Carrot Cake

2 cups sugar
1½ cups oil
4 egg yolks
3 cups grated carrots
1 teaspoon vanilla
2 cups flour
4 egg whites, stiffly beaten
1 tablespoon cinnamon
1 teaspoon baking soda
1 teaspoon salt
2 cups confectioner's sugar
8 oz. cream cheese
2 teaspoons vanilla
1 cup chopped nuts

Edith Thompson Adams
SED '42
Marlboro, Massachusetts

Preheat oven to 350°. Grease a 13x9 inch pan. Combine sugar, oil and egg yolks. Stir in carrots and vanilla. Mix well. Stir in flour, cinnamon, soda and salt. Fold in egg whites and nuts. Pour into pan. Bake 30 to 40 minutes. Cool and frost. Can be frozen. Makes about 18 pieces.

Frosting
In a bowl, cream cheese. Beat with sugar and vanilla until smooth.

Carrot Cake

People tend to go nuts about this when they first taste it. The recipe gets passed around a lot.

Beulah Freeman Katz
Friend of Boston University
Brookline, Massachusetts
Patricia Sproule
Department of
Speech Pathology
Sargent College
of Allied Health Professions
Diane M. Dodendorf
SON '72
Omaha, Nebraska
Cheryl L. Germain
CLA '74
Little Falls, New Jersey
Janet Converse
Staff
School of Education

2 cups flour

1 cup sugar

1 cup grated raw carrots

¾ cup salad oil

½ cup coarsely chopped walnuts

½ cup raisins

2 eggs, beaten

1 teaspoon baking powder

1 teaspoon cinnamon

½ teaspoon vanilla

¼ teaspoon salt

Preheat oven to 350°. Grease a 9x5 inch loaf pan. In a bowl, combine flour, sugar, carrots, oil, walnuts, raisins, eggs, cinnamon, vanilla and salt. Pour into pan. Bake 1 hour. Serve from pan or remove and cool on rack. Can be frozen. Serves 8.

Frosting

½ cup butter

8 oz. cream cheese

1 lb. confectioner's sugar

Cream butter and cheese and beat in sugar until smooth. *Variation:* Add 8 oz. can drained, crushed pineapple.

Canned Carrot Cake

2 cups sugar
2 cups white flour
1 cup oil
3 eggs
2 teaspoons cinnamon
2 teaspoons baking soda
2 teaspoons vanilla
1 teaspoon salt
2 cups shredded carrots
1 cup chopped walnuts
1 8 oz. can crushed pineapple, drained
3½ oz. canned carrots

Rebecca J. Gourley
SAR '74
Cookbook Committee
Medfield, Massachusetts

Frosting

½ cup butter
8 oz. cream cheese
1 lb. confectioner's sugar
1 teaspoon vanilla

Preheat oven to 350°. Beat flour, sugar, oil, eggs, cinnamon, baking soda, vanilla and salt together. Mix well. Stir in shredded carrots, walnuts, pineapple and canned carrots. Grease a 9x13 inch pan and bake 30 minutes or until test knife comes out dry. Cool. For frosting, beat cream cheese, butter and vanilla until smooth. Beat in sugar to spreading consistency. Can be frozen.

Chocolate Cake

Judy Spellissey SFA '75
West Chelmsford,
Massachusetts

¾ cup butter

1¾ cups sugar

2 eggs

1 teaspoon vanilla

2 cups flour

¾ cup cocoa

1¼ teaspoons baking soda

½ teaspoon salt

1⅓ cups water

Preheat oven to 350°. Grease and flour 2, 8 inch cake pans. Cream butter and sugar until light and fluffy. Add eggs and vanilla. Beat 1 minute. Combine flour, cocoa, baking soda and salt. Add to creamed mixture. Pour into prepared pans and bake 35 to 40 minutes. Cool and frost. Can be frozen. Serves 6 to 8.

Sour Cream Chocolate Cake

Patti A. Marcus SAR '72
Cookbook Committee
Brighton, Massachusetts

½ cup butter

2 cups sugar

2 eggs

½ cup sour cream

2 teaspoons vanilla

2 cups flour

¾ teaspoon salt

1 teaspoon baking soda

½ cup cocoa

¾ cup water, boiled

Preheat oven to 350°. Grease 2, 9 inch cake pans. Cream butter with sugar, add eggs and beat until light and fluffy. Mix in sour cream and vanilla. Combine flour, salt and baking soda. Mix cocoa with cold water to make a paste. Add boiling water. Add flour and cocoa alternately, beginning and ending with flour, to egg and cream mixture. Pour into pans, bake 30 minutes. Frost with butter cream. Can be frozen. Serves 6 to 8.

Bittersweet Chocolate Scottish Tweed Cake

½ cup butter
½ cup sugar
2 cups sifted cake flour
3 teaspoons baking powder
pinch of salt
1 cup milk
1 teaspoon vanilla
3 1 oz. squares unsweetened baking chocolate, grated
3 egg whites
½ cup sugar

One of the desserts served at the annual meetings of the Gastronomes of Cape Breton, Nova Scotia. It was contributed by a marine biologist who lives in the Margaree Lighthouse, Cape Breton Island.

Douglas Parker SFA '67
Senior Designer
University Relations

Preheat oven to 350°. In a bowl, cream butter and sugar. Sift cake flour with baking powder and salt. Add dry ingredients to creamed mixture alternately with milk combined with vanilla, beginning and ending with dry ingredients. After each addition, beat until smooth. Blend chocolate into batter. Beat egg whites until foamy. Add sugar 1 tablespoon at a time, beat until stiff and carefully fold into batter. Pour into 3, 8 inch greased and floured cake pans or 2, 9 inch pans. Bake for 20 to 25 minutes or until a toothpick inserted in center comes out clean. Cool slightly. Turn cake out of pans. Cool thoroughly on wire racks. Frost between layers and on top and sides.

Frosting

¾ cup softened butter
3 egg yolks
2½ cups sifted powdered sugar

Beat together butter and egg yolks. Blend powdered sugar into mixture until smooth.

Chocolate Topping

3 oz. semi-sweet chocolate chips
2 tablespoons water

Melt chocolate chips in top part of double boiler. Add water and stir until smooth, pour over top of cake allowing a small amount to drip down sides of cake.

Cranberry Cake

Audrey Oshansky
Parent
Utica, New York

2½ cups flour

½ teaspoon salt

½ teaspoon baking soda

1 cup sugar

2 well rounded teaspoons baking powder

¾ cup oil

2 eggs, well beaten

1 cup buttermilk

1 cup fresh cranberries

1 cup chopped pitted dates

1 cup chopped walnuts

grated rinds of 2 oranges

½ cup orange juice

½ cup sugar

Preheat oven to 350°. Grease and flour 9 inch tube pan. Sift flour, add salt, soda, sugar and powder. Sift again. Beat eggs and oil together in a separate bowl. Add dry ingredients alternately with buttermilk to eggs. Add whole cranberries, chopped dates and walnut pieces. Stir in orange rinds. Bake 1 hour. When done, mix orange juice and sugar until sugar dissolves. Baste hot cake. Cool. Can be frozen. Serves 8.

Chocolate Chip Date Cake

Suzanne Pachter Wallach
SON '69
Cookbook Committee
Miami, Florida

1 cup chopped dates

1½ cups water, boiled

1½ teaspoons baking soda

¾ cup butter or shortening

1 cup sugar

2 eggs

1¾ cups flour

¾ teaspoon baking soda

½ teaspoon salt

1 6 oz. package chocolate chips

¼ cup sugar

Preheat oven to 350°. Grease and flour an angel cake pan. In a bowl, combine dates, soda and water. Let cool 30 minutes. Cream butter and sugar, add eggs and beat well. Combine flour, baking soda and salt. Add to mixture, then add cooled date mixture. Pour batter into pan. Sprinkle chocolate chips over cake, then sprinkle sugar over the bits. Bake 50 minutes to 1 hour or until cake begins to pull away from sides. Remove from oven and cool completely before removing from pan. Can be frozen. Serves 8.

Date Cake

1 8 oz. package pitted dates, cut into pieces
1 teaspoon baking soda
1 cup water, boiled
1 cup sugar
2 tablespoons shortening
1 egg, beaten
1 teaspoon lemon extract
1½ cups flour
¼ teaspoon salt
4 teaspoons butter
2 cups confectioner's sugar
¼ teaspoon salt
1 teaspoon vanilla
light cream or milk

Virginia Tierney
PAL '36/SED '68
Director
Office of Equal Opportunity
National Alumni Council
Pat Garrity CBS '81
Staff

Preheat oven to 325°. Grease a 8x8 inch pan. Place dates in a bowl, sprinkle with baking soda and pour on water. In another bowl, mix sugar, shortening, egg and lemon extract. Add liquid from dates alternately with flour and salt. Fold in dates. Bake 1 hour. Cool. Cream butter, add 1 cup confectioner's sugar, salt and vanilla. Then beat in remaining sugar. Add cream as needed to make a smooth spreadable mixture. Spread on cake. Can be frozen. Makes 16 pieces.

Log Roll Cake

Gidon Apteker
Former Pastry Chef
The Colonnade Hotel
Boston, Massachusetts

Cake

6 *large eggs, separated*

¼ *cup sugar*

¾ *cup cake flour*

2 *tablespoons water*

3 *tablespoons oil*

1 *teaspoon baking powder*

vanilla, to taste

¼ *cup sugar*

pinch of cream of tartar

pinch of salt

Filling

½ *cup heavy cream*

1 *oz. confectioner's sugar*

5 *oz. sweet chocolate*

4 *oz. sweet butter*

8 *oz. granulated sugar*

rum, to taste

Preheat oven to 400°. Grease an 11x16 inch jelly roll pan, line with wax paper and butter and flour. In a bowl, beat yolks, sugar, flour, water, oil, baking powder and vanilla. Beat 5 minutes with electric mixer. Beat egg whites until soft peaks form, then add sugar, cream of tartar and pinch of salt. Beat until stiff. Fold into yolk mixture. Pour into prepared pan and bake about 10 minutes or until top springs back. Cool and peel off wax paper. In a saucepan, heat cream, sugar and chocolate, stirring until smooth. Chill. Cream butter with sugar until fluffy. Beat in chilled chocolate and add rum. Spread on cake, roll and place on serving platter. Sprinkle with confectioner's sugar. Can be frozen. Serves 6.

Pineapple Upside-Down Cake

⅓ cup butter
½ cup brown sugar
1 lb. 4 oz. can sliced pineapple
pecan halves and cherries
1⅓ cups flour
1 cup sugar
2 teaspoons baking powder
½ teaspoon salt
⅓ cup softened butter
⅔ cup milk
1 teaspoon vanilla
½ teaspoon lemon extract
1 egg
whipped cream

Mildred Thomas
SED '36/'38
Penney Farms, Florida

Preheat oven to 350°. Melt butter in heavy 9 or 10 inch pan. Sprinkle brown sugar evenly over butter. Arrange pineapple in attractive pattern on the butter-sugar coating. Sprinkle with pecan halves and cherries. In mixing bowl, stir flour, sugar, baking powder and salt. Add butter, milk, vanilla and lemon extract. Beat 2 minutes at medium speed. Scrape sides and bottom of bowl constantly. Add egg. Beat 2 more minutes, scraping bowl frequently. Pour batter over fruit. Bake 40 to 50 minutes. Immediately turn upside down on serving plate. Leave pan over cake a few minutes. Serve warm with whipped cream. Serves 8.

Pineapple Meringue Cake

Dorothy Keefer PAL '46
Registrar
School of Medicine

| ¼ cup butter |
| 1 cup sugar |
| 2 eggs, separated |
| 1 cup sifted cake flour |
| 1 teaspoon baking powder |
| ⅛ teaspoon salt |
| ⅓ cup milk |
| ½ teaspoon vanilla extract |
| ½ cup drained crushed pineapple |
| ½ cup heavy cream, whipped |

Preheat oven to 350°. Grease and flour 8 inch cake tin. Cream butter until light and fluffy. Beat in ½ cup sugar. Beat in egg yolks. Sift together cake flour, baking powder and salt. Add this alternately with milk and vanilla to creamed mixture, beating until smooth. Pour into cake tin. Beat egg whites until stiff. Gradually beat in ½ cup sugar, 1 tablespoon at a time. Beat until stiff and glossy. Spread meringue on cake. Bake 25 minutes or until done. Remove from oven. Cool in pan on rack. Cut into squares and serve topped with crushed pineapple combined with whipped cream sweetened with 1 tablespoon sugar. Keeps two days. Serves 6 to 8.

Pecan Cake

This dessert is very light and great after any meal. Of course, you don't need to have a meal first to enjoy it.

Mrs. Joseph Pliskin
Joseph Pliskin
Professor
Department of Quantitative Methods
School of Management

| 6 eggs, separated |
| 10 tablespoons sugar |
| 7 oz. chopped pecans |
| 3 tablespoons bread crumbs |
| 1 orange, grated with peel |

Preheat oven to 350°. Beat egg yolks and ½ sugar until light and fluffy. Add nuts, crumbs and orange. Beat egg whites with remaining sugar until stiff. Carefully fold into nut mixture. Pour into greased and floured bundt pan and bake until a skewer comes out clean, about 45 minutes. Can be frozen. Serves 8.

Fruit Cocktail Pudding Cake

1 cup flour
1 cup sugar
¼ teaspoon salt
1 teaspoon baking soda
1 egg, beaten until frothy
1 can diet fruit cocktail
¼ cup chopped walnuts
¼ cup brown sugar

Judy Green Kessler
CLA '58
Boston, Massachusetts

Preheat oven to 375°. Combine flour, sugar, salt and soda. Add egg. Mix in fruit cocktail with juice. Pour into greased 9x9x2 inch square pan. Sprinkle with nuts and sugar. Bake until toothpick comes out clean, about 40 minutes. Serve warm with ice cream or whipped cream. Can be frozen. Serves 8.

Pound Cake

½ lb. butter, room temperature
1⅔ cups sugar
5 eggs
2 cups cake flour
grated rind of 1 lemon
dash salt
1 teaspoon vanilla or 1 teaspoon fresh lemon juice

This is just so simple. Through the years, I've used it to cap off every type of meal.

Leah F. Gould   PAL '37
Cookbook Committee
Elberon, New Jersey

Preheat oven to 300°. Grease 2, 8x3 inch loaf pans, line with wax paper and grease again. Cream butter and sugar thoroughly. Beat in eggs 1 at a time, beating thoroughly between each addition until batter is foamy. Fold in flour, grated rind, salt and vanilla. Pour into pans, filling no higher than 1 inch below the top. Bake 1 hour. Cool. Can be frozen. Serves 8 to 16.

Rum Pound Cake

Betsy Wilson
John P. Wilson
Associate Dean
School of Law

1½ cups butter
3 cups sugar
5 eggs
1 cup milk
1 tablespoon rum
3 cups flour
1 teaspoon baking powder
pinch of salt

Grease and flour 2 loaf pans or a bundt pan. Cream butter and sugar thoroughly, beat in eggs 1 at a time. Add milk and rum. Fold in flour, baking powder and salt. Pour into prepared pans. Put into cold oven. Turn to 325° and bake 1 hour 15 minutes. Cool. Can be frozen.

The Budy Family Busy Day Whole Wheat Pound Cake

While the pound cake is baking, find a quiet place and slowly sip the cup of white wine. Relax, your cake will be a delightful end to dinner.

Andrea Hollander Budy
DGE '66/SED '68
2nd Competition
Poetry Winner
Mountain View, Arkansas

1 cup softened butter
1 cup dry white wine
¾ cup maple syrup or raw honey
juice of 1 lemon
4 eggs
¼ teaspoon baking powder
1¼ cups whole wheat pastry flour *(Note: Pastry flour is ground from spring wheat; bread flour is ground from winter wheat and is more coarse.)*

Preheat oven to 325°. Grease a 9x5x3 inch loaf pan. Cream butter and maple syrup for 5 minutes. Add lemon juice. Add eggs, beating well. Combine baking powder with pastry flour. Stir the dry mixture into the liquid mixture until well mixed. Pour into pan and bake for 1 hour and 10 minutes. Can be frozen. Serves 8.

Pumpkin Cake

2 cups stewed pumpkin
2 cups sugar
4 eggs
1 cup oil
3 cups flour
1 tablespoon baking powder
2 teaspoons baking soda
2 teaspoons cinnamon
2 teaspoons vanilla
1 teaspoon salt
1 cup chocolate chips
1 cup chopped walnuts
raisins (optional)

Neila Straub SED '70
Beverly, Massachusetts

Preheat oven to 350°. Grease a 10 inch tube pan. Combine pumpkin, sugar, eggs and oil and stir in flour, baking powder, soda, cinnamon, vanilla and salt. Beat well. Add chocolate chips and walnuts. Pour into pan. Bake 1 hour and 15 minutes. Can be frozen. Serves 8.

Raisin-Spice Cake

1 cup sugar
1 cup raisins
1 cup water
½ cup butter
½ cup chopped nuts
1 teaspoon cinnamon
1 teaspoon clove
1 cup flour
½ cup whole wheat flour
1 teaspoon baking powder

Rita J. Aisner GRS '72
Framingham, Massachusetts

Preheat oven to 350°. Grease an 8 inch baking pan. In medium saucepan over medium heat, cook sugar, raisins, water, butter, nuts, cinnamon, clove and salt. Cool. Add flours and baking soda. Blend well. Bake 25 minutes. Frost with cream cheese frosting. Cut into squares. Can be frozen. Serves 8.

Sood Paklava
(Armenian Walnut Cake)

Mary Ishkanian
Friend of Boston University
Lynn, Massachusetts

5 cups flour
4 teaspoons baking powder
1 cup chopped walnuts
1 lb. margarine, melted
1 cup milk
whole walnuts
1½ cups sugar
1 cup water

Preheat oven to 400°. Heat margarine in a saucepan. Add milk slowly, then mix in flour, baking powder and nuts with a wooden spoon. Pour into greased 9x13 inch baking dish. Bake for 40 minutes. Cut into squares and garnish with walnuts. After 15 minutes rescore to make sure cake is well cut. Bring sugar and water to a boil and pour over cake. When the cake is cool, dust with powdered sugar, if desired. Keeps one week. Serves 8.

Texas Sheet Cake

Great for a crowd. This will serve 15 to 20 guests.

Sandra J. Levine SED '59
Cookbook Committee
Newtonville, Massachusetts

2 cups flour
2 cups sugar
½ lb. butter
1 cup water
4 tablespoons unsweetened cocoa
2 extra large eggs
1 teaspoon baking soda
1 teaspoon vanilla
½ teaspoon salt

Preheat oven to 350°. Grease and flour a 9x13 inch pan.
In a bowl, combine flour and sugar. In a saucepan, bring
butter, water and cocoa to a boil. Mix with flour. Stir in
eggs, soda, vanilla and salt. Beat well. Pour into pan and
bake 35 to 40 minutes. Frost as desired or top with
chocolate bits and let melt. Can be frozen. Serves 8.

Sheet Cake

2	cups flour
2	cups sugar
½	lb. butter
1	cup water
3	tablespoons cocoa
½	cup buttermilk
1	teaspoon salt
1	teaspoon vanilla
1	teaspoon soda
1	teaspoon cinnamon
2	eggs, beaten
6	tablespoons milk
¼	lb. butter
3	tablespoons cocoa
1	lb. powdered sugar
1	cup nuts

Phyllis Cook PAL '47
Union, Iowa

Preheat oven to 350°. Grease and flour 9x13 inch pan.
Mix flour and sugar in a large bowl. Bring the butter,
water and cocoa to a boil. Pour over flour mixture. Add
buttermilk, salt, vanilla, soda, cinnamon and eggs. Bake
for 25 minutes. In a saucepan, bring milk, butter and
cocoa to a boil. Add sugar and nuts. Beat well. Spread on
warm cake. Can be frozen. Serves 8 to 12.

Sour Cream Cake

Shelly Tiber
Abe Tiber SMG '70
Cookbook Committee
Haifa, Israel

½ lb. butter

1½ cups flour

1 teaspoon baking powder

¾ cup sugar

1 teaspoon vanilla

2 eggs

¾ cup butter

¾ cup sugar

2 eggs

1 teaspoon vanilla

1 pint sour cream

½ cup chopped nuts

Preheat oven to 350°. Grease 2, 8 inch pans. In a bowl, combine butter, flour, sugar, eggs, baking powder and vanilla. Mix well. Press ⅔ of mixture in bottom of 1 pan and ⅓ into bottom of another. Bake until golden, about 10 minutes. In a bowl, mix butter, sugar, eggs and vanilla. Stir in sour cream and nuts. Pour onto layer of dough. Crumble the remaining ⅓ of dough and sprinkle on top. Freeze until firm. Serves 8.

Yellow Delicate Cake

Diane Robbins CLA '64
National Alumni Council
Manderville, Louisiana

½ cup butter

¼ cup sugar

⅔ cup milk

2 cups flour

½ teaspoon salt

1 teaspoon vanilla extract

1 teaspoon lemon extract

2 teaspoons baking powder

3 eggs

Preheat oven to 350°. Grease and flour an 8 cup pan. Cream butter and sugar until light and fluffy. Sift flour, baking powder and salt. Add flour to mixture alternately with milk. Add extracts and eggs, 1 at a time. Beat well. Pour into pan. Bake 1 hour. Cool. Frost with butter cream. Can be frozen. Serves 6 to 8.

New York Cheesecake

1¼ cups graham cracker crumbs
6 tablespoons butter, melted
2 tablespoons sugar
24 oz. cream cheese
4 eggs
1 cup sugar
2 teaspoons vanilla
1 pint sour cream
3 tablespoons sugar
berries (optional)

Vera Melnechuk **SED '79**
La Jolla, California

Preheat oven to 350°. In a bowl, combine cracker crumbs, butter and sugar. Press into the bottom of a 9 inch spring form pan. In a bowl, beat cheese until smooth. Beat in eggs 1 at a time. Beat in sugar and vanilla until smooth. Pour into pan and bake for 35 minutes or until cracks appear on the top. Raise heat to 450°. Beat sour cream and sugar until sugar has dissolved. Pour over the cake. Bake 7 minutes. Cool. Top with berries, if desired. Keeps two days. Serves 8 to 10.

Cheesecake

1¾ cups graham cracker crumbs
½ cup butter, melted
¼ cups nuts
½ teaspoon cinnamon
3 eggs
1 lb. cream cheese
1 cup sugar
1 teaspoon vanilla
3 cups sour cream

Judy Spellissey SFA '75
West Chelmsford,
Massachusetts

Preheat oven to 350°. In a bowl, combine crumbs, butter, nuts and cinnamon, reserving 5 tablespoons for topping. Press mixture into bottom of a 9 inch springform pan. Beat eggs, cheese, sugar and vanilla until smooth. Blend in sour cream and pour into crust. Top with reserve crumbs and bake for 1 hour. Chill 4 to 5 hours. Keeps one week refrigerated. Serves 8.

New York Ricotta Cheese Cake

Marie LaPorta
Waitress at the Castle

1 *lb. cream cheese*

1 *lb. ricotta cheese*

1½ *cups sugar*

3 *medium eggs, room temperature*

3 *tablespoons flour*

3 *tablespoons cornstarch*

¼ *cup butter, melted, cooled*

2 *teaspoons vanilla*

1 *pint sour cream*

Mix cheeses together. Add sugar gradually. Beat in eggs 1 at a time. Add flour and cornstarch. Mix well. Blend in melted butter and vanilla. Fold in sour cream. Pour into ungreased 10 inch springform pan. Bake at 325° for 1 hour, shut off the oven. Do not open oven door. Leave cake for 2 more hours. Keeps three days. Makes 12 servings.

The World's Best Cheesecake

Dr. Matthew Witten
CLA '72
Cookbook Committee
Los Angeles, California
Janice Bernstein SED '75
Brighton, Massachusetts

1½ *cups graham cracker crumbs*

¼ *cup sweet butter, melted*

3 *tablespoons sugar*

½ *teaspoon ground cinnamon*

3 *8 oz. packages cream cheese, room temperature*

1¼ *cups sugar*

6 *eggs, separated*

16 oz. *dairy sour cream*

⅓ *cup all-purpose flour*

2 *teaspoons vanilla*

grated rind of 1 lemon

juice of 1 lemon

Preheat oven to 350°. Grease 9 inch springform pan. Mix together crumbs, butter, sugar and cinnamon until well blended. Use all but ⅓ cup of crumbs to coat inside of the pan. Refrigerate. Beat cream cheese until soft. Add sugar and beat until light and fluffy. Beat in yolks 1 at a time mixing thoroughly each time. Add sour cream, flour, vanilla, lemon rind and lemon juice. Beat egg whites until they form stiff peaks. Fold into cheese mixture. Pour into pan and bake 1 hour and 15 minutes or until top is golden brown. Turn off oven and let cheesecake set in oven 1 extra hour. Sprinkle remaining crumbs on top. Refrigerate overnight. Keeps four days. Serves 8 to 12.

Cheesecake

1½ cups graham cracker crumbs	
5 tablespoons butter, melted	
4 eggs, separated	
1 cup sugar	
1 tablespoon flour	
1 teaspoon vanilla	
¼ teaspoon salt	
4 8 oz. packages cream cheese	
3 cups sour cream	

Lillian Peplan
Staff
Development Office

Preheat oven to 325°. Combine crumbs and butter, reserving 2 tablespoons of crumbs for topping. Press into a 9 inch round cake pan with detachable bottom. Beat egg whites until fluffy. Add 1 cup sugar. Beat yolks and blend into whites. Add flour, vanilla, salt, cream cheese and sour cream. Beat well and pour into pan. Bake 45 minutes. Refrigerate at least 24 hours. Bake longer for a drier cake. Top with crumbs. Serves 8.

Chocolate Cheesecake

Sylvia Luck
Parent
Waban, Massachusetts

18 chocolate wafers
¼ cup butter, melted
¼ teaspoon cinnamon
1½ lbs. softened cream cheese
1 cup sugar
3 eggs
8 oz. semi-sweet chocolate, melted
2 teaspoons cocoa
1 teaspoon vanilla
2 cups sour cream
whipped cream (optional)

Preheat oven to 350°. Crush enough wafers to make 1 cup crumbs. Mix butter, crumbs and cinnamon. Press mixture on bottom of 8 inch springform pan. Chill. In a large bowl, beat softened cream cheese until fluffy and smooth, then beat in sugar. Add eggs 1 at a time, beating after each addition. Beat in melted chocolate, cocoa and vanilla, blending thoroughly. Beat in sour cream. Pour into pan and bake 1 hour and 10 minutes. Cake will still be runny but becomes firm as it chills. Cool at room temperature, then chill in refrigerator at least 5 hours before serving. Garnish with whipped cream, if desired. Keeps four days refrigerated. Serves 12.

Low Cal Cheesecake

Rebecca J. Gourley
SAR '74
Cookbook Committee
Medfield, Massachusetts

8 oz. farmer cheese
2 envelopes gelatin
8 slices pineapple, juice reserved
4 packets artificial sweetener
1 teaspoon vanilla

Soften gelatin in 2 tablespoons pineapple juice. Boil rest of juice and mix with gelatin. In a blender, combine farmer cheese, pineapple, juice, sweetener and vanilla. Pour into 7 inch pie plate and put in refrigerator. Chill until set. Keeps two days. Serves 6.

Yogurt Cheesecake

¼ cup butter
1 egg yolk
1 cup sifted flour
2 tablespoons cold water
2⅔ cups plain whole milk yogurt
2⅔ cups low fat cottage cheese
8 large eggs
1⅔ cups sugar
1 teaspoon vanilla
½ cup sifted flour

Elnora Austell
Staff

Preheat oven to 400°. Mix butter and egg yolk with 1 cup flour and add water to form dough. Roll about ⅓ of dough, fit in bottom of 9 inch springform pan, leave off sides. Bake 10 minutes or until golden. Cool. Raise heat to 475°. Fit sides of pan to bottom. Grease sides. Roll out remaining dough and line sides of pan. In a processor, blend yogurt and cheese until smooth. Beat together eggs, sugar, vanilla and flour. Stir in yogurt mixture. Pour into crust and bake at 475° for 10 minutes. Lower heat to 250° and bake about 1 hour until custard is set. Cool on rack. Refrigerate overnight. Top with fresh fruit or fresh fruit and glaze. Keeps four days refrigerated. Serves 6 to 8.

Cafe Budapest Dobos Torte

Elvira Slezak
Pastry Chef
Chuck Hemmerlin
Day Chef
Cafe Budapest
Boston, Massachusetts

8 eggs
2 cups sugar
8 oz. unsweetened chocolate, melted
2 tablespoons butter
1½ lbs. butter, room temperature
instant coffee, to taste
8 eggs
1 cup sugar
pinch of salt
1¼ cups flour
2 cups sugar

In a large saucepan, beat eggs with 2 cups sugar until light. Beat in chocolate and butter. Heat over low heat until smooth. Cool. Cream butter, add chocolate mixture and coffee to taste. Beat until smooth. Chill until spreadable. Preheat oven to 325°. In a large bowl, beat eggs and 1 cup sugar until they are light. Add salt, fold in flour. Line 3, 8x16 inch baking sheets with waxed paper and spread batter ¼ inch thick. Bake until done, about 15 minutes. Cool. Cut lengthwise into 4x16 inch strips. In a skillet, cook 2 cups sugar over low heat until dissolved, then boil until golden brown (do not get too dark). Pour sugar over 1 cake layer. Heat a knife to score 20 slices in cake. Set aside. Repeat process for 4 layers and assemble cake. To finish, spread fifth layer with butter cream and stock. Pour sugar over sixth layer and place on top. Freeze 30 minutes. Square off sides of cake and spread remaining cream on sides. Serve. Keeps three days refrigerated. Serves 20.

Suzanne's Chocolate Mousse Cake

Sponge cake

4 eggs, separated
⅓ cup sugar
⅓ cup flour
1 tablespoon orange juice
1 teaspoon orange rind

Preheat oven to 350°. Grease a 16x11 inch jelly roll pan, line with wax paper and grease the paper. In a bowl, beat yolks and sugar until mixture forms ribbons. In another bowl, beat egg whites until stiff peaks form and then beat in 1 tablespoon orange juice and 1 teaspoon orange rind. Fold ¼ of whites into yolk mixture gently but thoroughly. Pour remaining yolk mixture on whites and sift flour over mixture. Fold together until no traces of white show. Pour into jelly roll pan and bake for 15 minutes or until lightly browned. Loosen the paper from the sides of pan and invert the cake onto aluminum foil. Let cake cool and peel off the paper.

Suzanne Pachter Wallach
SON '69
Cookbook Committee
Miami, Florida

Mousse

⅔ *cup sugar*

6 *eggs*

8 *oz. semi-sweet chocolate, melted, cooled*

2 *cups heavy cream*

In a heavy saucepan, combine sugar and ¼ cup water. Boil syrup until it threads. Separate 5 eggs. Beat the egg yolks and 1 whole egg on low speed. Add syrup in a thin stream. Beat mixture at medium speed for 10 minutes. Fold in chocolate and chill mixture for 10 minutes or until stiff but not set. Whip cream and fold into chocolate mixture.

To assemble: Use a 15x4½x2½ inch loaf pan. Cut 2 long sections of sponge cake; 1 to line bottom of pan and 1 to cover top. Brush generously with Tia Maria. Cut the rest of the cake to line pan. Brush with Tia Maria. After lining pan and reserving long strip for top, fill with chocolate mousse. Place long strip over top. Cover with plastic wrap and refrigerate overnight. Next day invert on serving platter. Place strips of wax paper under cake to catch excess icing.

Frosting

½ *cup Tia Maria*

6 *oz. semi-sweet chocolate*

¼ *cup butter*

½ *teaspoon oil*

Melt chocolate in a double boiler. Remove from the pan and add softened butter in pieces and stir until all pieces are melted. Add vegetable oil and stir. Frost cake. Can be garnished with chocolate curls or glacéed fruits. Can be frozen. Serves 15.

Japonais au Chocolat

This is a super extravaganza for special occasions.

Betty Niederman
Staff
School of Nursing

Torte

2½ cups whole hazelnuts

1½ cups sugar

⅔ cup sifted flour

8 egg whites

Preheat oven to 350°. Grease and flour 2 cookie sheets. Mark off 2, 8 inch circles on each, using a cake pan for guide. Save about 20 whole hazelnuts to decorate top of cake and grind rest. Reserve about ¼ cup ground nuts to use on top layer. Mix remaining nuts, 1 cup sugar and flour. Beat egg whites until stiff. Beat in remaining ½ cup sugar until smooth. Mix with nut combination gently and spread a very thin even layer within the marked circles. Bake 10 to 12 minutes and remove from pan immediately with a broad spatula. Bake 7 of these layers. Cool.

Cream Filling

1 cup heavy cream

2 tablespoons confectioner's sugar

1½ teaspoons unflavored gelatin

1 tablespoon cold water

2 tablespoons water, boiled

1 tablespoon grated orange rind

Beat cream and sugar together. Sprinkle gelatin over cold water to soften and then stir in boiling water until dissolved. Mix gently into whipped cream along with orange rind. Chill.

Chocolate Filling

4 oz. unsweetened chocolate

½ cup butter or margarine

1 cup confectioner's sugar

8 egg yolks

Melt chocolate over hot water. Work butter or margarine until creamy, then mix in sugar and egg yolks alternately until filling is smooth and fluffy. Stir in chocolate last of all. Alternate layers of chocolate filling and cream between cooled layers of cake. Do not put on top layer.

Glaze

6 oz. semi-sweet chocolate	
1 tablespoon vegetable oil	
3 tablespoons corn syrup	
2 tablespoons milk	

Melt chocolate and shortening together over hot water. Stir in syrup and milk. Dip 20 whole hazelnuts in glaze carefully and let stand until hard. Pour remaining glaze over entire top layer of torte. Sprinkle ¼ cup of ground nuts over ½ the top and arrange glazed hazelnuts around the rim. Place top layer on top of torte layers. Allow cake to mellow in refrigerator at least 8 hours before serving. Keeps two days refrigerated. Serves 6 to 8.

Baklava

1½ lbs. phyllo dough	
4 cups finely chopped walnuts	
½ cup granulated sugar	
1 tablespoon cinnamon	
¾ to 1 lb. butter or margarine, melted	
1 lb. honey	
½ cup water	
1 teaspoon clove	
1 teaspoon cinnamon	

To insure good Baklava, the phyllo dough must not dry out. Keep it covered with a lightly dampened dish towel.

Dr. Linda Nelson
CLA '74
Cookbook Committee
Lansdale, Pennsylvania

Preheat oven to 250°. Grease a 9x11 inch rectangular pan and layer 8 sheets of phyllo dough, buttering each sheet with a pastry brush. Add 1 unbuttered sheet of phyllo dough. Mix nuts, sugar and cinnamon together and spread ½ of mixture evenly over ninth layer. Add another 10 sheets of buttered phyllo dough, then add 1 unbuttered sheet and spread remaining nuts. Finish adding rest of phyllo dough buttering each sheet. Cut halfway through baklava in a diamond pattern. Bake 2 hours. Simmer honey, water, cinnamon and clove ½ hour. Cool to room temperature. Remove baklava from oven and pour syrup over pastry. Cool and serve. Keeps at room temperature for four days. Makes 50 pieces.

Commonwealth Torte

A simple and very elegant
dessert

Eileen Schell GRS '59/'64
Secretary of Consumer Affairs
Commonwealth
of Massachusetts

Meringue

4 egg whites

pinch of salt

¼ teaspoon cream of tartar

1 cup sugar

1 cup finely ground walnuts

Preheat oven to 250°. Beat egg whites with a pinch of
salt until stiff but not dry. Beat in cream of tartar. Add
¾ cup sugar by tablespoons. Beat constantly until the
meringue is thick and smooth. Fold in ¼ cup additional
sugar. Fold in walnuts. Spread mixture on 4, 8 inch
round brown or parchment papers. Bake for about
15 minutes or until dry. Turn the layers and dry about
5 minutes longer.

Filling

¼ cup butter

1 cup packed brown sugar

¼ cup milk

1¼ to 2 cups sifted confectioner's sugar

⅓ cup Rice Krispies

⅓ cup raisins

⅓ cup coconut

Melt butter in saucepan. Add brown sugar. Boil over low
heat, stirring constantly for 2 minutes. Add milk, stirring
until the mixture comes to a boil. Remove from heat and
cool. Slowly add confectioner's sugar, beating well until
the filling has the consistency of peanut butter. Sprinkle
Rice Krispies, coconut and raisins evenly over the filling.
Spread filling on each layer and the top. Do not frost
sides. Decorate the top by making 3 concentric rings of
sprinkled coconut, Rice Krispies and raisins. Allow torte
to ripen 24 hours. Keeps 48 hours refrigerated. Serves 8.

Boston Cream Pie

½ cup butter
2½ cups sifted cake flour
3 teaspoons baking powder
½ teaspoon salt
1½ cups sugar
¾ cup and 2 tablespoons milk
1 teaspoon vanilla extract
2 eggs
cream filling
confectioner's sugar

Cynthia Elyce Rubin
GRS '70
Cookbook Committee
Charlestown, Massachusetts

Preheat oven to 375°. Grease 2, 9 inch layer pans. Sift in flour, baking powder, salt and sugar. Add ¾ cup milk and vanilla. Mix until dry ingredients are dampened. Continue to beat until thoroughly mixed. Add eggs and remaining milk. Beat well. Pour into prepared pans. Bake 20 to 25 minutes. Turn out on cake racks. Cool. Put cream filling between the layers and sprinkle top with confectioner's sugar.

Cream Filling

½ cup sugar
2½ tablespoons cornstarch
¼ teaspoon salt
1½ cups milk
2 egg yolks, beaten
1 teaspoon vanilla extract

In heavy saucepan, mix sugar, cornstarch and salt. Add ½ cup milk, and stir over low heat until smooth and thickened. Remove from heat, stir in egg yolks. Return to heat and cook 2 minutes longer, stirring constantly. Cool and add vanilla.

Croque en Bouche

This is a Scandinavian specialty served during the winter holidays.

Richard Lucas
Executive Chef
Hotel Sonesta
Cambridge, Massachusetts

Cream Puffs

2 cups water

½ cup unsalted butter

2 cups flour

8 eggs

1 tablespoon sugar

pinch of salt

In a saucepan, bring water, salt and butter to a full boil. Add flour and sugar. Cook, stirring on high flame until mixture leaves the sides of the pan. Put into heavy duty mixer on low speed and add eggs 1 at a time. When smooth, the dough is ready. While still warm, pipe the dough through a pastry bag onto greased baking sheets into 2 inch mounds. Bake at 400° for 20 minutes or until cooked through. Makes 80 to 150 depending on size. Can be frozen.

Filling

8 egg yolks

2 cups sugar

⅔ cup flour

4½ cups milk, scalded

¼ cup vanilla extract

In a saucepan, mix egg yolks with sugar until light. Beat in flour. Stir in milk and cook over a low flame for 10 minutes until thickened. Cool. Stir in vanilla, pipe into puffs. Keeps two days refrigerated. Makes 1½ quarts.

To Assemble

cream puffs filled with pastry cream

3 cups sugar

mandarin oranges

almonds, sliced

½ cup cold water

Heat sugar and water until sugar dissolves. Boil until it turns a caramel color. Using this caramel, stick the cream puffs together to form a circle on a platter. Continue sticking puffs together, filling the center and building to form a cone. Dip oranges and almonds into caramel and decorate the cone. Do not get caramel on your fingers, it burns. Keep a bowl of ice water at hand to plunge your hand in if the caramel should get onto it. Keeps about six hours depending on humidity. Serves 20.

Mushroom Meringues

2 *egg whites*
⅛ *teaspoon cream of tartar*
½ *teaspoon almond extract*
⅔ *cup sugar*
¼ *cup semi-sweet chocolate*

For gift giving, arrange this dessert on a bed of toasted coconut.

Mary Etta Cousino
Friend of Boston University
Brighton, Massachusetts

Preheat oven to 350°. Grease and flour a large cookie sheet. Beat egg whites, cream of tartar and almond extract with electric mixer at high speed until foamy. Sprinkle in sugar, 1 tablespoon at a time, beating until sugar dissolves and meringue forms stiff peaks. Spoon meringue into pastry bag fitted with a (No. 5) large plain tip. Press into 1¼ inch rounds holding bag vertical and close to sheet to make mushroom caps. Smooth top of each if needed. Hold pastry bag vertical and pull straight up while piping meringue 1 inch long for stems. Bake for 30 minutes or until firm but not brown. Cool slightly on cookie sheet on wire rack. Loosen carefully with a small spatula; remove to wire rack. Cool completely. Melt chocolate in a cup over hot water. Working carefully, make a small hole in the underside of each cap with the tip of a knife. Spoon a little melted chocolate into the hole, then press stem firmly into chocolate. Let stand until chocolate is firm. Sprinkle tops with cocoa, if desired. Store in a tightly covered container in a dry place. Keeps in tight container two weeks. Makes about 24.

Oatmeal Cookies

This is really my
husband's recipe.

Marion Gorham
SON '52/'56
National Alumni Council
Holyoke, Massachusetts

½ cup corn oil
1 egg
2 tablespoons milk
1 tablespoon orange peel
1 cup brown sugar
1 cup raisins or chopped prunes
1½ cups rolled oats
1 cup sunflower seeds
¾ cup whole wheat flour
¾ cup cornmeal
1 teaspoon baking powder
1 teaspoon baking soda

Preheat oven to 350°. Mix oil, egg and milk. Add orange
peel, raisins and brown sugar. Stir well. Stir oats, sunflower seeds, flour, cornmeal, baking powder and soda
together in a bowl. Mix dry ingredients into wet ingredients. Batter should be thick. Spoon onto cookie sheet.
You may need to use your fingers to assist in shaping but
don't flatten too much. Bake approximately 20 minutes
or until brown. Can be frozen. Makes 48 to 60 depending on size.

Orange Oatmeal Cookies

Mary Ellen Cuenir
SED '73/SFA '78
Lynnfield, Massachusetts

1 cup flour
½ teaspoon baking soda
½ teaspoon salt
½ cup butter
1 cup light brown sugar
1 egg
2 tablespoons orange juice
1 tablespoon grated orange peel
1 cup instant oatmeal
1 cup chopped walnuts
1 cup raisins

Preheat oven to 350°. Sift flour with salt and soda. Set
aside. Cream butter and sugar. Add egg and beat until
fluffy. Beat in orange juice and peel. Add flour mixture.
Blend until just combined. Stir in oats, nuts and raisins.
Drop on greased cookie sheet. Bake 15 to 18 minutes.
Can be frozen. Makes 4 dozen 2½ inch cookies.

Sour Cream Oatmeal Cookies

¼ cup butter
1 cup brown sugar
1 egg
½ cup sour cream
1 teaspoon vanilla
1¼ cups flour
⅔ cup oatmeal
½ cup nuts
½ cup raisins
1 teaspoon baking powder
1 teaspoon cinnamon
¼ teaspoon nutmeg
¼ teaspoon baking soda
¼ teaspoon salt

Diane M. Dodendorf
SON '72
Omaha, Nebraska

Preheat oven to 425°. In a bowl, cream butter and sugar.
Add egg, sour cream and vanilla. Stir in flour, oatmeal,
nuts, raisins, baking powder, cinnamon, nutmeg, baking
soda and salt. Mix well. Drop onto greased cookie sheets.
Bake 8 to 10 minutes. Makes about 24.

Fruit Bars

My 93 year old neighbor, Marguerite Durkee, who once modeled for Auguste Rodin, was interested in "Cooking By Degrees" and brought this for us to sample. We rate it 4½ stars ☆☆☆☆☆

Helen Crawford Bander
SED '31
Cookbook Committee
Paris, Arkansas

| 1¾ cups oats |
| 1¾ cups flour |
| 1 cup sugar |
| 1 teaspoon soda |
| 1 cup butter |
| 2 cups cooked prunes or applesauce |

Preheat oven to 375°. Grease a 9x6 inch pan. Set aside. In a bowl, combine oats, flour, sugar and soda. Cut in butter to form dough. Sprinkle a little more than ½ on the bottom of the pan and spread with prunes or applesauce. Cover with remaining oatmeal mixture. Bake 20 minutes or until golden. Cool. Can be frozen. Makes 27, 1x2 inch bars.

Mandelbrot

If you like your mandelbrot soft instead of dunkable, do not return to oven after slicing.

Sterne Barnett CBA '35
Cookbook Committee
Chestnut Hill, Massachusetts

| 1 cup sugar |
| ¼ cup oil |
| ¼ teaspoon lemon rind |
| ½ teaspoon almond extract |
| 2 eggs, well beaten |
| 2 cups flour |
| ½ cup sliced almonds |
| 1½ teaspoons baking powder |
| ½ teaspoon salt |
| ½ cup sugar |
| 1 teaspoon cinnamon |

Preheat oven to 325°. Mix sugar and oil. Beat in eggs until light and add lemon rind and almond extract. Add ½ cup flour and almonds. Stir in baking powder and salt. Mix thoroughly. Shape into 2 long loaves with help of spatula or knife because mixture is too soft to handle. Place on greased cookie sheets. Combine sugar and cinnamon and sprinkle on top. Bake 30 minutes. Cut into diagonal strips while still warm. Place on baking sheet and toast in oven until golden. Orange peels, crystallized ginger, walnuts, candied cherries or maraschino cherries may be added to the basic recipe.

Date Dropped Swirls

8 oz. dates, halved
½ cup hot water
⅔ cup butter
2 cups brown sugar
2 eggs
2 cups all-purpose flour
1 teaspoon soda
½ teaspoon salt

Mildred Thomas
SED '36/'38
Penney Farms, Florida

Preheat oven to 350°. Put dates in a saucepan and pour hot water over them. Simmer. In a bowl, cream butter and sugar. Add eggs and beat until light and fluffy. Sift flour, soda and salt. Add slowly to creamed mixture. Swirl and fold dates into the creamed mixture. Drop by teaspoonfuls on greased cookie sheet. Bake 12 to 15 minutes. Can be frozen. Makes about 3 dozen 2 inch cookies.

Hobnail Cookies

½ cup butter
1 cup firmly packed brown sugar
1 egg, beaten
1 teaspoon vanilla
1½ cups sifted flour
1 teaspoon cinnamon
½ teaspoon salt
½ teaspoon soda
½ cup raisins

Sandra J. Levine SED '59
Cookbook Committee
Newtonville, Massachusetts

Preheat oven to 375°. Cream butter and sugar. Add beaten egg and vanilla. Sift flour, cinnamon, salt and soda. Beat into butter mixture. Stir in raisins. Drop in small balls on greased sheet and bake 12 to 15 minutes until brown. Can be frozen. Makes 35 small or 25 large cookies.

Applejacks

Mary Ellen Cuenir
SED '73/SFA '78
Lynnfield, Massachusetts

1 *cup light brown sugar*
½ *cup butter*
1 *egg*
1½ *cups sifted flour*
1 *teaspoon nutmeg*
½ *teaspoon soda*
½ *teaspoon salt*
1½ *cups chopped, peeled apples*

Preheat oven to 375°. Cream sugar and butter until light and fluffy. Beat in egg. Beat in flour, nutmeg, soda and salt until well blended. Stir in apples. Drop in balls on greased cookie sheet. Bake 12 to 15 minutes until golden. Can be frozen. Makes about 3 dozen 3 inch cookies.

Date Bars

Peg Wallace LAW '76
Brookline, Massachusetts

1 *cup sugar*
½ *cup butter, melted*
2 *eggs, well beaten*
¾ *cup flour*
¼ *teaspoon baking powder*
⅛ *teaspoon salt*
1 *cup finely chopped dates*
1 *cup finely chopped nuts*
confectioner's sugar

Preheat oven to 350°. In a bowl, combine sugar, butter and eggs. Mix well. Beat in flour, baking powder and salt. Stir in dates and nuts. Pour into greased 9x13 inch baking pan. Bake 20 minutes. Cut into 1x2 inch bars. Roll bars in confectioner's sugar while still warm. Keeps one week in airtight container. Makes 54 bars.

Cheddar Cheese Streusel Raisin Bars

1½ cups seedless raisins
¾ cup water
¾ cup brown sugar
1½ tablespoons cornstarch
1 teaspoon grated lemon peel
juice of ½ lemon
½ teaspoon ground cinnamon
pinch of clove
pinch of nutmeg
pinch of ginger
½ cup flour
¾ cup brown sugar
1½ cups shredded sharp Cheddar cheese
¾ cup butter

Cookbook Committee

Preheat oven to 350°. In a 1½ quart saucepan, bring water and raisins to a boil. Stir in sugar, cornstarch, lemon peel, juice, cinnamon, clove, nutmeg and ginger. Cook until thickened and clear. Set aside. In a bowl, combine flour and sugar. Cut in cheese and butter to make a crumbly mixture. Press ⅔ of mixture in bottom of 9x13 inch cake pan. Spread filling over top and sprinkle on remaining dough. Bake 30 minutes until crisp and brown. Cool. Can be frozen. Makes about 54 bars.

Chewy Bars

¼ lb. butter
1 cup graham cracker crumbs
6 oz. butterscotch bits
6 oz. chocolate bits
1 cup shredded coconut
1 14 oz. can condensed milk
1 cup chopped walnuts

This recipe is about 22 years old. It's one of those pour-it-together, easy desserts that comes out tasting great.

Carol M. Winer CBA '58
Cookbook Committee
Framingham, Massachusetts

Preheat oven to 350°. In a 9x13 inch baking pan, melt butter. Add the graham cracker crumbs, butterscotch, chocolate, coconut, milk and walnuts. Bake 25 to 30 minutes. Cool. Can be frozen. Makes 50 squares.

Mardi Gras Brownies

Virginia Tierney
PAL '36/SED '68
Director
Office of Equal Opportunity
National Alumni Council

6 oz. butterscotch bits
¼ cup butter
¾ cup flour
⅓ cup packed light brown sugar
1 egg
1 teaspoon baking powder
½ teaspoon vanilla
¼ teaspoon salt
1 cup mini marshmallows
6 oz. semi-sweet chocolate bits
¼ cup chopped nuts

Preheat oven to 350°. Grease an 8x8 inch baking dish. In a 3 quart saucepan, melt butterscotch bits and butter, stirring constantly. Remove from heat. Beat in flour, sugar, egg, baking powder, vanilla and salt. Fold in marshmallows, chocolate bits and nuts. Spread in pan and bake 20 to 25 minutes. Do not overbake. Center will be jiggly but will firm when cool. Can be frozen. Makes approximately 32.

Chocolate Slices

Virginia Tierney
PAL '36/SED '68
Director
Office of Equal Opportunity
National Alumni Council

½ cup butter
¼ cup sugar
4 teaspoons cocoa
1 teaspoon vanilla
1 egg
2 cups graham cracker crumbs
1 cup coconut
½ cup chopped walnuts
1 cup confectioner's sugar
2 tablespoons butter
1 teaspoon vanilla
milk
6 oz. semi-sweet chocolate, melted

In a saucepan, heat butter, sugar, cocoa and vanilla until
sugar is dissolved. Remove from heat, beat in crumbs,
coconut and walnuts. Press into a greased 8x8 inch pan.
In a bowl, mix sugar, butter, vanilla and milk until
smooth. Spread over dough. Pour chocolate on icing.
Chill in refrigerator and cut into squares. Keeps one
week refrigerated. Can be frozen. Makes approximately
32 slices.

Mud Bars

1 cup butter
¼ cup cocoa
4 eggs
2 cups sugar
1½ cups flour
2 teaspoons vanilla
pinch of salt
½ teaspoon baking powder
1 package mini marshmallows
1½ cups evaporated milk
½ cup butter
1 lb. confectioner's sugar
1 teaspoon vanilla
½ cup cocoa
1 cup chopped nuts (optional)

Louise Ablondi Bonar
SMG '58
Brighton, Massachusetts

Preheat oven to 350°. In a small saucepan, melt butter
with cocoa. In a bowl, beat eggs and sugar until they
form a ribbon. Add the cocoa mixture and stir in the
flour, vanilla, salt and baking powder. Pour into a
greased and floured 9x13 inch baking pan. Bake for
30 minutes or until a cake tester comes out clean. Immediately sprinkle marshmallows over top and let melt. In a
bowl, beat milk, butter, sugar, vanilla and cocoa until
creamy. Spread over marshmallows and sprinkle with
nuts if desired. Makes about 26 bars.

Chocolate Surprise Cookies

These are my husband's
favorites.

Gail Goodman Hamilton
SON '66/'68
Cookbook Committee
Winston-Salem,
North Carolina

| 3 cups sifted flour |
| 1 teaspoon soda |
| ½ teaspoon salt |
| 1 cup butter |
| 1 cup sugar |
| ½ cup finely packed brown sugar |
| 2 eggs |
| 1 teaspoon vanilla |
| 9 oz. solid chocolate wafers |
| 54 walnut halves |

Preheat oven to 350°. Sift flour, soda and salt together.
In a bowl, cream butter and sugar until light and fluffy.
Beat in eggs and vanilla. Add flour and mix well. Cover
and refrigerate 2 hours. Use 1 teaspoon of dough to
enclose chocolate wafer. Place on baking sheet, top with
walnut halves. Bake 10 to 12 minutes or until golden.
Can be frozen. Makes 54 cookies.

Chocolate Chip Bars

Elaine Richman **SED '66**
Cookbook Committee
Brookline, Massachusetts

| ½ cup butter |
| 1 cup sugar |
| 2 eggs, separated |
| 1 teaspoon vanilla |
| 1½ cups flour |
| 1 teaspoon baking powder |
| 2 egg whites |
| 1 cup packed brown sugar |
| ½ cup chopped nuts |
| ½ cup chocolate chips |

Preheat oven to 375°. Cream butter and sugar until light and fluffy. Add egg yolks and vanilla. Beat together. Sift in flour and baking powder and blend well. Spread in 8x8 inch or 8x10 inch pan. Beat egg whites stiff. Gradually add brown sugar. Fold in nuts and chips and spread over batter. Bake 20 minutes. Can be frozen. Makes 32 bars.

The Best Chocolate Chip Bars

½ lb. butter
1½ cups sugar
½ cup molasses
1 teaspoon vanilla extract
2 large eggs
1 tablespoon water
1 teaspoon salt
½ teaspoon baking soda
2 to 2½ cups sifted flour
1 12 oz. package semi-sweet chocolate chips
½ lb. softened cream cheese
½ cup chopped nuts (optional)
½ cup raisins (optional)
½ cup peanut butter

Sharon Friedman
DGE '68/SED '70
Sharon, Massachusetts

Preheat oven to 350°. In a large mixing bowl, cream margarine, sugar and molasses. Mix in vanilla, eggs and water. Sift salt, baking soda and ½ of the flour into mixture. Mix well. Add remaining flour until dough is stiff. Add chips and mix well. In a greased 8x8x2 inch baking dish, spread ½ mixture on bottom. Spread a layer of cream cheese on top of dough. Sprinkle with nuts and raisins, if desired. Spread layer of peanut butter. Carefully spread remaining dough onto peanut butter. Bake 15 to 20 minutes. When done, cool 15 minutes. Can be frozen. Makes 32.

Chocolate Crinkle Cookies

Amy Glick Korman
CLA '74
Pittsburgh, Pennsylvania

2 cups sugar

4 oz. chocolate, melted

½ cup vegetable oil

4 eggs

2 teaspoons vanilla

2 cups sifted flour

2 teaspoons baking powder

½ teaspoon salt

1 cup confectioner's sugar

Preheat oven to 350°. Combine sugar, chocolate and oil together. Blend in eggs 1 at a time until well mixed. Add vanilla. Stir in sifted flour, baking powder and salt. Chill several hours or overnight. Drop teaspoonfuls of dough into confectioner's sugar. Roll around and shape into balls. Place about 2 inches apart on greased baking sheet. Bake 10 to 12 minutes. Can be frozen. Makes about 50 cookies.

Florentines

Maureen Simmons
Friend of Boston University

¼ lb. butter

½ cup sugar

5 tablespoons honey

2 tablespoons heavy cream

3 cups sliced blanched almonds

½ cup cut up glacéed cherries

6 oz. semi-sweet chocolate, melted

Preheat oven to 350°. Combine butter, sugar, honey and cream in a 1 quart saucepan. Simmer on low heat for 15 minutes until golden. Remove from heat, stir in almonds and cherries. Spoon heaping teaspoons of batter 2 inches apart onto baking sheet lined with parchment paper. Bake 10 minutes. Remove from oven, cool and transfer to flat surface. Spread underside of each cookie with chocolate. Invert cookies on rack until chocolate cools. Keeps one week in airtight container. Makes 50 cookies.

Peanut Butter Candy Balls

½ cup peanut butter

½ cup honey

2½ tablespoons or ¼ cup instant dry skim milk

½ cup wheat germ

½ cup raisins

½ cup chopped nuts

½ cup chocolate chips

toasted sesame seeds

ground nuts

wheat germ

coconut

confectioner's sugar

Ruth Albert
DGE '63/SED '65/'69
Brockton, Massachusetts

Combine peanut butter, honey and dry skim milk. Mix well. Fold in wheat germ, raisins, nuts and chocolate chips. Shape teaspoonfuls of the mixture into balls. Roll in sesame seeds, nuts, wheat germ, coconut or confectioner's sugar. Refrigerate. Keeps one week in refrigerator. Makes about 18.

Variation: Add any or all of the following: ½ cup chopped dates, sunflower seeds or coconut.

Rum Balls

2½ cups finely crushed vanilla wafers

1 cup confectioner's sugar

1 cup finely chopped walnuts

⅓ cup rum or brandy (use Bacardi 151)

1 tablespoon corn syrup

2 teaspoons cocoa

granulated sugar

confectioner's sugar or cocoa

Lisa Radtke
*Department of
Physical Therapy
Sargent College of
Allied Health Professions*

Combine wafers, sugar, walnuts, rum, corn syrup and cocoa. Mix thoroughly. Shape into 1 inch balls. Roll in sugar or cocoa. Keep in tightly covered box for 1 week. Can be frozen. Makes 24 to 36.

Blueberry Squares

Mildred Thelen
PAL '33/GRS '42
Lynn, Massachusetts

| 1 cup butter |
| 2 cups sugar |
| 4 eggs |
| 3 cups flour |
| 1 teaspoon vanilla |
| 1 can blueberry pie filling |

Preheat oven to 375°. Grease and flour an 11x16 inch jelly roll pan. Cream butter and sugar until light and fluffy. Beat in eggs 1 at a time. Stir in flour and vanilla. Spread ¾ of batter in bottom of pan, top with filling. Dot filling with remaining batter. Bake 35 to 45 minutes until golden and set. Cool in pan. Can be frozen. Makes about 4 dozen 2 inch squares.

Cheese Squares

Libby Cohen SED '77
Cape Elizabeth, Maine

| ⅓ cup light brown sugar |
| 5 tablespoons butter |
| 1 cup flour |
| ¼ cup ground nuts |
| ½ lb. cream cheese |
| ½ cup white sugar |
| 1 tablespoon milk |
| ½ tablespoon vanilla |
| 1 tablespoon lemon juice |
| 1 egg |

Preheat oven to 350°. Cream brown sugar and butter. Add flour and nuts, mix well. Set aside 1 cup. Press remaining mixture in 8 inch square cake pan. Bake 12 to 15 minutes. Cream the cream cheese and white sugar. Add egg, milk, vanilla and lemon juice. Mix well. Pour into baked crust. Sprinkle with reserved topping. Bake 25 minutes. Refrigerate. Keeps refrigerated for four days. Makes 16, 2 inch squares.

Butterscotch Squares

2 cups packed brown sugar	
1½ cups flour	
¾ cup chopped nuts	
½ cup butter	
2 eggs	
2 teaspoons baking powder	
1 teaspoon vanilla	
pinch of salt	

Elizabeth McIlwraith
PAL '26
Bridgewater, Massachusetts

Preheat oven to 350°. In a bowl, combine sugar, flour, nuts, butter, eggs, baking powder, vanilla and salt. Mix well. Press into greased 9x13 inch pan. Bake 30 minutes. Can be frozen. Makes 54.

Fruit Pie Filling Squares

¾ cup butter
1 cup sugar
2 eggs
2 cups flour
1 teaspoon baking powder
1 teaspoon vanilla
1 can pie filling

Cherry filling is best for this recipe. Try not to use blueberry.

Elizabeth McIlwraith
PAL '26
Bridgewater, Massachusetts

Preheat oven to 350°. Cream butter and sugar. Add eggs 1 at a time. Beat in flour, baking powder and vanilla. Spread ½ mixture in greased 9x10 inch cake pan. Spread filling over mixture, spoon remaining dough over filling. It does not have to cover completely. Bake 35 to 40 minutes. Can be frozen. Makes almost 2 dozen 2 inch squares.

Lemon Squares

MaryAnn Gannam
Nicholas Gannam
CLA '40/GRS '41
National Alumni Council
San Francisco, California
Mary Sears Mattfield
SED '55
2nd Competition
Poetry Winner
New Bedford, Massachusetts
Marie Foss
Friend of Boston University
Elizabeth Latour Freeman
CLA '61
Waltham, Massachusetts

1 *cup flour*

½ *cup butter, melted*

¼ *cup confectioner's sugar*

1 *cup sugar*

2 *tablespoons flour*

½ *teaspoon baking powder*

grated rind of 1 lemon

juice of 1 lemon

2 *eggs*

Preheat oven to 350°. In a bowl, combine flour, butter and sugar. Mix well and press into bottom of 9 inch square cake pan. Bake 15 minutes or until firm. In a bowl, combine sugar, flour and baking powder. Stir in lemon rind, juice and eggs. Mix well. Pour over crust. Bake 25 minutes. Cool before cutting. Can be frozen. Makes 16, 2 inch squares.

Swedish Crescent Cookies

Marilyn Peters
Friend of Boston University

1 *cup softened butter*

1½ *cups confectioner's sugar*

1¾ *cups sifted flour*

1 *cup chopped nuts, almonds, pecans and/or filberts*

¼ *teaspoon salt*

2 *teaspoons vanilla extract*

Preheat oven to 300°. Cream butter, gradually beating in ½ cup sugar, flour, nuts and salt. Chill well. Shape into crescents, using ½ tablespoon dough for each and place on cookie sheets. Bake 18 to 20 minutes. While still warm, roll cookies in remaining sugar and vanilla. Can be frozen. Makes about 36.

Tea Cookies

⅔ cup butter

1¼ cups sugar

2 eggs, well beaten

3 cups flour

2 teaspoons baking powder

1 teaspoon salt

grated rind of 1 orange

1 tablespoon orange juice

granulated sugar

These aren't too sweet, and they are great to serve with tea or coffee.

Leah F. Gould PAL '37
Cookbook Committee
Elberon, New Jersey

Preheat oven to 325°. Cream butter and sugar. Add eggs. Sift flour, baking powder and salt together. Add to butter with rind and juice. Mix to smooth dough. Chill in refrigerator, then roll out as thinly as possible on a lightly floured board. Sprinkle with sugar very lightly, place on baking sheets and bake 12 to 15 minutes. Can be frozen. Makes 6 to 8 dozen cookies.

Butterballs

1 cup butter

¼ cup honey

2 cups sifted flour

½ teaspoon salt

2 teaspoons vanilla

1 cup finely chopped nuts

confectioner's sugar

Lorraine Wysoskie Hurley
SED '67/'69
Chairwoman
Cookbook Committee
Newtown, Connecticut

Preheat oven to 300°. Cream butter and add honey, flour, salt and vanilla. Mix well and add chopped nuts. Form into very small balls on a greased baking sheet. Bake 40 to 45 minutes. Roll in powdered sugar while still hot. Cool. Roll again in sugar.

Czechoslovakian Cookies

Janice Bernstein SED '75
Brighton, Massachusetts

½ lb. butter
1 cup sugar
2 egg yolks
2 cups flour
1 cup chopped walnuts
6 to 8 oz. jam

Preheat oven to 325°. Grease an 8 inch square cake pan. Cream butter and sugar until light and fluffy. Add egg yolks and blend well. Gradually add the flour and mix thoroughly. Fold in nuts. Spoon ½ the batter into the cake pan, spreading evenly. Top with jam, cover with remaining cookie dough. Bake 1 hour or until lightly browned. Remove from oven, cool and cut into 1 to 2 inch bars. Can be frozen. Makes 32.

Coconut Shortbread Cookies

These cookies are not overly sweet. They have a chewy texture and an incredible taste.

Barbara Tomashefsky
Abbott CLA '59
Cookbook Committee
Hudson, New Hampshire

1 cup softened butter
6 tablespoons granulated sugar
2 cups flour
1 cup firmly packed coconut
½ cup toasted wheat germ
1 teaspoon vanilla

Preheat oven to 350°. Beat butter and sugar until pale and fluffy. Work in flour, coconut, wheat germ and vanilla. Divide dough in half and put each piece on a sheet of waxed paper about 20 inches long. Shape each mound of dough into a roll about 14 inches long. Wrap waxed paper around each roll and place in freezer, 30 minutes. Cut rolls into ¼ inch thick rounds and place on ungreased baking sheets. Bake 12 to 14 minutes or until cookies are lightly browned. Can be frozen. Makes about 40 cookies.

Penuche Cookies

1½ cups raisins

1 cup water

3½ cups flour

1½ cups sugar

1 cup butter

2 eggs

2 teaspoons baking soda

1 teaspoon clove

1 teaspoon nutmeg

1 teaspoon cinnamon

1 teaspoon vanilla

dash salt

½ cup butter, melted

1 cup brown sugar, melted

¼ cup milk

1¾ to 2 cups confectioner's sugar

Brian W. Foster CLA '68
National Alumni Council
University City, Missouri

Preheat oven to 400°. In a saucepan, cook raisins in water until thick. Combine with flour, sugar, butter, eggs, baking soda, clove, nutmeg, cinnamon, vanilla and salt. Mix well. Drop by teaspoonfuls onto baking sheets. Bake for 15 minutes. In a saucepan, combine butter and brown sugar. Simmer 2 minutes. Stir in milk and bring to a full boil, stirring. Set over pan of cold water and stir until cool. Stir in confectioner's sugar. Spread on cookies. Can be frozen. Makes about 72 cookies.

Mexican Wedding Cakes

I don't know why these
are called Mexican.
There's really nothing
Mexican about them.

Carolyn Payne
Cookbook Committee
Coordinator
All-University Functions

1 cup flour
1 cup ground pecans
3 tablespoons sugar
1 teaspoon vanilla
1 teaspoon salt
confectioner's sugar
¼ lb. softened butter

Preheat oven to 350°. Cream butter and sugar. Blend
in vanilla, nuts and salt. Add flour. Mix well and shape
into small balls. Place on baking sheet and bake about
20 minutes until lightly browned. Roll in confectioner's
sugar while still warm.

Mrs. Lee's Plum Cakes

Plum is an old word for
raisins and other dried
fruits. A good example is
Plum Pudding. Today,
these cakes would be
called cookies.

Joyce Davies
Don Davies
Professor
Department of
Humanistic, Developmental
& Organizational Studies
School of Education

6 oz. butter
6 oz. sugar
1 egg
1 egg yolk
6 oz. currants
2 tablespoons flour
1 teaspoon grated nutmeg
3 cups flour less 2 tablespoons
½ teaspoon baking powder
¼ teaspoon salt
2 teaspoons rosewater, cognac, rum or orange
liqueur

Preheat oven to 350°. In a bowl, cream butter and sugar.
Add egg and egg yolk. Dust currants with flour and add
to mixture with nutmeg, flour, baking powder and salt.
Mix well. Add flavoring. Mix well. Grease a cookie
sheet. Drop tablespoons of dough onto the sheet and
smooth tops with the back of a spoon. They should be
about ½ inch thick. Bake 30 minutes or until golden.
Serve hot or cold. Can be frozen. Makes 72.

Möhn Cookies

¼ lb. butter
2 eggs
¾ cup sugar
2 tablespoons poppy seeds
1 tablespoon sour cream
¼ teaspoon salt
2 cups flour
2½ teaspoons baking powder
3 tablespoons lemon juice
grated rind of 1 lemon
sugar
½ cup chopped nuts

Bert M. Hirshberg
Cookbook Coordinator

Preheat oven to 350°. Cream butter and sugar. Beat in eggs, poppy seeds, sour cream and salt. Beat in flour, baking powder, lemon juice and lemon rind. Drop by teaspoonfuls onto greased baking sheets. Flatten with a moist fork. Sprinkle with sugar and chopped nuts. Bake 12 to 15 minutes or until golden. Can be frozen. Makes 4 dozen.

Pecan Teatime Tassies

3 oz. softened cream cheese
½ cup softened butter
1 cup sifted flour
¾ cup brown sugar
dash salt
1 egg
1 tablespoon butter
1 teaspoon vanilla
⅔ cup chopped pecans

**Jessie Whittier
Sumner G. Whittier
HON '60**
Ellicott City, Maryland

Preheat oven to 325°. Blend cheese and butter. Add flour. Chill for 1 hour. Press into 12, 2 inch tart pans. In a bowl, beat sugar, salt, egg, butter and vanilla until smooth. Distribute ⅓ cup pecans in bottom of tarts. Fill with filling and top with remaining pecans. Bake 20 to 30 minutes. Can be frozen. Makes 12.

Cookies in a Hurry

Sandy Trainor
Friend of Boston University

24 *graham crackers*

½ *cup packed brown sugar*

½ *cup margarine*

½ *cup chopped walnuts*

½ *teaspoon vanilla*

¼ *teaspoon ground cinnamon*

Preheat oven to 275°. Arrange crackers on cookie sheet. Combine butter and sugar in 1½ quart saucepan. Bring to boil over medium heat, stirring constantly. Stir and boil gently for 5 minutes. Remove from heat. Stir in nuts, vanilla and cinnamon. Immediately drizzle mixture over the crackers. Spread evenly and bake for 10 minutes. Cool on wire rack. Keeps one week in airtight container. Makes 24.

Cheese Rugglachs
(Nut Filled Crescents)

Elayne R. Baer MET '78
Forest Hills, New York

½ *lb. cream cheese*

½ *lb. butter*

2½ *to 3 cups flour*

6 *to 9 tablespoons cold water*

1 *teaspoon vanilla*

½ *teaspoon sugar*

¼ *teaspoon salt*

1 *cup sugar*

½ *cup crushed walnuts*

1½ *tablespoons cinnamon*

Preheat oven to 375°. Combine cheese, butter, flour, water, vanilla, sugar and salt to form a dough. Moisten dough with 6 tablespoons of water adding more if needed. Shape into a flat cake. Wrap in waxed paper. Chill in refrigerator for 24 hours. The cake can be frozen for 6 months. In a bowl, combine sugar, walnuts and cinnamon. Divide dough into quarters. Roll each quarter into a large circle ¹⁄₁₆ inch thick. Cut into wedges 1½ inches wide at widest point. Sprinkle with nut mixture, roll from wide end to the point and place on a baking sheet. Bake 20 minutes or until golden. Can be frozen. Makes about 48.

Mama's Taglich

2 cups flour
4 eggs, beaten
2 tablespoons oil
½ teaspoon baking powder
¼ teaspoon ginger
1 lb. honey
1 lb. sugar
¼ teaspoon ginger
½ cup water
raisins
½ cup water, boiled
chopped nuts, coconut, ginger

Mix flour, eggs, oil, baking powder and ginger into a soft dough. Let rest, covered for at least ½ hour. Combine honey, sugar and ginger in a large pot. Add ½ cup water. Roll dough into a pencil-like strip and knot with a raisin in the center. Repeat until all the taglich are made. Bring mixture in pot to boil and slowly drop the taglich in 1 by 1 so that boiling does not stop. Cover and lower heat. Simmer 1 hour. When taglich are a lovely brown, remove from heat and pour boiling water into pot, stirring with long-handled wooden spoon. Sprinkle with ginger. Taglich may be served wet, that is, dripping with honey, or dry, rolled in chopped nuts or coconut.

Not many people make these anymore, but I bet that if you do someone will say,"My mother used to make these."

Sterne Barnett CBA '35
Cookbook Committee
Chestnut Hill, Massachusetts

Fudge Vasbinder

½ cup butter
4 cups sugar
1 can evaporated milk
20 to 22 large marshmallows
12 oz. chocolate morsels
1½ teaspoons vanilla
1 teaspoon salt

In a 2 quart saucepan, cook butter, sugar and milk, stirring until a soft ball forms. Stir in marshmallows and chocolate until dissolved. Stir in vanilla and salt. Beat vigorously for 5 minutes. Pour into greased 9x3 inch pan. Chill. Keeps two weeks in refrigerator. Makes about 100 pieces.

Grace Vasbinder, a 70 year old real estate agent, literally rescued my wife and me when we arrived penniless in Buffalo. She found us our first apartment and made us this fudge.

Dr. Matthew Witten
CLA '72
Cookbook Committee
Los Angeles, California

Chocolate Fudge

Elizabeth M. Lanigan
SMG '53
Reading, Massachusetts

2 oz. unsweetened chocolate

3 tablespoons butter

2 cups sugar

1 cup evaporated milk

3 tablespoons marshmallow topping

½ cup walnuts

1 teaspoon vanilla

In a 1 quart saucepan over low heat, melt chocolate and butter. Mix until smooth. Add sugar and milk and cook over medium heat until it forms a soft ball (238° on a candy thermometer). Add marshmallow, walnuts and vanilla. Beat until soft. Pour into a greased 8 inch square pan and let harden. Cut into 1 inch squares. Keeps one week. Makes 64 pieces.

Apple Pie

Anna E. Bessette
SON '63/'65
Attleboro, Massachusetts

2 frozen pie crust shells

8 McIntosh apples, peeled, diced

1 cup granulated sugar

½ cup light brown sugar

juice of 1 lemon

½ teaspoon cinnamon

½ teaspoon nutmeg

⅛ teaspoon ground clove

¼ cup honey

2 teaspoons instant coffee

⅛ cup water, boiled

¼ cup sugar

⅛ cup milk

2 teaspoons butter

Preheat oven to 350°. Grease a 9 inch pie plate, place 1 shell into plate and fill with sliced apples. Top with sugars, lemon juice, cinnamon, nutmeg and clove. Combine honey, coffee and water. Dribble over the top. Dot with butter. Add top crust and pinch edges of crusts together. To brown top crust, dissolve sugar in milk. Pat on top crust. Slash top crust 3 times with sharp knife. Bake 1 hour. Keeps two days. Serves 6 to 8.

Foolproof Flaky Piecrust

4 cups flour
1¾ cups vegetable shortening
1 tablespoon sugar
1 egg
½ cup water
1 tablespoon vinegar
2 teaspoons salt

Elaine Spivack Katz
SAR '76
Cookbook Committee
Oak Lawn, Illinois

With pastry blender, mix together flour, shortening, sugar and 1 teaspoon salt. In a bowl, beat egg, water, vinegar and 1 teaspoon salt. Combine the 2 mixtures, stirring with a fork until all ingredients are moistened. Then with hands, mold dough into flat cake. Chill at least 15 minutes before rolling into desired shape. Dough can be left in the refrigerator up to three days, or frozen until ready to use. Makes 5, 9 inch pie shells.

Swedish Apple Pie

6 apples, peeled, cored, sliced
1 tablespoon sugar
1 teaspoon cinnamon
1 teaspoon nutmeg
1 cup sugar
1 cup flour
¾ cup butter, melted
1 egg
¼ cup chopped nuts
pinch of salt

If you ever wanted a fool-proof way to make an apple pie, this is it.

Irene E. Beach
Staff
School of Medicine

Preheat oven to 350°. Place apples in a 10 inch pie plate. Sprinkle with sugar and cinnamon. In a bowl, combine sugar, flour, butter, egg, nuts and salt. Sprinkle over apples. Bake for 50 to 60 minutes. Best served warm. Serves 6 to 8.

Apfelpita *(Viennese Apple Pie)*

My mother's recipe. Be
sure to cut it with a sharp
knife because it's quite
fragile.

Eva R. Kashket
Professor
Department of Microbiology
School of Medicine

2 cups flour

1 cup sugar

½ cup unsalted butter

2 egg yolks

3 tablespoons sour cream

grated rind of 1 lemon

5 baking apples, peeled, ¼ inch slices

½ cup sugar

¼ cup honey

½ cup seedless raisins

2 to 3 tablespoons lemon juice

2 to 3 tablespoons rum or white wine

1 teaspoon cinnamon

½ cup unflavored bread crumbs, toasted

Preheat oven to 350°. In a bowl, combine the flour, sugar, butter, egg yolks, sour cream and lemon rind. Mix together to form a soft dough. Put ⅔ of the dough into the bottom and up the sides of a 10 inch pie tin with a removable bottom. Set aside remaining dough. In a saucepan, combine the apple slices with the sugar, honey, raisins, lemon juice, rum and cinnamon. Cook until half done. Pour into the prepared pastry. With the palms of your hands, shape the remaining dough into ropes and place in a lattice pattern over the apples. Sprinkle the spaces with the bread crumbs. Bake for 1¼ hours. Remove from the pan and serve in slices. Best served warm. Serves 8.

Apple Tart

1 1/2 cups flour
1/2 cup sugar
1/4 cup butter
pinch of salt
7 to 8 large apples, peeled, cored, sliced
1/2 cup sugar
2 tablespoons instant tapioca
3/4 teaspoon cinnamon
1/4 teaspoon nutmeg

Carla Marcus Schair
SED '70
Scarborough, Maine

Preheat oven to 425°. Combine flour, sugar, butter and salt until crumbly. Reserve 1 cup of mixture and put remainder in bottom of a 9 inch pie plate. In a bowl, combine apples, sugar, tapioca, cinnamon and nutmeg. Mix and put into pie plate. Bake 20 to 25 minutes. Sprinkle with reserved crumbs. Bake 25 minutes longer or until golden. Best served warm. Serves 6 to 8.

Kentucky Festival Pie

1/4 cup butter
1 cup sugar
3 eggs
3/4 cup honey
1 teaspoon vanilla
1/4 teaspoon salt
1/2 cup chocolate bits
1/2 cup chopped nuts
2 tablespoons bourbon
1 8 inch unbaked pie crust
1 cup heavy cream, whipped, sweetened, flavored to taste

Gail Goodman Hamilton
SON '66/'68
Cookbook Committee
Winston-Salem,
North Carolina

Preheat oven to 375°. Cream butter and sugar gradually. Add beaten eggs, honey, vanilla and salt. Stir well. Pour into pie shell and bake 40 to 50 minutes. Can be frozen. Serve warm with whipped cream. Serves 8.

Black Russian Pie

Powerful! It conquers rev-
olutionary tastebuds.

Carolyn Goldstein
SMG '80
Roslyn Harbor, New York

30 chocolate wafers, crushed

1/4 cup butter

2 tablespoons Kahlua

1/2 cup milk, boiled

2 envelopes unflavored gelatin

1/3 cup Kahlua

2 eggs

1/2 cup sugar

2/3 cup vodka

1 1/2 cups heavy cream, whipped

In a bowl, combine wafer crumbs, butter and Kahlua.
Spread on bottom and sides of 10 inch chilled pie plate.
Chill for 30 minutes. In a blender or processor, sprinkle
gelatin over hot milk. Process to dissolve gelatin. Add
Kahlua, sugar and vodka. Mix well. Strain into mixing
bowl and chill until it thickens, stirring occasionally.
Fold cream gently into mixture. Pour into crumb crust
and chill for a few hours. Garnish with chocolate curls.

Chocolate Cheese Pie

Genevieve Ginwala
Professor
Graduate General
Course Unit
School of Nursing

8 oz. cream cheese

1/2 cup white sugar

6 oz. semi-sweet chocolate, melted, cooled

1/2 cup light brown sugar

2 eggs, separated

dash salt

2 cups heavy cream, whipped

1 teaspoon vanilla

1 10 inch pie crust, baked

Beat cream cheese and sugar until smooth. Beat in egg
yolks. Add cooled chocolate to cheese mixture. Beat egg
whites until stiff with salt and brown sugar. Fold into
cheese mixture. Beat cream until stiff, add vanilla. Fold
1/2 of cream into the chocolate mixture. Pour into pie
crust. Spoon remaining cream over the top of the pie.
Chill overnight to set. Can be frozen. Serves 6 to 8.

Chocolate Velvet Pie

6 eggs, separated

12 oz. semi-sweet chocolate

1½ cups milk, boiled

¾ cup sugar

2 tablespoons coffee

butter

½ cup graham cracker crumbs

¼ cup rum

2 cups heavy cream

My sister says this is the most divine pie you'll ever taste. I'm in total agreement.

Carla Kindt SED '75
Development Office
Bill Beckett
SED '76/SSW '78

Preheat oven to 400°. In blender or processor, blend yolks, chocolate, milk, sugar and coffee until smooth. Grease 9 inch pie pan well and dust with cracker crumbs. Beat egg whites with salt until stiff. Fold 1½ cups chocolate into whites. Bake 5 minutes, then reduce heat to 350° for 25 minutes more or until center is firm. Cool 1½ hours. Center will fall. In a small saucepan, soften gelatin in rum. Stir over low heat until melted and blend with remaining chocolate. Cool to room temperature, mix with cream until blended. Beat until double in volume. (It will not be the consistency of whipped cream.) Chill until it holds shape and turn into pie shell. Chill or freeze. Serves 6 to 8.

Frozen Chocolate Pie

1 package Social Tea cookies, crushed

⅓ cup butter, melted

3 eggs

12 oz. semi-sweet chocolate chips

1 pint heavy cream, whipped

2 tablespoons rum

Adele Melrose
Paul Melrose
Parents
Newton Centre,
Massachusetts

Preheat oven to 375°. Mix crumbs and butter and press into fluted pie plate. Bake 10 minutes, cool. Melt chocolate chips in double boiler. Cool. Beat 1 egg and 2 yolks together. Stir in chocolate. Set aside. Beat egg whites until stiff. Fold into chocolate mixture with egg white and rum into cream. Pour into pie shell. Freeze. For mocha pie, add 1 tablespoon instant coffee to melted chocolate. Serves 6 to 8.

Cheese Tarts

Audrey Oshansky
Parent
Utica, New York

| 2 cups graham cracker crumbs |
| ¼ lb. butter, melted |
| 6 teaspoons sugar |
| 1 lb. farmer cheese |
| 1 lb. cream cheese |
| 1 cup sugar |
| 2 eggs |
| 1 tablespoon lemon juice |
| 2 teaspoons vanilla |
| berries (optional) |

Preheat oven to 350°. Place 2 cupcake liners in each insert of cupcake tins. In a bowl, combine crumbs, butter and sugar. Mix well. Distribute in papers and use a glass to press down and part way up sides. In a processor, blend cheeses, sugar, eggs, lemon juice and vanilla. Mix until well blended. Fill cups ⅝ full. Bake 11 to 12 minutes. Cool and refrigerate. Top with fresh cherries, blueberries or strawberries, if desired. Keeps three to four days refrigerated. Makes 26 to 28 average size or 75 small tarts.

Chess Pie

J. Kenneth Scott SFA '56
New York, New York

| 1⅓ cups sugar |
| ½ cup butter |
| 1 tablespoon cornmeal |
| ⅓ cup cream |
| 1 teaspoon white vinegar |
| 3 eggs |
| 1 teaspoon vanilla |
| 1 9 inch unbaked pie shell |

Preheat oven to 350°. Cream sugar and butter. In a bowl, beat in cornmeal, cream and vinegar. Add eggs 1 at a time, beating well after each. Blend in vanilla. Pour into unbaked pastry shell. Bake 50 minutes. Cool ½ to 2 hours before cutting. Can be frozen. Serves 6 to 8.

Cranberry Pie

2 cups fresh cranberries	
1 cup sugar	
½ cup chopped walnuts	
2 eggs	
1 cup flour	
¾ cup butter, melted	

Cheryl Connery
John Connery CLA '69
Vice President
General Alumni Association
Melrose, Massachusetts

Preheat oven to 350°. Grease a 10 inch plate. Sprinkle cranberries in and cover with ½ cup sugar and nuts. Combine eggs, ½ cup sugar, flour and butter. Beat well. Pour over cranberries. Bake for 1 hour. Serve hot or cold, plain or with topping. Keeps two days. Serves 6 to 8.

Summer Fruit Tart

1 9 or 10 inch pastry shell, baked
3 to 4 medium peaches
½ cup blueberries
½ cup granulated sugar
3 eggs
⅓ cup sifted flour
1 cup milk, scalded
1 teaspoon vanilla or other flavoring
¼ cup red currant jelly
1 teaspoon sugar
1 tablespoon kirsch

Any other fruits of your choice may be used in this refreshing summer dessert.

Peg Mitchell
Assistant Director
Reunions
Mildred Campbell
Friend of Boston University
Brookline, Massachusetts

In a saucepan, beat sugar into egg yolks until pale yellow. Beat in flour. While beating, pour in milk. Put pan over low heat and cook, stirring until it just reaches a boil and thickens. Do not scorch. Remove from heat and add flavoring. Dot top of custard with softened butter to prevent formation of a skin. Chill. Place cooled custard in baked pie shell. Arrange sliced peaches on top and sprinkle with blueberries or other fruits. In a saucepan, combine jelly, sugar and kirsch. Bring to a boil and cook until slightly thickened. Brush over fruits while still warm. Keeps refrigerated two days. Serves 6 to 8.

Walnut Tassy

This recipe makes 48 to 60 depending on the thickness of the crust. Use small cupcake tins with a capacity of about 1 tablespoon.

Cheryl Connery
John Connery CLA '69
Vice President
General Alumni Association
Melrose, Massachusetts

1 cup butter, melted
2 cups flour
6 oz. cream cheese
3 eggs
2¾ cups light brown sugar
dash salt
½ teaspoon vanilla
2 cups chopped walnuts

Preheat oven to 350°. Combine butter, flour and cheese to make a dough. Pinch off small bits of dough and press into wells of ungreased tiny cupcake tins. In a bowl, mix eggs, sugar, salt, vanilla and walnuts. Fill pastry shells. Bake 25 to 30 minutes or until golden. Can be frozen. Makes 48 to 60.

Grasshopper Pie

Barbara Goulson
Arceneaux PAL '54
Cookbook Committee
Jacksonville, Florida

12 chocolate wafers, crushed
¼ cup butter, melted
26 large marshmallows
½ cup milk
½ pint heavy cream, whipped
1 jigger Crème de Menthe
1 jigger Crème de Cacao

Combine crumbs and butter. Press into 9 or 10 inch pie plate and chill. In the top of double boiler, melt marshmallows and milk. Set aside until cool. Fold in whipped cream and liqueurs. Add extra green food coloring if needed. Pour mixture into pie shell. Refrigerate 3 to 4 hours. Can be frozen. Serves 6 to 8.

Edna's Green Grape Pie

1	cup crushed coconut cookies
1	cup flour
⅓	cup butter, melted
1	egg yolk
2½	cups seedless green grapes
⅓	cup rum or brandy
1	egg white
3	tablespoons sugar

Charlotte Edna Boutwell
SED '25
*2nd Competition
Poetry Winner
Stoneham, Massachusetts*

Preheat oven to 400°. In a bowl, mix crumbs, flour, butter and egg yolk until the mixture holds together. Press into bottom and sides of a 9 inch pie plate. Bake 10 minutes. Cool. Meanwhile, wash grapes and soak in rum for 1 hour. Preheat oven to 325°. Beat egg whites until soft peaks form and beat in sugar 1 tablespoon at a time until stiff. Fold grapes into meringue gently. Pour into shell and bake 15 to 20 minutes or until the meringue is a delicate gold. Keeps 24 hours. Serves 6 to 8.

Alaskan Ice Cream Pie

1	9 inch pie shell, baked
1	pint vanilla ice cream
1	pint peppermint stick ice cream
4	egg whites
1	cup sugar
1	cup fudge sauce

Edith Thompson Adams
SED '42
Marlboro, Massachusetts

Preheat oven to 450°. In a pie shell, spread a layer of vanilla ice cream and another layer of peppermint. Beat egg whites until soft peaks form. Beat in sugar gradually until stiff. Spread meringue over entire surface and bake until brown. Serve with fudge sauce. Can be frozen after baking. Serves 6 to 8.

Key Lime Pie

Cheryl Germain CLA '74
Little Falls, New Jersey

3 *egg yolks*

1 *can condensed sweetened milk*

½ *cup strained lime juice*

1 *9 inch pie shell, baked*

1 *cup heavy cream, whipped, sweetened, flavored to taste*

In a bowl, beat egg yolks and milk. Add juice and beat until thick. Pour into pie shell and chill for 1 hour. Cover with whipped cream before serving. Keeps two days refrigerated.
   Variation: Top with meringue and bake 10 to 15 minutes at 350°. Serves 6 to 8.

Key Lime Chiffon Pie

Nancy Seebert SON '68
Day's Creek, Oregon
Nancy Barton SED '77
Rehoboth Beach, Delaware

1 *envelope plain gelatin*

1 *cup sugar*

⅛ *teaspoon salt*

4 *eggs, separated*

½ *cup lime juice*

¼ *cup water*

2 *teaspoons grated lime rind*

1 *9 inch pie shell, baked*

2 to 3 *drops green food coloring (optional)*

1 *cup heavy cream, whipped, sweetened, flavored to taste*

Mix gelatin, ½ cup sugar and salt in double boiler. Beat in egg yolks, lime juice and water. Cook over boiling water stirring constantly until gelatin is dissolved, about 5 minutes. Remove from heat and stir in grated rind. Chill, stirring constantly until the mixture mounds when dropped from spoon. Beat egg whites stiff, beat in remaining sugar. Fold into gelatin mixture with food coloring. Pour into baked pie shell. Chill until firm. Serve with whipped cream. Keeps two days refrigerated. Serves 8.

Pecan Pie

1 cup light corn syrup
3 eggs, slightly beaten
½ cup brown sugar
¼ teaspoon salt
½ teaspoon vanilla
1 cup pecans, broken
1 9 inch pie shell, unbaked

Edith Thompson Adams
SED '42
Marlboro, Massachusetts

Preheat oven to 450°. In a bowl, mix corn syrup, eggs, salt, vanilla and broken nuts. Pour into pie shell. Bake 10 minutes. Lower heat to 350°. Bake 35 minutes. Cool. Can be frozen. Serves 6 to 8.

Lemon Meringue Pie

2 eggs, separated
1 cup sugar
1 cup water, boiled
2 tablespoons cornstarch
¼ cup lemon juice
rind of 1 lemon
1 tablespoon butter
dash salt
1 9 inch pie shell, baked
½ cup sugar

Mildred Thomas
SED '36/'38
Penney Farms, New Jersey

Preheat oven to 350°. Mix together 2 egg yolks, sugar, water, cornstarch, juice and rind. Cook in double boiler until thick. Add salt and butter. Cool. Pour into baked pie shell. Beat egg whites to soft peak stage and add remaining ½ cup sugar gradually, beating until stiff. Put on top of pie. Brown in oven 12 to 15 minutes. Chill. Keeps two days refrigerated. Serves 6.

Lemon Kiss Tart

Carol Lowe
Philip L. Lowe
Former Member
Board of Visitors
School of Management

8 eggs, separated
½ teaspoon cream of tartar
1¾ cups sugar
6 tablespoons lemon juice
2 tablespoons lemon rind
dash salt
1 pint heavy cream, whipped
1 cup heavy cream, whipped
1 cup fresh strawberries
sweet butter

Preheat oven to 300°. In a bowl, beat egg whites to soft peak stage and gradually add cream of tartar and 1 cup sugar. Beat until very stiff. Grease a 10 or 11 inch glass pie plate with sweet butter and spread in egg whites. Bake for 1 hour. Let cool in oven. In a double boiler, beat remaining sugar and egg yolks until thick and pale yellow. Add lemon juice and rind. Cook, stirring constantly. Cool. Fold in whipped cream and put in meringue shell. Refrigerate at least 24 hours. Before serving, top with whipped cream and strawberries. Can be frozen. Serves 6 to 8.

Heavenly Pie

Mrs. Daniel L. Marsh
Wife of Daniel L. Marsh
Former President
Boston University
Excerpted from
''The International Cuisine''
1957

1½ cups sugar
¼ teaspoon cream of tartar
4 eggs, separated
3 tablespoons lemon juice
3 tablespoons finely grated lemon rind
1 pint heavy cream

Sift together 1 cup sugar and cream of tartar. Beat egg whites until stiff. Gradually add sugar mixture and blend thoroughly. Use to line bottom and sides of greased 9 or 10 inch pie plate, not too close to the rim. Bake at 275° for 1½ hours. Cool and set aside. Beat egg yolks slightly; stir in remaining sugar, lemon rind and juice. Cook in top of double boiler until very thick, about 8 minutes. Remove and cool. Whip cream, combine ½ with lemon-egg mixture and fill shell. Cover with remaining whipped cream and chill for 24 hours. Serves 6 to 8.

10 Breads

Breads

10

Onion Boards

2⅓ to 3 cups flour, (all white or half white and half wheat)
1 package yeast
2 teaspoons sugar
1½ teaspoons salt
1 cup warm water
¼ cup butter, melted
2 onions, chopped
paprika
poppy seeds

Marilyn Joress
Development Office

Preheat oven to 375°. Mix 1 cup flour, yeast, sugar and salt in mixing bowl. Add water and beat at medium speed for 2 minutes. Add ½ cup flour and beat at high speed for ½ minute. Add enough additional flour by hand to make a dough that is not sticky. Cover and let rise for 20 minutes. Punch down and divide in half. Grease 2, 9 inch pie plates and press in dough. Butter top of dough lightly and refrigerate for 2 to 24 hours. Spread top with melted butter, onion, paprika and poppy seeds. Bake for 25 minutes. Can be frozen. Makes 12 to 18 servings.

Spice Muffins

Helen Crawford Bander
SED '31
Cookbook Committee
Paris, Arkansas

½ cup butter
1 cup brown sugar
2 eggs, beaten
1¾ cups flour
½ teaspoon cinnamon
½ teaspoon nutmeg
1 tablespoon baking powder
1 cup milk

Preheat oven to 400°. In a bowl, cream butter and sugar until light and fluffy. Beat in eggs, flour, cinnamon, nutmeg and baking powder. Stir in milk. Pour into greased muffin pans. Bake until golden and cooked through, about 25 minutes. Can be frozen. Makes 12.

Bran Muffins

Jessie Danielsen
Dr. Albert V. Danielsen
Honorary Trustee
Wellesley Hills,
Massachusetts

2 cups buttermilk
1½ cups sugar
½ cup oil
2 eggs, beaten
2½ cups flour
2½ teaspoons baking soda
2 cups All-Bran
1 cup Bran Buds
½ cup dates or raisins
1 cup boiling water

Mix buttermilk, oil, sugar and eggs. Add flour and soda. Stir in All-Bran, Bran Buds and boiling water. Let stand covered overnight in refrigerator. Preheat oven to 400°. Bake in greased muffin pans 20 to 25 minutes. Bake only as many as required. Batter will keep for two months. Muffins can be frozen. Makes 12, 3 inch muffins.

Popovers

2 eggs
1 cup milk
1 cup flour
¼ teaspoon salt

Judy Spellissey SFA '75
*West Chelmsford,
Massachusetts*

Preheat oven to 450°. Beat eggs, milk, flour and salt together in a bowl. Half fill greased pans or glass cups. Place in oven for 30 minutes. Lower heat to 350° for 10 minutes. Remove and poke a hole in each popover on the side. Serve immediately. Makes 12.

Apple Bread

½ cup butter
1 cup sugar
2 eggs
2 cups flour
1 teaspoon baking soda
½ teaspoon salt
1 teaspoon vinegar
2 tablespoons milk
1¾ cups peeled, chopped apples
½ cup chopped nuts
¼ cup currants (optional)
2 tablespoons flour
1 tablespoon sugar
1 teaspoon cinnamon
1 tablespoon butter

**Ernestine J. Dakin Rose
SED '40/'41/'70**
Lynnfield, Massachusetts

Preheat oven to 350°. Cream butter and sugar. Add eggs and beat well. Sift together flour, soda and salt. Mix vinegar and milk. Add dry ingredients to creamed mixture alternately with milk mixture, beginning and ending with dry ingredients. Stir in apples and nuts. Add currants if desired. Pour into greased 9x5x3 inch loaf pan. Combine flour, sugar, cinnamon and butter. Sprinkle over batter. Bake 1 hour. Can be frozen. Makes 1 loaf.

Apricot-Date Loaf

Bernice Lipman
Friend of Boston University
Wayland, Massachusetts

1 1/2 cups sugar

1 cup dates

1 cup dried apricots

1/4 cup butter

2 teaspoons baking soda

1 3/4 cups water, boiled

2 eggs, slightly beaten

2 1/2 cups sifted bread flour

1 cup chopped nuts

Preheat oven to 350°. Grease a 9x5x3 inch loaf pan. In a bowl, combine sugar, dates, apricots, butter and baking soda. Pour on water and stir. When cool, beat in eggs, flour and nuts. Bake 1 hour or until tests done. Can be frozen. Serves 8.

Banana Bread

I can definitely say this is the best banana bread I've ever tasted. It stays moist because of the sour cream.

Camille Anthony
William Anthony
Director, Research and
Training Center
in Mental Illness
Sargent College
of Allied Health Professions

1 1/2 cups sugar

1/4 lb. butter

3 eggs

6 tablespoons sour cream

3 bananas, mashed

1 3/4 cups flour

1 teaspoon baking powder

1 teaspoon soda

1/2 cup nuts

Preheat oven to 325°. Cream sugar and butter. Add eggs, sour cream and bananas. Blend in flour, baking powder, soda and nuts. Pour into greased 9x5x3 inch loaf pan. Bake 1 hour. Can be frozen. Makes 1 loaf.

Banana Nut Bread

½ cup butter
1 cup sugar
2 eggs, beaten
3 ripe bananas, mashed
2 cups flour
1 teaspoon baking soda
½ teaspoon baking powder
½ teaspoon salt
3 tablespoons milk
½ teaspoon vanilla
½ cup chopped nuts

Cheryl L. Germain
CLA '74
Little Falls, New Jersey

Preheat oven to 350°. Cream butter and sugar together. Add eggs and banana. Beat well. Beat in flour, soda, baking powder, salt, milk and vanilla. Mix well and stir in nuts. Pour into greased and floured 9x5x3 inch loaf pan. Bake about 1 hour. Cool well and store overnight before cutting. Can be frozen. Makes 1 loaf.

Nut Bread

3 cups flour
2 cups chopped pecans or walnuts
1 cup sugar
3 teaspoons baking powder
1 teaspoon salt
1¾ cups milk

This dry bread keeps well and may be sliced paper thin for tea sandwiches.

Elizabeth B. deTrevino
20th Century Archives
Mugar Library

Preheat oven to 350°. Mix all dry ingredients. Stir in enough milk to form a rather stiff paste. Put into a greased 9x5x3 inch loaf pan. Let stand for 20 minutes, then bake until a toothpick inserted in center comes out dry, 1 hour. Makes 1 loaf.

Date Nut Bread

Obviously, this is a very popular recipe.

Mrs. Justin Lee Altshuler
Dr. Justin Lee Altshuler
Henry M. Goldman
School of Graduate Dentistry
Mary Ellen Cuenir
SED'73/SFA'78
Lynnfield, Massachusetts
Elizabeth McIlwraith
PAL'26
Bridgewater, Massachusetts
Daphne S. Palmer
Friend of Boston University
Nancy Seebert SON'68
Day's Creek, Oregon

1 cup chopped dates
3/4 cup chopped walnuts
1 1/2 teaspoons baking soda
1/2 teaspoon salt
3/4 cup boiling water
1/4 cup butter
2 eggs, lightly beaten
1 1/2 cups sifted flour
1 cup sugar
1/2 teaspoon vanilla

Preheat oven to 350°. Combine dates, nuts, soda and salt in a large mixing bowl. Add boiling water and butter. Let stand 15 minutes. Stir to blend. Add flour, sugar and vanilla. Stir into date mixture. Do not overmix. Bake in greased and floured 9x5x3 inch loaf pan. Bake 1 hour. Test with toothpick. If done, pick will come out clean. Cool before removing from pan, loosening sides. Cool several hours. Can be frozen. Makes 1 loaf.

Boston Brown Bread

Today, Boston brown bread and baked beans are a typical Saturday night supper, but New England farmers ate them for breakfast.

Sterne Barnett CBA '35
Cookbook Committee
Chestnut Hill, Massachusetts

1 cup white flour
1 cup whole wheat flour
1 cup cornmeal
1 teaspoon baking powder
2 tablespoons lemon juice
3/4 teaspoon baking soda
2 cups milk
3/4 cup dark molasses
1 cup raisins (optional)

Add lemon juice to milk and let stand 10 minutes. Mix flours, cornmeal, soda, baking powder and salt together. Add milk and molasses. Stir in raisins, if desired. Mix well. Fill 3 greased 1 lb. coffee cans half full. Cover tightly with foil or greased cheese cloth. Place on rack or trivet in kettle. Pour boiling water to a level halfway up cans. Steam 3 hours. Keep water boiling and add more as needed. Remove cans; uncover. Remove bread. Can be frozen. Makes 3 to 5 loaves.

Nonesuch Cornbread

2 cups yellow cornmeal
2 cups regular white flour
1 teaspoon salt
8 teaspoons baking powder
2 cups whole milk
2 eggs
4 tablespoons vegetable oil
1 cup Barbados molasses
1 teaspoon ground nutmeg
1 cup seedless raisins

Guaranteed to knock your hat off

Merritt Paul Skaggs
CLA '49
River Edge, New Jersey

Preheat oven to 425°. In a bowl, combine the cornmeal, flour, salt, baking powder, milk, eggs, oil, molasses, nutmeg and raisins. Mix until batter is smooth. Fold into a greased 20x14 inch pan. Bake 30 minutes. It is done when knife emerges clean. Serves 6.

Cranberry Bread

2 cups flour
1 cup sugar
1½ teaspoons baking powder
1 teaspoon salt
½ teaspoon baking soda
rind of 1 orange, grated
juice of 1 orange
2 tablespoons butter, melted
¾ cup boiling water
1 egg, beaten
1 cup fresh cranberries, halved
¾ cup chopped walnuts or pecans

Sharon Gamsin DGE '69
Cookbook Committee
New York, New York

Preheat oven to 325°. Sift flour, sugar, baking powder, soda and salt together. Combine orange rind, juice, butter and water. Add egg to flour mixture and mix well. Add liquid mixture. Mix lightly. Add berries and nuts. Bake in greased 9x5x3 inch loaf pan for 1 hour. Keep 24 hours before serving. Can be frozen. Makes 1 loaf.

Glorified Gingerbread

A favorite while studying

Dr. Ann Baker Jenkins
CLA'50/GRS'52
*Collegium of
Distinguished Alumni
Mendham, New Jersey*

2 cups flour
1 cup granulated sugar
½ cup butter
½ teaspoon ginger
½ teaspoon cinnamon
1 cup sour milk
2 tablespoons molasses
1 egg
1 teaspoon soda
pinch of salt

Preheat oven to 350°. Grease and flour 9 inch square baking pan. In a bowl, combine flour, sugar, butter, ginger and cinnamon. Crumble as for pie crust. Set aside ½ cup. Make a well in remainder. Add sour milk, molasses, egg, soda and salt. Mix well. Put into prepared pan and sprinkle with dry mixture. Bake 30 to 35 minutes. Cool. Can be frozen. Serves 8.

Gingerbread

Top this with applesauce and whipped cream.

Elizabeth McIlwraith
PAL'26
Bridgewater, Massachusetts

2 cups flour
1 cup sugar
1 cup sour cream
1 egg
4 tablespoons molasses
3 tablespoons butter, melted
1 teaspoon soda
1 teaspoon cinnamon
1 teaspoon ginger
½ teaspoon baking powder
½ teaspoon nutmeg
½ teaspoon clove
¼ teaspoon salt

Preheat oven to 350°. Grease a 9x13 inch baking pan. Combine flour, sugar, egg, sour cream, molasses, butter, soda, cinnamon, ginger, baking powder, nutmeg, clove and salt. Mix well. Pour into prepared pan. Bake for 35 to 40 minutes. Cool. Can be frozen. Serves 8.

Irish Soda Bread

4 cups white self-rising flour
2 cups whole wheat flour
½ teaspoon baking soda
pinch of salt
1 teaspoon sugar
2 tablespoons butter
1⅔ cups milk

Preheat oven to 325°. Mix flours together in bowl. Add soda, salt, sugar and butter. Mix together. Add milk to mixture and stir together with care. Knead well. Form bread loaf and place on flat baking pan. Cook in oven for 1 hour or until done. Can be frozen. Makes 1 large loaf.

Phyllis Ratcliffe Hamilton
CLA'62
Libertytown, Maryland

Lemon Bread

6 tablespoons butter
1 cup sugar
2 eggs
1½ cups flour
1 teaspoon baking powder
dash salt
rind of 1 lemon, grated
1 cup milk
½ cup chopped walnuts
juice of 1 lemon
½ cup sugar

Preheat oven to 325°. Cream butter and sugar. Beat in eggs until light and fluffy. Stir in flour, baking powder, salt and lemon rind. Stir in milk and nuts and mix well. Pour into a greased 9x5x3 inch loaf pan. Bake 1 hour. Mix lemon juice and sugar until sugar is dissolved. Pour over bread and let stand for at least 4 hours before serving. Can be frozen. Makes 1 loaf.

Tastes even better the next day

Anna E. Bessette
SON'63/'65
Attleboro, Massachusetts
Stanlee Lipkin-Quaytman
CLA'72
Cookbook Committee
Baltimore, Maryland

Irish Raisin Bread

Elizabeth A. Kelley
SON'71
West Roxbury,
Massachusettts

4 cups flour
1 cup sugar
4 teaspoons baking soda
½ teaspoon salt
1½ to 2 cups milk
1 tablespoon vinegar
2 eggs, beaten
3 tablespoons butter, softened or melted
2 cups raisins

Preheat oven to 350°. Mix flour, sugar, baking soda and salt. Add vinegar to milk to sour it. Add eggs, butter, milk and raisins to dry ingredients. Knead lightly on floured board or mix with a spoon until a soft dough is formed. (Add the extra ½ cup milk if too dry.) Shape into round loaf. Placc in dccp, greased 9 inch round pan. Mark a cross on top with sharp knife. Bake 1 hour or until bread tests done. Can be frozen. Makes 1 large loaf.

Pumpkin Tea Bread

As with any tea bread, this one improves with age.

Barbara Lanciani SED'66
Cookbook Committee
Leominster, Massachusetts

3 cups sugar
1 cup salad oil
3 eggs
15 oz. canned pumpkin
3 cups flour
1 teaspoon baking soda
½ teaspoon salt
½ teaspoon baking powder
1 teaspoon clove
1 teaspoon cinnamon
1 teaspoon nutmeg

Preheat oven to 350°. Blend sugar and oil. Add eggs and pumpkin. Mix well. Stir in flour, baking soda, clove, cinnamon, nutmeg, salt and baking powder. Pour into greased tube cake pan. Bake 1 hour and 15 minutes. Cool bread in pan. Freezes well. Makes 1 cake.

Spicy Zucchini Nut Bread

3 eggs	
2 cups sugar	
1 cup oil	
1 tablespoon vanilla	
2 cups raw grated zucchini, drained	
3 cups flour	
3 teaspoons cinnamon	
2 teaspoons baking soda	
1 teaspoon salt	
½ teaspoon baking powder	
1 cup finely chopped walnuts	

Diane M. Dodendorf
SON'72
Omaha, Nebraska
Phyllis Forman **SFA'75**
New York, New York

Preheat oven to 350°. Beat eggs until frothy. Beat in sugar, oil and vanilla until mixture is thick and lemon colored. Stir in zucchini. Stir in flour, cinnamon, soda, salt and baking powder. Blend well. Fold in nuts. Pour batter into 2 greased and floured 8x3x2 inch bread pans. Bake 1 hour. Can be frozen. Makes 2 small loaves.

Orange Graham Cracker Loaf

2⅔ cups graham cracker crumbs	
½ teaspoon baking soda	
½ teaspoon baking powder	
½ teaspoon salt	
½ cup orange juice	
½ cup butter	
½ cup sugar	
3 eggs, beaten	
rind of 1 orange, grated	
1 cup chopped walnuts	
1 cup raisins	

Mary Ellen Cuenir
SED'73/SFA'78
Lynnfield, Massachusetts

Preheat oven to 350°. Butter a 9x5x3 inch loaf pan. Combine crumbs, soda, powder and salt. In another bowl, combine juice, butter, sugar, eggs and rind. Add to dry mixture. Stir in nuts and raisins. Bake 50 minutes. Cool. Can be frozen. Serves 8.

Apricot and Cheese Coffee Cake

Barbara Tomashefsky
Abbott CLA '59
Cookbook Committee
Hudson, New Hampshire

| 1 package dry yeast |
| 1/4 cup warm water |
| 1/4 cup butter, melted |
| 1/4 cup sugar |
| 1/4 cup milk, room temperature |
| 1 egg, room temperature |
| 1/2 teaspoon vanilla |
| 1/4 teaspoon salt |
| 2 to 2 1/2 cups flour |
| 1 egg, lightly beaten |
| 8 oz. small curd cottage cheese |
| 1/4 cup sugar |
| 1/8 teaspoon cinnamon |
| 1 tablespoon flour |
| 16 or 17 oz. can apricot halves, drained |

Preheat oven to 350°. Dissolve yeast in warm water. Add butter, sugar, milk, egg, vanilla and salt. Stir until well blended. Add 1 cup flour and beat at medium speed for 2 minutes, scraping sides occasionally. With spoon, stir in 1 more cup of flour, until a soft dough is formed. Turn dough onto well floured surface, knead until smooth and elastic, using more flour as needed. Place in buttered bowl and turn over to butter top. Cover and let rise in a warm place, until doubled in bulk, about 1 hour. Grease a 9 inch springform pan. Punch dough down; pat evenly into pan, covering bottom and pushing dough up about 2 inches around side. Cover and let rise for 30 minutes. While dough rises again, combine egg, cottage cheese, sugar, cinnamon and flour. Place canned apricots on paper towels to drain. When dough has risen, lightly pat down dough only on bottom of pan. Cover with apricots. Spoon cheese filling over apricots. Bake 55 to 60 minutes until cheese is set. Let cool on wire rack 10 minutes before removing side of springform pan. Cut into wedges. Can be frozen. Makes 12 servings.

Swedish Coffee Bread

2 cups milk, scalded
1 cup sugar
½ cup butter
1 teaspoon salt
6 cardamom seeds
2 packages yeast
1 egg
6 cups flour

Elaine Hatch Laverty
CBA '72
Philadelphia, Pennsylvania

Preheat oven to 375°. In a bowl, combine milk, sugar, butter, salt and cardamom. Stir until butter is melted. Stir in yeast and egg. Stir in flour, using enough to make a medium dough. Knead until smooth and elastic. Let rise in covered greased bowl until doubled in size, about 1½ hours. Punch down and shape into a large braid or small rolls. Place on greased baking sheet. Let rise until doubled in size. Bake until golden: 45 minutes for braid; 20 to 25 minutes for rolls. Can be frozen. Makes 1 large braid or 16 rolls.

Sour Cream Coffee Cake

¼ lb. butter
1 cup sugar
2 eggs
1 teaspoon vanilla
1½ cups flour
1½ teaspoons baking soda
1 cup sour cream, room temperature
1½ teaspoons cinnamon
¼ cup sugar
1 cup chopped nuts

Stanlee Lipkin-Quaytman
CLA '72
Cookbook Committee
Baltimore, Maryland

Preheat oven to 350°. Grease 9x5x3 inch loaf pan. In a bowl, cream butter and sugar until light and fluffy. Beat in eggs and vanilla. Add flour and baking soda. Stir in sour cream and mix well. In another bowl, combine nuts, sugar and cinnamon. Pour ½ the batter into pan. Sprinkle on ½ the nut and spice combination and remainder of batter. Top with remaining ingredients. Bake 45 minutes. Cool. Can be frozen. Serves 6 to 8.

Coffee Ring

Mildred Thomas
SED '36/'38
Penney Farms, Florida

½ cup shortening
1 cup sugar
2 eggs
1 cup sour milk
2 cups flour
1 teaspoon baking powder
1 teaspoon soda
1 teaspoon vanilla
½ cup chopped nuts
1 teaspoon cinnamon
¼ cup brown sugar

Preheat oven to 350°. Cream butter and sugar. Add eggs, milk, flour, baking powder, soda and vanilla. Put ½ batter in greased 9 inch tube pan. Combine nuts, sugar and cinnamon and sprinkle over batter. Add rest of batter and sprinkle the remainder of the topping. Bake 45 minutes. Can be frozen. Makes a 9 inch tube cake.

Yogurt Coffee Cake

Rita Aisner GRS '72
Framingham, Massachusetts

8 tablespoons butter
1 cup sugar
2 eggs
¾ cup yogurt
½ teaspoon baking soda
1½ cups flour
2 teaspoons baking powder
1 cup raisins
¼ teaspoon cinnamon
¼ cup flour
½ cup brown sugar
1 tablespoon butter, melted
½ teaspoon cinnamon

Preheat oven to 350°. Butter and flour 9 inch cake tin. In
a large bowl, cream butter and sugar together. Add eggs
1 at a time, beating well after each. Stir together yogurt
and baking soda. Sift flour and baking soda together.
Add yogurt to dry ingredients, alternately, mixing well.
Spoon ½ of the batter into cake tin. Cover batter with
raisins and ¼ teaspoon cinnamon. Add rest of batter.
Mix together the flour, brown sugar, melted butter and
cinnamon. Sprinkle over batter. Bake for 1 hour. Cool.
Can be frozen. Serves 6 to 8.

Z'ydowski Kieks Dokawa

1 pint sour cream
2 teaspoons baking soda
½ lb. butter
2 cups sugar
4 eggs
1 tablespoon vanilla
4 cups flour
1 teaspoon salt
1 teaspoon baking powder
½ cup sugar
½ cup chopped nuts
2 teaspoons cinnamon

A Jewish cake to eat with
coffee

**Sonia K. Piekos Keirstead
CLA '62**
Tallahassee, Florida

Preheat oven to 350°. Grease a 9 inch loaf pan. Mix sour
cream and soda together. In a bowl, combine butter,
sugar, eggs and vanilla. Beat well. Add flour, salt, baking
powder and mix well. Beat in sour cream. Put ⅓ of batter in pan. Combine sugar, nuts and cinnamon. Mix
well. Sprinkle ⅓ on top of batter. Add another ⅓ of
batter, ⅓ of topping, etc. Bake 1 hour. Can be frozen.
Serves 6 to 8.

Kummelweck Rolls

These are often called Kieser rolls. They make great deli sandwiches.

Dr. Matthew Witten
CLA'72
Cookbook Committee
Los Angeles, California

4½ to 5½ cups flour
2 tablespoons sugar
2 teaspoons salt
1 package active dry yeast
3 tablespoons softened butter
1½ cups hot tap water
1 egg white, room temperature
melted butter
2 tablespoons kosher salt
2 tablespoons caraway seeds

Preheat oven to 375°. In a large bowl, mix 1⅓ cups of the flour, sugar, salt and undissolved yeast. Add softened butter. Gradually add tap water to dry ingredients and beat 2 minutes at medium speed of electric mixer, scraping bowl occasionally. Add egg white and enough flour to make a thick batter. Beat at high speed 2 minutes, scraping bowl occasionally. Stir in enough additional flour to make a soft dough. Turn out on a lightly floured board. Knead dough until smooth and elastic, about 8 to 10 minutes. Place in buttered bowl, turning dough to butter the top. Cover bowl; let dough rise in warm place free of drafts until double in bulk, about 45 minutes. Punch down dough. Place on floured board. Knead gently for 1 or 2 minutes. Break dough into 2 ounce pieces, a little less than ¼ cup. Form the pieces into balls. Let them stand covered on the board 15 minutes. Brush a small amount of melted butter on the top of each ball. Using a ½ inch dowel, press across each round firmly. Then make another indentation at right angles to the first crease, forming 4 equal segments. Pick up each creased round. Gently squeeze it together compressing the quarters somewhat. Turn face down on greased baking sheet. Repeat with each roll. Cover and let them rise again until double, about 35 minutes. Mix salt with caraway seeds. Rub through the fingers to combine the flavors. Turn each risen roll face up. With a pastry brush, lightly brush the top of the roll with water. Sprinkle well with caraway mixture. Bake 30 minutes. Can be frozen. Makes 1½ dozen.

Classic Rolls

2	cups water
1	cup butter
½	cup sugar
1	tablespoon salt
2	packages dry yeast
½	cup very warm water
2	eggs, beaten
7	cups flour

Preheat oven to 375°. In a saucepan, combine water, butter, sugar and salt. Heat until butter is melted and sugar is dissolved. Cool to lukewarm. Proof yeast in warm water. Combine eggs with butter mixture and stir well. Add flour, 1 cup at a time, beating well after each addition. Turn into a buttered bowl and turn to butter the top. Refrigerate overnight. Next day, roll out and shape as desired, Parker House or cloverleaf. Place on buttered baking sheet and let rise until doubled. Bake 15 to 20 minutes. Can be frozen. Makes 2 dozen rolls. Dough can also be used for sweet rolls.

This is a good basic recipe that can be used to make cinnamon rolls.

Margaret Wilkerson
Cookbook Committee

Fluffy Baking Powder Biscuits

1	cup flour
2	teaspoons baking powder
½	cup milk
3	tablespoons mayonnaise
2	teaspoons salt
2	teaspoons sugar

Preheat oven to 400°. In a bowl, combine milk and mayonnaise. Lightly stir in flour, baking powder, salt and sugar to form a medium dough. Pat out onto a floured board about ¾ inch thick. Cut into biscuits. Put onto greased baking sheet. Cut into biscuits. Put onto greased baking sheet. Bake 20 to 25 minutes. Best served immediately. Can be frozen. Makes 12, 2½ inch biscuits.

Gail Goodman Hamilton
SON '66/'68
Cookbook Committee
Winston-Salem,
North Carolina

Excellent for breakfast
served with jam, sweet
butter and café au lait.

Dr. Edward S. Gross
MED '68
West Newton, Massachusetts

Croissants

Equipment
Cookie sheets

Rolling pin: Preferably a piece of closet rod 1¾ inches in diameter by 24 inches long, carefully sanded smooth. This permits a light touch in rolling and lessens the likelihood of running butter.

Rolling boards: 2 sheets of lucite, 16x10x½ inches or ⅝ inches thick. These can be obtained at plastics supply houses and cut from scrap. Place in the freezer when not in use.

Ingredients

3	cups unbleached flour (extra flour for dusting board)
1	cup milk
2	packets dry active yeast
¾	lb. unsalted butter
1	tablespoon sugar
	for glaze: 1 egg, beaten with 1 teaspoon milk

This method for making the familiar French breakfast roll is more a technique than a recipe, enabling the baker to go from ingredients to table in 1 to 1½ hours instead of the more usual overnight approach with twice-risen dough. It depends upon the use of cold plastic boards for rolling out dough. These are cooled to freezer temperature so as to prevent melting and running of the butter between the dough layers as the dough is worked. The low temperatures also prevent rising of the dough which occurs only at the end in the oven.

Preheat oven to 400°. Place both rolling boards in freezer. Prepare and proof yeast. Combine yeast and water at 110°. Add sugar, stir together and watch for bubbles to form. Make dough by processing yeast, flour and 2 tablespoons butter cut in small pieces in processor or mixing bowl. Add milk until a smooth, firm, almost rubbery ball is produced. Knead for 5 to 10 minutes and place covered, in refrigerator, 10 minutes. While dough rests, unwrap butter and work it between sheets of waxed paper or a plastic bag until it becomes pliable but not runny. Shape into a block ½ inch thick and set aside at room temperature. Remove 1 rolling board from freezer, dust liberally with flour and place dough on it. Roll out dough until it extends beyond edges of board. Place ½ of butter in center and fold ⅓ of length of dough over butter, pinching edges to seal. Place second half of butter on top of the first fold and fold other end of dough over the stack of butter and dough.

Turn dough combination 180° so open end faces you. Roll out on the board until it fills the board and has a roughly rectangular shape. Repeat fold in thirds, like a folded letter. This is a "fold" and will be repeated. Place rolling board in freezer. Remove other rolling board from the freezer and dust liberally with flour. Place dough on it, open end facing you. Roll and fold. Repeat. Roll dough out to 1¼ inch thick. Cut dough into 3 roughly equal parts and place in refrigerator for 10 minutes. Return rolling boards to freezer. Grease baking sheet. Remove 1 portion of dough and a rolling board. Roll out dough to fill board almost exactly. Cut dough into 12 triangles. Roll triangles up into cylinders, starting from their shorter edge to the point opposite, gently pulling dough as you roll to lengthen the resulting cylinder to 5 or 6 inches and tuck in point firmly. Bend this cylinder into a croissant with the point inside the curve. Place on baking sheet. Brush tops of croissants with glaze. Bake 15 to 18 minutes until golden brown and crisp. Can be frozen. Makes 48.

Montana Range to Range Cinnamon Buns

Dr. Kathleen Cronin
SED'74
National Alumni Council
Great Falls, Montana

⅓ *cup milk, scalded*

2 *tablespoons sugar*

2 *tablespoons butter*

½ *teaspoon salt*

1 *package dry yeast*

¼ *cup warm water*

1 *egg, beaten*

¼ *teaspoon grated lemon rind*

2 *cups flour*

⅔ *cup brown sugar*

1 *teaspoon cinnamon*

3 *tablespoons butter*

¼ *cup dark corn syrup*

½ *cup raisins*

¾ *cup pecans*

Preheat oven to 325°. Combine milk, sugar, butter and salt. Stir until butter is melted. Cool to lukewarm. Sprinkle yeast over water. Stir in milk mixture, egg and lemon rind. Beat in flour, 1 cup at a time. Turn onto a board and knead until smooth and elastic. Butter a large bowl; turn dough over in bowl to coat all sides; cover and let rise in warm place until doubled, about 1 hour. Combine sugar and cinnamon. Butter a 9 inch square cake pan with ½ the butter. Pour on ½ the corn syrup and sprinkle with ½ the sugar mixture. Roll out the dough on a lightly floured board into an 8x16 inch rectangle. Spread with remaining butter, syrup and sugar. Sprinkle with raisins and pecans. Roll firmly. Cut into 16, 1 inch pieces. Place cut side down in pan. Cover and let rise until doubled in bulk. Bake 35 to 40 minutes. Let stand for 1 minute. Unmold onto plate and serve. Best served warm. Can be frozen. Makes 16.

Glazed Orange Rolls

1 recipe basic sweet dough (see below)
½ cup softened butter
1 cup sugar
rinds of 2 oranges, grated
½ cup sugar
¼ cup light corn syrup
¼ cup water
rind of 1 orange, grated

This sweet dough is soft and makes light, tender breads. Because it is rich, it doesn't require much kneading.

Barbara B. Baumgardner
Jeffrey Baumgardner
Curator of Observatory

Preheat oven to 425°. Roll dough into a rectangle ¼ inch thick. Cream butter, sugar and grated orange peel. Spread mixture evenly over the dough. Roll dough up as for a jelly roll and chill. Cut chilled dough into 1 inch slices and place in greased muffin pans or 1 inch apart on greased baking sheets. Allow rolls to rise in a warm place until almost doubled in bulk. Bake 10 to 14 minutes. Simmer sugar, corn syrup and water for 10 minutes. Add the grated orange peel. Cool syrup slightly before glazing the warm rolls. Can be frozen. Makes about 2 dozen.

Basic Sweet Dough

¼ cup butter
1 teaspoon salt
¼ cup sugar
1 cup milk, scalded, cooled to lukewarm
1 package active dry yeast
¼ cup warm water
1 egg, slightly beaten
4 cups sifted flour
softened butter

Place the butter, salt and sugar in a large bowl; add milk, stirring to dissolve the sugar and salt and to melt the butter. Soften the yeast in the warm water and add, along with the beaten egg, to the milk mixture. Stir in 3½ cups of flour, 1 cup at a time, beating vigorously to blend. Scrape dough from the sides of the bowl and brush the top of the dough and the sides of the bowl with the softened butter. Cover dough and let rise in a warm place about 2 hours or until almost doubled in bulk. Turn out on a well floured board and knead lightly, adding flour until the dough is no longer sticky (do not use more than ¼ to ½ cup flour on the board). Shape and bake as suggested in the recipe.

The Boston University Cookbook

Pretzels

Kids love to help with this recipe. Have your apparatus and your ingredients readily accessible because quickness is the key.

Dr. Matthew Witten
CLA'72
Cookbook Committee
Los Angeles, California
Barbara Tomashefsky
Abbott CLA'59/SED'62
Cookbook Committee
Hudson, New Hampshire

2 cups milk, scalded

1 envelope dry yeast

½ cup very warm water

½ cup sugar

1½ teaspoons salt

¼ cup butter

6¾ cups flour

¾ teaspoon baking powder

3 teaspoons salt

1 egg

1 teaspoon water

4 teaspoons Kosher salt

Preheat oven to 400°. Heat milk until lukewarm. Sprinkle yeast over water in large bowl; stir to dissolve. Add sugar, salt and butter. Beat in 3 cups flour to make smooth batter. Cover and let rise in warm place until doubled in volume, about 45 minutes. Stir down batter and mix in baking powder. Stir in 3 cups flour, 1 cup at a time. Turn dough out onto a well floured board; knead until smooth and elastic. Use only as much flour as needed to prevent dough from sticking. Roll dough out to 10x16 inch rectangle. With a sharp knife, cut into 20 strips 16x½ inch. With palms of hands roll strips out to 24 inches long and shape into pretzel. Let rise uncovered on lightly floured board for 30 minutes. When nearly ready dissolve 1 tablespoon of salt in 2 quarts boiling water. Using large slotted spatula, lower pretzels 1 at a time into water for 2 seconds. Lift out, tilt and drain. Place ½ inch apart on greased baking sheet. Beat egg with water; brush over each pretzel. Sprinkle with salt. Bake 18 to 20 minutes. Can be frozen. Makes 20.

Index

Index

A

Acorn squash with applesauce, *180*

Adobo, chicken and pork, *106*

Agro dolcie (sweet and sour zucchini), *183*

Alaskan ice cream pie, *327*

Alaskan baked swordfish, *79*

Almendrado (Mexican dessert), *238*

Antipasto, eggplant, *9*

Apfelpita (Viennese apple pie), *320*

Appetizers, *2–40*

– *baba ganooj (eggplant spread), 10*

– *baked stuffed clams, 28*

– *Barbara's raw vegetable dip, 3*

– *barbecued chicken wings, 31*

– *beef roll-ups, 21*

– *bibelkase, 6*

– *broiled stuffed mushrooms, 23*

– *caponata, 8*

– *caviar mold, 12*

– *champignons grand'mere (stuffed mushrooms), 24*

– *cheese ball, 7*

– *cheese-clam log, 14*

– *cheese cocktail cookies, 22*

– *cheese puffs, 21*

– *chili con queso (hot dip), 22*

– *Chinese chicken wings, 31*

– *choomis and chapati (chickpea spread and flat bread), 14*

– *clams casino, 27*

– *clam stuffed shells, 27*

– *crab meat fondue, 28*

– *crab meat won ton, 29*

– *cranberry herring spread, 15*

– *cucumber and mussels vinaigrette, 16*

– *curried cream cheese dip, 4*

– *curry and chili sauce dip, 5*

– *curry dip, 4*

– *dill dip, 5*

– *eggplant antipasto, 9*

– *golden cooler, 39*

– *herbed cheese spread, 6*

– *herring dip, 15*

– *hot buttered rum cider, 38*

– *hot cheese puffs, 22*

– *hot chili pepper spread, 7*

– *hot salami and cheese in phyllo triangles, 36*

– *Jane's herring stuff, 15*

– *kipper spread, 17*

– *kugeli, 26*

– *kuo-teh (potstickers), 34*

– *liverwurst ball, 20*

– *low cal curry dip, 4*

– *marinated carrots, 11*

– *marinated mushrooms, 10*

– *miniature Reuben sandwiches, 36*

– *minted lemon orange iced tea, 39*

– *mock blintz appetizers, 21*

– *mock Kahlua (coffee liqueur), 38*

– *onion olé, 25*

– *Parmesan rounds, 23*

– *pâté de foie de porc (pork liver pâté), 18*

– *Peruvian causa (potato balls), 12*

– *pickled eggplant, 9*

– *pini cheese spread, 5*

– *pistachio-gruyère cheese spread, 7*

– *red headed pâté, 19*

– *rumaki, 32*

– *salmon balls, 17*

– *salmon mousse, 16*

– *saté ajam (Indonesian skewered chicken), 30*

– *Scotch eggs, 40*

– *seafood stuffed mushrooms, 24*

– *shrimp toast, 37*

– *southern cheese log, 6*

– *spiced pecans, 37*

– *stuffed grape leaves, 20*

– *Swedish meatballs, 33*

– *sweet and sour chicken wings, 32*

– *sweet and sour meatballs, 33*

– *tabbouleh (Middle Eastern salad), 13*

– *taramosalata (Greek caviar dip), 13*

– *terrine de campagne (country pâté), 18*

– *white wine clam puffs, 69*

– *zucchini artichoke squares, 25*

– *zucchini sticks, 26*

Apple

– *apfelpita (Viennese apple pie), 320*

– *bread, 335*

– *cake, Babe's, 263*

– *cake, German, 262*

– *cake, tea, 262*

– *fruit salad, 225*

– *kugel, 196*

– *latkes and cottage cheese, 240*

– *pie, 318*

– *pie, Swedish, 319*

– *pudding, orange noodle, 199*

– *pudding, Pearl's crispy, 252*

– *strudel, the Cafe Budapest, 239*

– *tart, 321*

Applejacks, *300*

Applesauce

– *acorn squash with, 180*

– *cake, 261*

Apricot

– *cheese coffee cake, 344*

– *chicken, 105*

Key to Boston University's
Schools and Colleges

Program in Artisanry PIA
School for the Arts SFA
College of Basic Studies CBS
*College of Business
  Administration CBA
Henry M. Goldman School
  of Graduate Dentistry SGD
School of Education SED
College of Engineering ENG
Graduate School
  (Arts and Sciences) GRS
School of Law LAW
College of Liberal Arts CLA
School of Management SMG
School of Medicine MED
Metropolitan College MET
School of Nursing SON
*College of Practical
  Arts and Letters PAL
School of Public
  Communication SPC
Sargent College of Allied
  Health Professions SAR
School of Social Work SSW
School of Theology STH
*Have been absorbed by
  other departments